Prentice Hall
LITERATURE

All-in-One
Workbook

The American Experience

PEARSON

Upper Saddle River, New Jersey
Boston, Massachusetts
Chandler, Arizona
Glenview, Illinois

ISBN-13: 978-0-13-366817-9
ISBN-10: 0-13-366817-7

11 16

CONTENTS

"Study the Masters" by Lucille Clifton
"For My Children" by Colleen McElroy

"The Tropics in New York" by Claude McKay
"From the Dark Tower" by Countee Cullen
"A Black Man Talks of Reaping" by Arna Bontemps

from Dust Tracks on a Road by Zora Neale Hurston

UNIT 5   Prosperity and Protest

from Hiroshima by John Hersey
"The Death of the Ball Turret Gunner" by Randall Jarrell

All-in-one-Workbook

Name _Ian Wilson_   Date _1/29/19_

Unit 1 Introduction
Names and Terms to Know

A. DIRECTIONS: *Write a brief sentence explaining each of the following names and terms. You will find all of the information you need in the Unit Introduction in your textbook.*

1. Jamestown: _Supposedly the "first" colony in Made in America._
2. Stamp Act: _____
   _____
3. The Puritan Ethic: _An American Value of hard work and self-discipline._
4. Olaudah Equiano: _A slave narrative that helped Americans Face their own history and do something about it._
5. John Adams: _The second President of the United States._
6. Jean de Crevecoeur _Frenchman believed democracy could inspire and unite._

B. DIRECTIONS: *Use the hints below to help you answer each question.*

1. What role did Puritanism play in the settlement of North America by Europeans?
   [Hints: What caused the Puritans to leave Europe? What was the "shining city on a hill"?]
   One way was somewhat the impulse to escape to a New World and build a free and uncorrupts society.

2. What were some differences between the New England and Southern colonies?
   [Hints: What was the economy of New England like? What was the economy of the Southern colonies like? How were their lifestyles different? What happened in 1619 in Virginia?]
   They differed in climate, crops, social organization, and religion.

3. How did Enlightenment ideas influence the new American society?
   [Hints: What was the "social contract"? How did Enlightenment ideas influence the colonists to seek independence from England?]
   Through the News distribution and our Declaration of Independence. It points to several views from a Christian standpoint.

Name _Ian Wilson_   Date _1/30/19_

Unit 1 Introduction

Essential Question 1: What is the relationship between place and literature?

A. DIRECTIONS: *Answer the questions about the first Essential Question in the Introduction, about the relationship between place and literature. All the information you need is in the Unit 1 Introduction in your textbook.*

1. *The Natural Environment of the New World*

   a. The natural world the settlers found was _in habited by several hundred Native American Tribes._

   b. The Native American attitude toward nature was _in many of their myths and legends. protect it._

2. *The Colonists and Nature*

   a. The colonists regarded nature as belonging _to the people and not people to the land_

   b. The religious colonists' dream for the New World was _that it would be a community built on religious principles._

   c. In contrast to their dream, the colonists' reality in the New World was _trying to stay alive._

   d. By the eighteenth century, the colonists' attitude had changed ~~to~~ from _worrying less about survival to worrying about self-government._

3. *The Attitudes toward Nature Expressed in the Literature*

   a. The religious colonists' "Errand into the Wilderness" was _a group of writings that describe a mission of combating against evil in uncivilized area._

   b. Later on, reason and technology made the natural world _a more hospitible place._

B. DIRECTIONS: *Complete the sentence stems based on the Essential Question Vocabulary words.*

1. In contrast to a city, a *wilderness* is _uncivilized_

2. Early Americans appreciated both the danger and the *splendor* of _the great unknown wilderness_

3. Some of the *terrors* that faced the early colonists were _starvation, disease, supply shortage, etc._

Name _Ian Wilson_   Date _2/1/19 I_

Unit 1 Introduction

Essential Question 2: What makes American literature American?

A. DIRECTIONS: *On the lines provided, answer the questions about the second Essential Question in the Introduction, about what makes American literature American. All the information you need is in the Unit 1 Introduction in your textbook.*

1. *Theme in Literature*

    a. A theme is _a central idea, message, or insight that a literary work reveals._

    b. Themes in literary works are revealed through _characters' words and actions, through details of setting and plot, imagery, language, and style._

2. *Three Early American Themes*

    a. In their writings about nature, early Americans expressed _the wilderness and gave details and revealed insights into its nature._

    b. The public writings of early Americans showed the unique combination of _Community and Independence._

    c. Most early American writing emphasized two values: _self-reliance and individualism._

3. *Uniquely American Aspects of These Themes*

    a. What qualities did early Americans associate with their land? _Unique, splendid, dangerous,_

    b. What was the attitude of early Americans toward the past and traditional European themes? _They didn't want to continue with the stories and traditions of Europe, they started to express things about their unique surroundings._

    c. What vision of themselves did early Americans express in their writings? _They wanted self-reliance and individualism, for themselves to be a new and unique people._

B. DIRECTIONS: *Complete the sentence stems based on the Essential Question Vocabulary words.*

1. Anita's *independence* made her very unlikely to _____

    _____

2. Raj's *optimism* led him to approach challenges expecting _good things to come out of it._

3. A sense of *community* developed in our class when _they helped each other, when they were in need._

Name _Ian Wilson_ Date _2/4/19_

Unit 1 Introduction

Essential Question 3: How does literature shape or reflect society?

A. DIRECTIONS: *On the lines provided, answer the questions about the third Essential Question in the Introduction, about the relationship between the writer and society. All the information you need is in the Unit 1 Introduction in your textbook.*

1. *Social and Political Forces Affecting Early American Literature*
   a. Puritan daily life, social relations, and lawmaking were all marked by _the impulse to escape to a New World._
   b. The Enlightenment is associated with the qualities of _the Declaration of Independence._
   c. Deep painful marks on American literature were left by relationships between Americans of European descent and _Native Americans._

2. *Major Roles of Early American Writers*
   a. Examples of early American writers as oral poets and historians include _de Cárdenas and Cabeza de Vaca._
   b. Examples of early American writers as preachers and lawmakers include _Cotton Mather, Johnathan Edwards, Thomas Paine, Patrick Henry, and Thomas Jefferson_
   c. Early American autobiographers include _Olaudah Equiano and Benjamin Franklin._

B. DIRECTIONS: *Complete the sentence stems based on the Essential Question Vocabulary words.*

1. When Lani finally learned to *govern* her impulses, she _stopped constantly eating sugar_
2. We celebrate our family's *heritage* by _shooting off fireworks._
3. The preacher's sermon interpreted the *doctrine* of _the Apostle Paul._

Unit 1 Introduction
Following-Through Activities

A. CHECK YOUR COMPREHENSION: *Use this chart to complete the Check Your Comprehension activity in the Unit 1 Introduction. In the middle column, fill in two key concepts related to each Essential Question. In the right column, list a group of people (Native Americans, Puritans, or early revolutionaries) connected with each concept.*

ESSENTIAL QUESTION	Key Concept	Group
Place and Literature	1. _____ 2. _____	1. _____ 2. _____
American Literature	1. *Self-determination* 2. _____	1. *Revolutionaries like Thomas Jefferson* 2. _____
Writer and Society	1. _____ 2. _____	1. _____ 2. _____

B. EXTEND YOUR LEARNING: *Use this graphic organizer to help plan your research for the Extend Your Learning activity.*

What type of spoken literature are you researching?			
What was the speaker's purpose?			
What form did the performance take?			
What types of language did the speaker use?			
What else do we know about how the performance looked and sounded?	Gestures	Movements	Vocalization

Name _Ian Wilson_   Date _2/86/19_

Contemporary Commentary
Susan Power Introduces "Museum Indians"

DIRECTIONS: *Use the space provided to answer the questions.*

1. In her commentary, what does Susan Power mean by the term *oral tradition?*

   That they are handed down stories from generation to generation and kept alive within a community.

2. What does the author mean when she says that the Native American origin myths are meant to be "flexible" and "interactive"?

   They need to be pictured and acted out in the mind.

3. According to the author, why is she herself not a traditional storyteller?

   She was very shy as a child and found it difficult to speak before an audience.

4. What aspects of Shakespeare's plays fascinated Susan Power when she was young? Why does she think that Shakespeare would have felt at home in the Native American world?

   She loved his rhythmic and poetic words, and dramatic plot lines. Native American stories and Shakespeare's are probably similar.

5. What does the author mean when she says that she could not find herself on the literary map?

   Because she couldn't see what type of literature she'd fit in to, without her tradition, per say.

6. Identify four specific contrasts between the oral tradition and the written tradition.

   Setting, story, culture, and storytelling setup.

7. The writer asserts that, in the essay "Museum Indians," she has tried to capture oral literature in printed words. Do you think this goal can be achieved? Why or why not? Briefly explain your answer.

   Maybe, she was descriptive in the text with what the title read. They were kind of like museum indians.

8. If you had a chance to interview Susan Power, what are two questions you might like to ask her?

   I really don't have any questions for her.

Susan Power
Listening and Viewing

Segment 1: Meet Susan Power

• What were some of Susan Power's earliest experiences with writing and literature?
• Describe your early experiences with books. How did these stories shape your attitude toward reading and writing?

_____

_____

_____

_____

Segment 2: Susan Power Introduces "Museum Indians"

• How does Susan Power use her personal experiences as the basis for her nonfiction piece "Museum Indians"?
• Why do you think it is important for Susan Power to write about the cultural activities of Native Americans?

_____

_____

_____

_____

Segment 3: The Writing Process

• Why does Susan Power read aloud and listen to her sentences while she is writing and editing?
• Do you think it is important to consider the sounds of words when writing? Explain.

_____

_____

_____

_____

Segment 4: The Rewards of Writing

• What does Susan Power hope readers can gain by reading her work?
• What do you think you can learn by reading books that offer insights into other cultures?

_____

_____

_____

_____

Name _Ian Wilson_   Date _12/5/19_

Literary Analysis: Origin Myths and Archetypes

Origin myths are traditional stories that recount the origins of earthly life. Passed down from generation to generation, these myths often explain such phenomena as the beginning of human life, the customs and religious rites of a people, the creation of natural landmarks, and events beyond a people's control.

Archetypes are patterns in literature found throughout the world. Many cultures have a trickster character that represents the world's ability to fool us, a mysterious guide who represents the belief that there are forces in the world to help us on quests, and so forth.

DIRECTIONS: *Complete the first three boxes in Chart 1 below by explaining briefly on the right how each phenomenon on the left came into being. In Chart 2, identify on the right the character that represents the archetype identified on the left and the myth in which it appears. Review each selection for help.*

Chart 1

Selection and Phenomenon	Explanation
"The Earth on Turtle's Back": the world	When Sky Woman fell, the animals tried to make earth for her to step on. They all dove down in the water to bring up earth and finally got it. It was placed on the turtle and became the world.
"When Grizzlies Walked Upright": Mount Shasta, beaver, otter, fish, birds, grizzly bears	When Sky Spirit's daughter tried to talk to Wind Spirit, she was blown away. She grew up with bears and made offspring with them. Sky Spirit cursed the bears.
from *The Navajo Origin Legend*: man, woman	Man and Woman were created from crops by the gods.

Chart 2

Archetype	Character That Represents the Archetype
1. the small, determined character whose courage saves the day	The Muskrat
2. the disobedient child	The Sky Spirits daughter
3. the being made up of two races	The daughter's and bear's children
4. source of nutrients	Crops.

Name   Ian Wilson   Date   2/8/19

"The Earth on Turtle's Back" (Onondaga)
"When Grizzlies Walked Upright" (Modoc)
from The Navajo Origin Legend (Navajo)
Reading Strategy: Recognize Cultural Details

One purpose of reading literature is to learn more about the culture that produces it. While you read a piece of literature, pay attention to cultural details—such as references to objects, animals, or practices that signal how people live, think, or worship—to gain cultural insight. For example, the cultural details in the three Native American myths indicate how the Native Americans lived as well as what they valued in life.

DIRECTIONS: *Read the following excerpts from the selections. Then, answer the questions that follow.*

"The Earth on Turtle's Back"

There was an ancient chief in the Skyland. His young wife was expecting a child, and one night she dreamed that she saw the Great Tree uprooted. The next day she told her husband the story.

He nodded as she finished telling her dream. "My wife," he said, "I am sad that you had this dream. It is clearly a dream of great power and, as is our way, when one has such a powerful dream we must do all we can to make it true. The Great Tree must be uprooted."

1. Explain what you can infer about the place of dreams in Native American culture from the excerpt from "The Earth on Turtle's Back."

They take them as signs of wonder and greatness.

"When Grizzlies Walked Upright"

After many years had passed, the mother grizzly bear knew that she would soon die. Fearing that she should ask of the Chief of the Sky Spirits to forgive her for keeping his daughter, she gathered all the grizzlies at the lodge they had built.

2. What does this excerpt from "When Grizzlies Walked Upright" tell you about the beliefs of Native Americans regarding the taking of responsibility for their actions?

They looked down on bears as devious creatures.

from The Navajo Origin Legend

It is the wind that comes out of our mouths now that gives us life. When this ceases to blow we die.

3. What does this excerpt from *The Navajo Origin Legend* tell you about why the Navajo believed that the wind was what gave life to people?

They believed that if there was no wind giving life, they would cease to live.

"The Earth on Turtle's Back" (Onondaga)
"When Grizzlies Walked Upright" (Modoc)
from **The Navajo Origin Legend** (Navajo)
Vocabulary Builder

Using the Latin Root *-trud-*, *-trus-*

A. DIRECTIONS: *The root -trud-, also spelled -trus-, comes from the Latin* trudere, *which means "thrust" or "push." Protruded refers to something that was "pushed out" from where it was supposed to be. Use each word in the list below to answer the questions below them.*

intruder   intrusive   extrude   obtrusive

1. Which word best describes a busybody who thrusts himself or herself into a situation and asks a lot of nosy questions? ___intrusive___

2. Which word best describes a showoff, or someone who pushes himself or herself out in a forward manner? ___extrude___

3. Which word names the act of pushing or sticking out? ___obtrusive___

4. Which word names someone who "pushes in," or trespasses? ___intruder___

Using the Word List

ancestors   depths   protruded   unconscious

B. DIRECTIONS: *On the line, write the letter of the definition before the word it defines.*

__B__ 1. depths
__D__ 2. unconscious
__A__ 3. protruded
__C__ 4. ancestors

A. stuck out
B. deep places
C. those from whom one descends
D. not able to feel or think

C. DIRECTIONS: *On the line, write the letter of the word or phrase that is most similar in meaning to the word in capital letters.*

__A__ 1. ANCESTORS:
  A. forefathers   **B.** descendants   **C.** offspring   **D.** neighbors
__D__ 2. PROTRUDED:
  A. reversed   **B.** curved   **C.** stood   **D.** jutted out
__C__ 3. DEPTHS:
  A. wounds   **B.** regions   **C.** pits   **D.** trees
__B__ 4. UNCONSCIOUS:
  A. giggling   **B.** asleep   **C.** puzzled   **D.** wakeful

Name _Ian Wilson_   Date _2/21/19_

"The Earth on Turtle's Back" (Onondaga)
"When Grizzlies Walked Upright" (Modoc)
from **The Navajo Origin Legend** (Navajo)
Grammar and Style: Coordinating Conjunctions

Coordinating conjunctions join words, phrases, and sentences. The main coordinating conjunctions are *and, but, or, so,* and *for.* Read these examples:

> The Sky Chief and his young wife were expecting a child.

> The Chief's young wife was expecting a child, and one night she dreamed that she saw the Great Tree uprooted.

In the first example, the coordinating conjunction *and* joins two phrases—*Sky Chief* with *his young wife.* In the second example, the coordinating conjunction *and* joins two complete sentences—*The Chief's young wife was expecting a child* with *one night she dreamed that she saw the Great Tree uprooted.*

A. PRACTICE: *Write on the line any coordinating conjunction you see in each item. Then, identify what the conjunction is joining—words, phrases, or two complete sentences.*

1. The birds and animals looked up as the woman fell from the sky.
   They wonded what was happening, "as"

2. The water birds dove down, but they could not reach the woman.
   It shows one aspect, which then changes to another.

3. The Sky Chief yelled, "You have wronged me, so from this moment you will walk on four feet."
   Cause and effect is shown here, you did this, now therefore...

4. The Sky Chief's daughter and a grizzly bear made the first Indians.
   Two sides are brought together

5. The Sky Chief punished the grizzlies, for he was angry.
   It described action and reason for action.

B. WRITING APPLICATION: *Use the coordinating conjunction in parentheses to combine each pair of sentences into a longer sentence. Write each new sentence on the lines provided.*

1. The grizzlies looked as they do today. They walked on two feet. (use *but*)
   They walked as they do today, but on two feet.

2. The daughter looked for the ocean. She fell out of the mountain. (use *and*)
   She looked for the ocean, and she fell out of the mountain.

3. The little girl could die. The grizzlies could save her. (use *or*)
   She could die or they could save her.

All-in-One Workbook
11

"The Earth on Turtle's Back" (Onondaga)
"When Grizzlies Walked Upright" (Modoc)
from **The Navajo Origin Legend** (Navajo)

Integrated Language Skills: Support for Writing

Before you write a short play based on one of the myths, gather your ideas into the graphic organizer below. First, choose an element of the original myth. Then, explain how you will keep or adapt the element in your play.

Retelling the Myth of _____

Elements of the Myth	How Will I Adapt the Myth?
Setting: Where does the myth take place?	Setting: How will I put this information into brief stage directions?
Characters: Who are the main characters?	How will I list the cast? How to describe each character in the stage directions? How to show the change from character to character in the play?
What do the characters say to one another? Give two examples.	How will I summarize the action and dialogue from the myth into stage dialogue?
What is the outcome of the myth?	How will I end the play? What scene will be the climax? What scene will provide the resolution?

Below or on a separate page, write a first draft of your drama. Concentrate on describing characters and setting in your stage directions. Concentrate on showing character behavior and advancing the plot in your dialogue. Then, choose a passage of dialogue from your play, and perform the passage with you and your classmates playing the parts.

Name _Ian Wilson_ Date _3/11/19_

from **The Iroquois Constitution**
Literary Analysis: Political Document and Symbols

A **political document** describes the structure of a political organization and the responsibilities of its members. For example, the Constitution of the United States sets out the duties and responsibilities of the three branches of the U.S. government. The division of the government into three branches was a major **symbol** for the framers. The three branches symbolized, or stood for, a government that would provide restrictions on the ability of any one branch to gain too much power. This was a rejection of the absolute power held by the monarchy of England, from which many of the colonists came.

DIRECTIONS: *Read the passages from* The Iroquois Constitution. *Then, answer the questions about the document and the symbols within it.*

I am Dekanawidah and with the Five Nations confederate lords I plant the Tree of the Great Peace. . . . Under the shade of this Tree of the Great Peace . . . There shall you sit and watch the council fire of the confederacy of the Five Nations, and all the affairs of the Five Nations shall be transacted at this place before you.

1. How many peoples, or nations, are represented in the document known as *The Iroquois Constitution?*

   Five Nations

2. What does the Tree of the Great Peace symbolize?

   When a candidate lord is to be installed he shall furnish four strings of shells (or wampum) . . . . Such will constitute the evidence of his pledge to the confederate lords that he will live according to the constitution of the Great Peace and exercise justice in all affairs. _p. 42 - LAST LINE_

   Unification, entirety, and justice?

3. What behavior does the constitution demand of a lord of the Iroquois confederacy?

   Honesty is highly demanded; being dishonorable is a serious wrong.

4. What do the four strings of wampum symbolize for a candidate lord? _TO DO WHAT?_

   It will constitute evidence of his pledge.

   We place at the top of the Tree of the Long Leaves an eagle who is able to see afar. If he sees in the distance any evil approaching or any danger threatening he will at once warn the people of the confederacy.

5. What does the eagle symbolize to the Iroquois people?

   The one who warns of danger.

6. How does the symbol of the eagle represent what the confederacy really used to warn them of approaching danger?

   Think about it like this, like an eagle protects its young, it protects us? (Maybe?)

Name _Ian Wilson_　　　　　　　　　　　　Date _3/11/19_

from The Iroquois Constitution
Reading Strategy: Analyze Author's Assumptions and Beliefs

When you read a document, you can often determine what the writer believes or assumes about how people should live or behave. For example, read the following passage from *The Iroquois Constitution:*

> If any man or any nation outside the Five Nations shall obey the laws of the Great Peace . . . they shall be welcomed to take shelter beneath the Tree of the Long Leaves.

This passage makes it clear that the author does not believe in excluding people or nations from the Iroquois Constitution. He says that as long as any persons or nations *outside* the Five Nations obey the laws, they are welcome. The author has an *inclusive* philosophy.

DIRECTIONS: *Read the passages from* The Iroquois Constitution. *Then, answer the questions about what each passage tells you about the author's assumptions or beliefs.*

> Whenever the confederate lords shall assemble, . . . they shall offer thanks to the earth . . . , to the streams of water, . . . to the maize and the fruits, . . . to the animals that serve as food and give their pelts for clothing, . . .

1. What does the author assume about the worth of the natural world?
   That it's very high, and we should be grateful.

> It shall be a serious wrong for anyone to lead a lord into trivial affairs, for the people must ever hold their lords high in estimation out of respect to their honorable positions.

2. What does the author believe is a necessary characteristic for lords to have in order to earn respect from the people?
   Not to be mislead by anyone.

> Cast not over your shoulder behind you the warnings of the nephews and nieces should they chide you for any error or wrong you may do, but return to the way of the Great Law which is just and right.

3. Does the author think young people have any opinions that are worth hearing, or does he think only the opinions of adults count?
   Everyone's opinions count. Just because their children, does not mean they're dumb.

4. What does the author assume about the lord's character?
   That they should be an honorable and respectable person.

Name ___Iai Wilson___ Date ___3/11/19___

from The Iroquois Constitution
Vocabulary Builder

Using the Word List

constitute   deliberation   disposition   oblivion   tempered

A. DIRECTIONS: *On the line, write the letter of the definition before the word it defines.*

D 1. tempered
E 2. oblivion
B 3. deliberation
A 4. disposition
C 5. constitute

A. inclination to believe, do, or choose something
B. careful consideration
C. form, or make up
D. made less harsh
E. condition of being completely forgotten

B. DIRECTIONS: *On the line, write the letter of the word or phrase that is most similar in meaning to the word in capital letters.*

A 1. DISPOSITION:
    A. gain   B. size   C. tendency   D. teamwork

D 2. DELIBERATION:
    A. anger   B. belief   C. action   D. thought

B 3. OBLIVION:
    A. unhappiness   B. state of being forgotten   C. hostility   D. welfare

C 4. CONSTITUTE:
    A. break down   B. compete   C. establish   D. rejoice

B 5. TEMPERED:
    A. mixed   B. softened   C. criticized   D. thanked

Integrated Language Skills: Support for Writing

A **found poem** is the rearrangement of material from another genre into poetic form. It uses the same punctuation, or lack of punctuation, as the original. Read this example:

Roots have spread out

From the Tree of the Great Peace,

one to the north,

one to the east,

one to the south

and one to the west.

The name of these roots

is

the Great White Roots

and their nature

is

peace

and

strength

Do you recognize it? It's the third paragraph in the passage from *The Iroquois Constitution.* But it has been arranged in different lines, which gives new emphasis to words and thoughts.

DIRECTIONS: *Read each of these passages from* The Iroquois Constitution. *Then, turn one of them into a found poem on the lines below. As long as you keep the same order of words and punctuation, you can divide up the lines however you wish. Use a second sheet of paper if you wish.*

We place at the top of the Tree of the Long Leaves an eagle who is able to see afar. If he sees in the distance any evil approaching or any danger threatening he will at once warn the people of the confederacy.

Look and listen for the welfare of the whole people and have always in view not only the present but also the coming generations, even those whose faces are yet beneath the surface of the ground—the unborn of the future nation.

On the tree's top is an eagle, who is able to see afar.

IF he sees threatening danger, the people are warned.

_____

_____

_____

_____

Name _I_m_Wilson_ Date _3/13/19_

"A Journey Through Texas" *from* **The Journey of Alvar Núñez Cabeza de Vaca**
by Alvar Núñez Cabeza de Vaca
"Boulders Taller Than the Great Tower of Seville" by García López de Cárdenas

Literary Analysis: Exploration Narratives/ Chronological Text Structure

The two selections you have just read are exploration narratives—explorers' firsthand accounts of their experiences. Such narratives generally focus on the difficulties that the explorers faced and the specific discoveries they made. They are also generally written in chronological order, the order in which events occurred.

DIRECTIONS: *Read the two excerpts from "Boulders Taller Than the Great Tower of Seville" and "A Journey Through Texas" below. Then, answer the questions.*

The men spent three days looking for a way down [the Grand Canyon] to the river; from the top it looked as if the water were a fathom [six feet] across. But, according to the information supplied by the Indians, it must have been half a league wide [1½ miles]. . . . [Three men], being most agile, began to go down. . . .They returned about four o'clock in the afternoon, as they could not reach the bottom because of the many obstacles they met, for what from the top seemed easy, was not so, on the contrary, it was rough and difficult. . . . from the point they had reached, the river seemed very large, and that, from what they saw, the width given by the Indians was correct.

1. What do you learn from this narrative about access to the Grand Canyon?
It is a difficult journey.

2. Base your answers to the next three questions on the following excerpts.

They [Indians] said we should travel up the river towards the north, on which trail for seventeen days we would not find a thing to eat, except a fruit called *chacan*, ...

After two days were past we determined to go in search of maize, and not to follow the road to the cows, since the latter carried us to the north, which meant a very great circuit, . . .

So we went on our way and traversed the whole country to the South Sea [Gulf of Mexico], and our resolution was not shaken by the fear of great starvation, which the Indians said we should suffer (and indeed suffered) during the first seventeen days of travel.

a. Whose estimate of the width of the Colorado river is correct, according to the narrative?
The Indians

b. How long did the explorers stay with the Indians? _Well, at least 17 days._
Over twenty days.

c. What did they do next, and how long did the first part of their trip take?
The got to the Gulf of Mexico, which was called the South Sea at the time. The first part was 17 days.

Name ___Ian Wilson___ Date __3/13/19__

"A Journey Through Texas" *from* The Journey of Alvar Núñez Cabeza de Vaca
by Alvar Núñez Cabeza de Vaca
"Boulders Taller Than the Great Tower of Seville" by García López de Cárdenas
Reading Strategy: Recognize Signal Words for Time

One way to make sense of a writer's work is to look for signal words that point out relationships among the ideas and events presented. In a narrative text that is presented in chronological order, look for signal words related to time.

DIRECTIONS: *Read each passage from the selections. Then, identify the signal words that help you answer the question, and write the answers on the lines.*

We followed the women to a place where it had been agreed we should wait for them. After five days they had not yet returned, and the Indians explained that it might be because they had not found anybody.

1. How long did the explorers wait for the Indian women to return?

   5 days, but they did not return.

On the same day many fell sick, and on the next day eight of them died!

2. How long after people fell sick did eight of them die?

   One day!

We asked them why they did not raise maize, and they replied that they were afraid of losing the crops, since for two successive years it had not rained, and the seasons were so dry that the moles had eaten the corn, . . .

3. For how long had the drought been going on when the explorers arrived at the Indian camp?

   Two years.

They set out from there laden with provisions, because they had to travel over some uninhabited land before coming to settlements, which the Indians said were more than twenty days away.

4. Would the explorers cross the uninhabited land before they reached the settlements, or after? How many days away were the settlements?

   More than twenty.

When they had traveled four additional days the guides said that it was impossible to go on because no water would be found for three or four days, that when they themselves traveled through that land they took along women who brought water in gourds, that in those trips they buried the gourds of water for the return trip, and that they traveled in one day a distance that took us two days.

5. According to the guides, how many days distant was water from the beginning of this journey?

   _3 or 4_

6. How were the Indians able to travel through this dry country two times faster than the explorers?

   Because they're natives, they'd know
   how the land works out better than anyone.

Name _Ian Wilson_____ Date _3/13/19_____

"A Journey Through Texas" *from* The Journey of Alvar Núñez Cabeza de Vaca
by Alvar Núñez Cabeza de Vaca
"Boulders Taller Than the Great Tower of Seville" by García López de Cárdenas
Vocabulary Builder

Using the Word List

~~advantageous~~   ~~entreated~~   ~~feigned~~   ~~subsisted~~   ~~successive~~   ~~traversed~~

A. DIRECTIONS: *On the lines provided, write the word from the Word List that best completes each sentence.*

1. The hikers ___traversed___ the field from one end to the other.

2. Too poor to buy meat, the family ___subsisted___ on beans and rice.

3. The duke wanted his daughters to make _X successive_ marriages that would bring more wealth and power to the family.

4. To avoid having to make a speech, Marcia ___feigned___ a sore throat.

5. The bush bloomed three times, but each _X advantageous_ bloom had fewer flowers.

6. The convict's wife ___entreated___ the king to show mercy and pardon her husband.

B. DIRECTIONS: *On the line, write the letter of the word that is most nearly* opposite *in meaning to the word in capital letters.*

_D_ 1. ENTREATED:
   A. purchased   B. refused   C. asked   (D. begged)

_A_ 2. SUCCESSIVE:
   (A. following)   B. leading   C. religious   D. hungry   ✓

_A_ 3. SUBSISTED:
   (A. survived)   B. perished   C. hid   D. helped

_C_ 4. FEIGNED:
   A. conscious   B. trapped   (C. pretended)   D. truthful

_A_ 5. TRAVERSED:
   (A. crossed)   B. assisted   C. regressed   D. silenced

_C_ 6. ADVANTAGEOUS:
   A. injured   B. unfavorable   (C. sincere)   D. puzzled

Name __Ian Wilson__   Date __3/13/19__

"A Journey Through Texas" *from* **The Journey of Alvar Núñez Cabeza de Vaca**
by Alvar Núñez Cabeza de Vaca
"Boulders Taller Than the Great Tower of Seville" by García López de Cárdenas
Integrated Language Skills: Support for Writing

Prepare to write your **explorer's journal** by collecting information about the Grand Canyon or another Southwest location. Enter your information into the chart below. Be sure to focus on specific details that readers can use to understand the nature of the location and what they can expect to find if they travel there.

The Grand Canyon [or other location]	
Location: In relation to Atlantic and Pacific Oceans, Gulf of Mexico	In the state of Arizona, near three bordering states, about 1,680 miles from the Gulf of Mexico
Surrounding Landforms: Rivers, Plains, Plateaus	The Colorado River, Pike's Peak (maybe)
Vegetation: Trees and Plants	Cacti, Tumbleweeds, Sego Lily, American Plum Tree, Wooly daisy.
Animals	Big horn Sheep, Bison, Elk, Mountain Lion, Hognosed skunk
Climate	Rocky, Dry
Difficulties in getting to and from the location	Nowadays, you can just drive there

On a separate page, write the first draft of your journal. Have a classmate read it and make comments to help you make your revision clearer and more concrete. Add descriptions of landforms, plants, and animals, as well as drawings if you wish. Add a simple map based on your chart and other research.

Name _Ian Wilson_   Date _3/13/19 I_

from Of Plymouth Plantation by William Bradford
Literary Analysis: Author's Purpose and Audience

To understand a nonfiction reading selection, it is helpful to identify the **author's purpose and audience**. What does he or she wish to achieve with the selection, and to whom is he or she writing? When William Bradford returned to England, he wrote about the events that occurred during the first journey to Plymouth and the settlement of the colony. He hoped that others would also want to journey to the New World.

Read this passage from the selection:

> Being thus arrived in a good harbor and brought safe to land, they fell upon their knees and blessed the God of heaven, who had brought them over the vast and furious ocean, and delivered them from all the perils and miseries thereof, again to set their feet on the firm and stable earth, their proper element . . .

This passage shows that Bradford is writing for an audience that has a deep belief in a God who will bless their endeavors and keep them safe. He is also writing to show that although the trip was perilous, the company made it to shore safely.

DIRECTIONS: *Read each passage from* Of Plymouth Plantation, *and then answer the questions.*

What could now sustain them but the spirit of God and his grace? May not and ought not the children of these fathers rightly say: *Our fathers were Englishmen which came over this great ocean, and were ready to perish in this wilderness; but they cried unto the Lord, and He heard their voice, and looked on their adversity, etc.*

1. Who is Bradford's audience in this passage? _Their descendants to come._
   _____

2. What is his purpose in writing this passage? _To point out that we should give_ _thanks to God for all He has brought us through, seeing our commitment, and helping us through the hard times._
   And of these in the time of most distress, there was but six or seven sound persons, who, . . . spared no pains, night nor day, but with abundance of toil and hazard of their own health, fetched them wood, made them fires, dressed them meat . . . ; in a word, did all the homely and necessary offices for them . . . ; and all this willingly and cheerfully, without any grudging in the least, showing herein their true love unto their friends and brethren. . . . And I doubt not but that their recompense [reward] is with the Lord.

3. What is his Bradford's purpose in writing this passage? _Recognition of those who_ _take care of their fellow man or woman._

4. Of what does he hope to convince his audience in this passage? _That we would probably_ _have failed without their help._

from **Of Plymouth Plantation** by William Bradford

Reading Strategy: Breaking Down Sentences

One way to understand complex passages in a selection is to break down sentences to help unlock their meaning. This strategy is especially useful for reading the work of writers from centuries past, who tend to write in long, complicated sentences. In the following passage from *Of Plymouth Colony*, notice how the vital information telling who and what has been underlined, while all the less essential material has been bracketed. Breaking down material in this way helps you analyze clarity of meaning.

> After they had enjoyed fair winds and weather for a season, they [were encountered many times with crosswinds, and] met with many fierce storms, [with which the ship was shrewdly shaken, and her upper works made very leaky; and one of the main beams in the mid ships was bowed and cracked,] which put them in some fear that the ship could not be able to perform the voyage.

DIRECTIONS: *Break down the following passages by bracketing less essential material and underlining the essential information that tells who and what.*

1. But that which was most sad and lamentable was that [in two or three months' time,] half of their company died, [wanting houses and other comforts;] being infected with the scurvy and other diseases, which this long voyage and their inaccommodate condition had brought upon them; so as there died sometimes two or three of a day, in the foresaid time; [that of one hundred and odd persons,] scarce fifty remained.

2. [But after they had sailed that course about half a day,] they fell amongst dangerous shoals and roaring breakers, [and they were so far entangled therewith as] they conceived themselves in great danger; and [the wind shrinking upon them withal,] they resolved to bear up again for the Cape, [and thought themselves happy to get out of those dangers before night overtook them,] as by God's providence they did.

3. [At length] they understood by discourse with him that he was not of these parts, but belonged to the eastern parts, where some English ships came to fish, with whom he was acquainted, [and could name sundry of them by their names,] amongst whom he had got his language.

from **Of Plymouth Plantation** by William Bradford
Vocabulary Builder

Using the Word List

adversity   calamity   habitation   peril   relent   subject to

A. *Many words have related forms with similar meanings. For example, peril means "danger"; a related form is the adjective perilous, which means dangerous. Using your understanding of the Word List words, circle the letter of the best answer to the following questions.*

1. Which word most likely means "residents"? ✓
   A. inhabitants   **B.** subjects   **C.** adversaries

2. Which word most likely means "placing in danger"?
   A. subjugating   **B.** imperiling   **C.** relenting

3. Which word most likely means "persistent" or "never-ceasing"?
   A. subjective   **B.** uninhabitable   **C.** relentless

B. DIRECTIONS: *On the line, write the letter of the definition before the word or phrase it defines.*

E 1. subject to		A. become more merciful
C 2. calamity		B. unfavorable circumstances ✓
D 3. habitation		C. disaster
A 4. relent		D. place to live; group of homes or
B 5. adversity		E. affected by something

C. DIRECTIONS: *On the line provided, write the word or phrase from the Word List that best completes each of the following sentences. Use each word only once.*

1. They fought the high seas and strong winds all day and feared the ship would break up, but then at dusk the winds began to ___relent___ and soon the ocean was calm again. ✓

2. The heavy rains poured for days, which was inconvenient for travel, but then landslides began to pour down the slopes and the situation turned into a ___calamity___.

3. The family experienced much financial ___adversity___ before they were able to get their business off the ground and start to show a profit.

Name **Ian Wilson**   Date **3/13/19**

from **Of Plymouth Plantation** by William Bradford
Integrated Language Skills: Support for Writing

Imagine that William Bradford could use a time machine to visit your period in history. Invite him to your school to speak about his experiences in Plymouth Colony. First, decide how you might introduce him. Who is he, and what did he' do that makes his experience valuable to you and your class? Write your introduction on the lines below.

Hello Class, My Name Is William Bradford. About 400 years ago, myself and the crew of the Mayflower sought religious Freedom. At the time, England was under the rule of King James Who said we must follow the Doctrine of the Church. After a hard struggle, we escaped England and Fled into the country of Holland, where we dwelt many years. Even with our religious Freedom in Holland, we weren't satisfied with our children growing up in the customs of the Dutch people. After much thought and consideration, we decided to head For a place which was known to all as "The New World." Through many dangers, and many struggles, God helped us through each deadly turn and made us a proud and Free people.

Now that Bradford has finished his talk, think of three questions you might ask him about his life, his experiences, his beliefs, and even what he thinks of the country today. Write your questions on the lines.

1. What do you think about our government today?
2. What do you think would help Fix our government?
3. Do you think our Government needs some Jesus?

Name _Ian Wilson_   Date _3/15/10_

"To My Dear and Loving Husband" by Anne Bradstreet
Literary Analysis: Puritan Plain Style—Syntax and Inversion

Just as the Puritans' style of life was spare, simple, and straightforward, so too was their writing style. The **Puritan Plain Style**, as it is called, is characterized by short words, direct statements, and references to ordinary, everyday objects.

In addition, the structure of the sentences was often flipped—that is, the subject came after the verb. See this example:

From far away came the sound of thunder.

This sentence is an inverted way of saying "The sound of thunder came from far away." Inverting sentences or lines is a more poetic way of making literal statements.

DIRECTIONS: *Answer the questions related to each of the following excerpts from "To My Dear and Loving Husband."*

If ever two were one, than surely we.
If ever man were lov'd by wife, then thee;

1. How would you invert these two lines to make them more literal?
   If two were ever one, we would be. If a man were loved by his
   wife, that man would be you.

I prize thy love more than whole mines of gold.

2. This line reflects the Puritan Plain Style in terms of its direct statement. Which other element of the style does it reflect?

   _____

My love is such that rivers cannot quench,

3. What common experience does the poet refer to in this line?
   Unending love towards each other

Then while we live, in love let's so persevere,
That when we live no more, we may live ever.

4. Which part of this passage is an exception to the Puritan Plain Style rule of short words?
   The 'live no more' part.

Name _Ian Wilson_   Date _3/19/19_

"To My Dear and Loving Husband" by Anne Bradstreet
Reading Strategy: Paraphrasing

The old-fashioned language and sophisticated imagery of Bradstreet's poem can make it difficult to understand. When confronted with a challenging poem or piece of prose, you will often understand it better if you **paraphrase,** or restate ideas in your own words.

Bradstreet's version:

If ever wife was happy in a man,

Compare with me ye women if you can.

Paraphrased:

No woman could be happier with her husband than I am.

DIRECTIONS: *On the lines provided, paraphrase the following excerpts from Bradstreet's poem.*

1. If ever two were one, then surely we.

We are one if two were one.

2. I prize thy love more than whole mines of gold,
   Or all the riches that the East doth hold.

I prize your love over gold and riches.

3. Then while we live, in love let's so persevere,
   That when we live no more, we may live ever.

While we live, let's persevere in love. That we may live when we die

"To My Dear and Loving Husband" by Anne Bradstreet
Vocabulary Builder

The Suffix *-fold*

A. DIRECTIONS: *The suffix -fold, which means "a specific number of times or ways," can be used to form both adjectives and adverbs. On the lines provided, write a sentence using each word below as the part of speech indicated.*

1. tenfold (use as an adverb) _I'll pay back everyone, tenfold_
   _____

2. multifold (use as an adjective) _He was one multifold man._
   _____

Using the Word List

> manifold   persevere   quench   recompense

B. DIRECTIONS: *On the line provided, write the word from the Word List that best completes each sentence.*

1. I expected no _recompense_ from my friend for the help I gave him.
2. There are _manifold_ reasons for studying the literature of the Puritans.
3. I will not quit; I will _persevere_ in my efforts to learn about the Puritans.
4. Anne Bradstreet said that nothing could _quench_ her love for her husband.

C. DIRECTIONS: *On the line, write the letter of the pair of words that expresses a relationship most like the relationship of the words in capital letters.*

_C_ 1. RECOMPENSE : PAYMENT ::
    A. spend : providence
    B. contest : win
    C. contract : agreement
    D. replacement : trade

_B_ 2. ONCE : MANIFOLD ::
    A. usually : abnormally
    B. uniform : varied
    C. briskly : quickly
    D. hundredfold : tenfold

_A_ 3. PERSEVERE : PROCRASTINATE ::
    A. try : attempt
    B. attempt: fail
    C. continue : dawdle
    D. dawdle : delay

_C_ 4. QUENCH : EXTINGUISH
    A. flood : drought
    B. burn : wood
    C. rejoice : celebrate
    D. buy : sell

"To My Dear and Loving Husband" by Anne Bradstreet

Integrated Language Skills: Support for Writing: Interpretive Essay

Before you write your **interpretive essay** on "To My Dear and Loving Husband," gather information from the poem in the graphic organizer below.

Elements from "To My Dear and Loving Husband"	
Images of material wealth	_____ _____ _____ _____
Value of her love for her husband	_____ _____ _____ _____
Comparisons of material wealth with wealth of love	_____ _____ _____ _____
Comparisons of wealth on earth with wealth of immortality	_____ _____ _____ _____

On a separate page, write an interpretive essay to analyze Anne Bradstreet's poem in terms of the images and comparisons you have gathered on your chart. Then, revise your essay to be sure the connection between material wealth and the wealth of her husband's love and the love of God is clear.

Name _Ian Wilson_   Date _3/19/19_

"Huswifery" by Edward Taylor
Literary Analysis: Conceit (Extended Metaphor)

A metaphor is a form of figurative language. It compares two unlike things, people, or objects, but does not use the words like or as, which are used in similes. Compare the two examples below.

My grief made my heart like a stone.   **My grief made my heart a stone.**

The second example is a metaphor, a comparison of a heart with a stone, but without using the words *like* or *as*. A **conceit** is an **extended metaphor,** a comparison developed throughout several lines or an entire poem. Edward Taylor's poem is an extended metaphor as he asks God to make him into a spinning wheel and a loom so that he can clothe himself in God's glory.

DIRECTIONS: *Read each passage from "Huswifery" and answer the questions.*

Make me, O Lord, Thy spinning wheel complete.
Thy holy word my distaff make for me.
Make mine affections they swift flyers neat
And make my soul Thy holy spoole to be.
My conversation make to be Thy reel
And reel the yarn thereon spun of Thy wheel.

1. Which complete device does the poet compare himself to in his metaphor in this stanza?
   A spinning wheel

2. Which part of the poet himself does he ask God to make into the spoole [spool] of the spinning wheel?
   His soul, the essence of being

3. As the poet develops his extended metaphor, he mostly asks God to make parts of the poet into a loom. Which part of the wheel does he compare with God's word in the metaphor?
   A distaff

Make me Thy loom then, knit therein this twine;
And make Thy holy spirit, Lord, wind quills;
Then weaver the web Thyself. The yarn is fine,
Thine ordinances make my fulling mills.
Then dye the same in heavenly colors choice.
All pinked with varnished flowers of paradise.

4. To what major device does the poet compare himself in this stanza?
   The reel

5. In Stanza 3, when the poet asks God to clothe all parts of him in the new apparel, to what does he compare the apparel he will be wearing?
   The Robes of glory

Name **Ian Wilson**   Date **3/20/19**

Reading Strategy: Adjust Reading Rate

The poem "Huswifery" is a complex poem. Its subject and style are difficult. It is full of unfamiliar words that are defined at the bottom of the page, so that the reader has to stop and look away from the poem momentarily. The poem's ideas are put in a specific order that must be followed closely if a reader is to understand the full message. For these reasons, it is reasonable to read such a poem slowly, and more than once, rather than skimming through it as if it were a popular ballad.

DIRECTIONS: *Read each line or passage from the poem and answer the questions.*

> Make me, O Lord, Thy spinning wheel complete.
> Thy holy word my distaff make for me.

1. Is the poet asking the Lord to make a spinning wheel for the poet to use? Or is he asking the Lord to make the poet himself into a spinning wheel? How can you be sure?

   He's using metaphor. Translating a spinning wheel's actions and making into how we act.

> Thine ordinances* make my fulling mills*.
> They dye the same in heavenly colors choice.
> All pinked* with varnished flowers of paradise.

2. This passage has three unfamiliar terms in it. How would you read this part and what would you do besides read the lines?

   Read it with close attention and pay attention to how you can rephrase?

> Make mine affections Thy swift flyers neat
> Then weave the web Thyself. The yarn is fine.

3. Which of the examples above might you read faster than the other? Why?

   The first one, because it has no period.

Name _Ian Wilson_   Date _3/20/19_

"**Huswifery**" by Edward Taylor
Vocabulary Builder

Using the Word List

    affections   apparel   judgment   ordinances

A. DIRECTIONS: *Decide whether each statement below is true or false. Circle T or F, and then explain your answer.*

1. If you have strong <u>affections</u>, you rarely show what you are feeling.
   T / F _False_

2. Marriage is one of the <u>ordinances</u> in many religions.
   T / F _True_

3. A student who does his or her homework before going to the movies shows good <u>judgment</u>.
   T / F _True_

4. People going on a winter hike should wear lightweight <u>apparel</u>.
   T / F _False_

B. DIRECTIONS: *On the line provided, write the word from the Word List that best completes each sentence. Use each word only once.*

1. The poet wished all of his _apparel_ to be clothed in God's glory.

2. The _affections_ she wore to the informal dance was much too formal.

3. The dog showed good _judgement_ when she backed away from the hissing cat.

4. The ceremony followed all the _ordinances_ of the church in which it was performed.

C. *Write sentences using the words indicated.*

1. apparel/judgment _She showed good judgement not wearing a_ _polyester apparel. The building had a fire!_

2. affections/judgment _I have judgement towards your affections._

_____

Name **Ian Wilson**   Date **3/22/19**

"Huswifery" by Edward Taylor
Integrated Language Skills: Support for Writing

To gather information for a **reflective essay,** first reread Edward Taylor's "Huswifery." Notice how the poet uses spinning and weaving as metaphors for the larger meaning of creating a work to glorify God. Think of something you do regularly to which you could attach another meaning. For example, in helping to clean up a park, you make a statement about the environment's value. In helping babysit a younger sibling, you make a statement about protecting younger people. Enter your information into the chart below.

Reflective Essay on _Video Editing_

Everyday activity	Video Editing
Details about how activity is completed	You cut and delete the unwanted parts of the video and modify or add in things that lure in your audience
Larger meaning of activity	We can relate it to show God makes us new.
How activity is symbolic of larger meaning	God takes what our lives once were, cuts out the bad parts, and makes us look better than what we were.

On a separate page, write a first draft of your reflective essay using the information from your chart. Then, revise your essay to be sure the connection between the everyday activity and the larger meaning is clear.

Name _____   Date _____

from **Sinners in the Hands of an Angry God** by Jonathan Edwards
Literary Analysis: Sermon (Persuasive Oratory)

A sermon is a speech given from a pulpit in a house of worship usually as part of a religious service. Jonathan Edwards delivered many sermons that dealt with "fire and brimstone," or the torments of hell. Although he delivered his words in a level and calm voice, his message often caused listeners to shriek with fright. In his sermons, Edwards used **persuasive oratory,** or language that would convince listeners of the truth of what he was saying.

DIRECTIONS: *Two forms of persuasive oratory are logical appeals and emotional appeals. Logical appeals speak to the listener's sense of reason, and are based on facts and evidence. Emotional appeals speak to the listener's feelings about a subject, and often use loaded words that convey strong positive or negative connotations. Read the following excerpts from* Sinners in the Hands of an Angry God *and answer the questions.*

The God that holds you over the pit of Hell, much as one holds a spider, or some loathsome insect over the fire, abhors you, and is dreadfully provoked: his wrath towards you burns like fire; he looks upon you as worthy of nothing else, but to be cast into the fire; he is of purer eyes than to bear to have you in his sight; you are ten thousand times more abominable in our eyes, than the most hateful venomous serpent is in ours . . .

1. Which form of persuasive oratory does Edwards use in this passage, logical or emotional?

   _____

2. To which emotion or emotions in his listeners does he appeal? _____

   _____

3. List some loaded words or phrases that Edwards uses to persuade his listeners of God's wrath and their unworthiness?

   _____

   _____

And now you have an extraordinary opportunity, a day wherein Christ has thrown the door of mercy wide open, and stands in calling and crying with a loud voice to poor sinners; a day wherein many are flocking to him, and pressing into the kingdom of God. Many are daily coming from the east, west, north and south;. . .

4. What behavior is Edwards trying to persuade his listeners to undertake in this passage?

   _____

5. To which emotions is he appealing in his listeners? _____

   _____

6. Which loaded words or phrases help to give this passage its persuasive character?

   _____

   _____

from **Sinners in the Hands of an Angry God** by Jonathan Edwards
Reading Strategy: Use Context Clues

When you come across an unfamiliar word in your reading, you can often determine its meaning from its **context**—the words, phrases, and sentences that surround it. For example, notice how the context provides clues to the meaning of *avail* in the sentence that follows:

But indeed these things are nothing; if God should withdraw his hand, they would *avail* no more to keep you from falling than the thin air to hold up a person that is suspended in it.

Since we know that "these things are nothing" and that "they would avail no more" than "thin air" to keep a person from falling, we can figure out that *avail* must mean "help."

DIRECTIONS: *As you read these sentences from* Sinners in the Hands of an Angry God, *use context clues to determine the meaning of each italicized word. Write your definition on the lines provided and explain how you used context clues to help determine the word's meaning.*

1. It is only the power and mere pleasure of God that holds you up. You are probably not *sensible* of this; you find you are kept out of Hell, but do not see the hand of God in it.

   _____

   _____

2. It is a great furnace of wrath, a wide and bottomless pit, full of the fire of wrath, that you are held over in the hand of that God, whose wrath is provoked and *incensed* as much against you, as against many of the damned in Hell.

   _____

   _____

3. You hang by a slender thread, with the flames of divine wrath flashing about it, and ready every moment to *singe* it, and burn it asunder.

   _____

   _____

4. He will not *forbear* the executions of his wrath, or in the least lighten his hand: there shall be no moderation or mercy.

   _____

   _____

5. There will be no end to this exquisite horrible misery. When you look forward, you shall see a long forever, a *boundless* duration before you, which will swallow up your thoughts and amaze your soul.

   _____

   _____

from **Sinners in the Hands of an Angry God** by Jonathan Edwards
Vocabulary Builder

The Latin Prefix *omni-*

A. DIRECTIONS: *The prefix* omni- *means "all" or "everywhere." Bearing that in mind, circle the letter of the best answer to the following questions.*

1. If laughter is *omnipresent*, where is it found?
   A. here
   B. there
   C. everywhere
   D. nowhere

2. Giraffes are *herbivorous*, eating only plants; cats are *carnivorous*, eating only meat. If monkeys are *omnivorous*, what do you think they eat?
   A. only plants
   B. only meat
   C. only bananas
   D. plants and meat

3. *Science* is from a root meaning "to know." What kind of narrator is an *omniscient* narrator?
   A. a character in the story who knows only his or her own thoughts
   B. someone outside the story who knows all the characters' thoughts
   C. someone outside the story who knows just one character's thoughts
   D. someone outside the story who knows no characters' thoughts

Using the Word List

constitution	induce	mediator	omnipotent	prudence

B. DIRECTIONS: *On the line, write the letter of the definition next to the word it defines.*

___ 1. prudence   A. all-powerful
___ 2. induce   B. physical makeup
___ 3. constitution   C. influence; persuade
___ 4. mediator   D. good judgment
___ 5. omnipotent   E. one who settles a dispute

C. DIRECTIONS: *For each pair of sentences, circle the letter of the sentence in which the italicized word is used correctly.*

1. A. The workers and management called in a *mediator* to help settle the strike.

   B. Our teacher commissioned a *mediator* to draw a painting of our class.

2. A. I wanted to *induce* my weight, so I stopped eating foods with sugar.

   B. Nothing could *induce* our dog to get into the tub for his bath.

3. A. The hiker showed extreme *prudence* when he tried to leap over the crevasse.

   B. Her *prudence* told Mari that she should stay out of the quarrel between her brothers.

from Sinners in the Hands of an Angry God by Jonathan Edwards

Grammar and Style: Correlative Conjunctions

Correlative conjunctions are pairs of connecting words that link similar kinds of words and word groups and connect ideas. In this example, the italicized words show the relationship between the two actions in the sentence.

Edwards told his parishioners that *not only* would they burn in Hell, *but* Hell would last forever.

Other pairs of correlative conjunctions include the following:

Either . . . or   *neither . . . nor*   *not only . . . but also*   *whether . . . or*   *just as . . . so*

A. PRACTICE: *Circle each pair of correlative conjunctions in the sentences below.*

1. Edwards' listeners were told that neither their good works nor their holy life could protect them from Hell unless they accepted Jesus Christ.

2. The churchgoers understood that either they accepted Jesus Christ or they would burn in Hell for all eternity.

3. Edwards' sermon said that just as God hated the loathsome spider, so he also found the parishioners unworthy.

4. Whether the churchgoers screamed in fright or sat silent in their seats, they were all terrified.

5. Edwards' sermon told his listeners that not only did God hold them up from falling into Hell, but also could drop them at any time.

B. Writing Application: *For each item, create a logical sentence by adding a pair of correlative conjunctions from the list above.*

1. _____ did Edwards terrify his congregation, _____ he praised the power of God.

2. _____ Edwards offered little hope of salvation to his flock, _____ he condemned their unworthiness.

3. _____ they accepted Jesus Christ in their hearts, he said, _____ they would burn in Hell.

4. The parishioners heard that they were condemned _____ they led good lives _____ not.

5. Edwards said that _____ good works _____ personal holiness could save his listeners.

from Sinners in the Hands of an Angry God by Jonathan Edwards
Integrated Language Skills: Support for Writing: Evaluation

First, review the persuasive techniques of imagery and theme that Jonathan Edwards uses in his sermon. Then, prepare for writing an **evaluation** by entering important information about each in the graphic organizer below.

Evaluation of Jonathan Edwards's sermon

Examples of Imagery from Edwards's Sermon

_____

_____

_____

Effective or Ineffective? Why?

_____

_____

Examples of Main Themes from Edwards's Sermon

_____

_____

_____

Effective or Ineffective? Why?

_____

_____

On a separate page, use the information from the graphic organizer to write a first draft of your evaluation. Then, revise it to be sure you have included only information related to why Edwards's techniques were either effective or ineffective for his audience.

"Speech in the Virginia Convention" by Patrick Henry
"Speech in the Convention" by Benjamin Franklin
Literary Analysis: Persuasive Speeches

Effective **speeches** often make use of these techniques to emphasize key ideas and make them more memorable: (1) **repetition** of an idea in the same words; (2) **restatement** of a key idea in different words; (3) **parallelism,** or repeated use of the same grammatical structures; and (4) **rhetorical questions,** or questions with obvious answers that are asked not because answers are expected but to involve the audience emotionally in the speech.

DIRECTIONS: *Reread Patrick Henry's speech, and look for examples of each technique. Record the examples on the chart below.*

Restatement

Repetition

Parallelism

Rhetorical Questions

Name _____ Date _____

"Speech in the Virginia Convention" by Patrick Henry
"Speech in the Convention" by Benjamin Franklin
Reading Strategy: Evaluating Persuasive Appeals

Orators who wish to persuade their listeners of some action or belief cannot use the same tactics for all audiences. Some audiences are friendly to what the speaker has to say. Some audiences are hostile, and still others are composed of both friendly and hostile listeners. A good orator will speak to both groups.

Read this example from Benjamin Franklin's "Speech in the Convention."

I confess, that I do not entirely approve of this Constitution at present;

Franklin is hardly introducing his speech as if he were at a pep rally for the audience's team. He starts out by acknowledging that he himself does not entirely approve of the Constitution. He knows there are people in the audience who are hostile and he wants to communicate to them immediately that he shares some of their misgivings.

DIRECTIONS: *Read each passage from either Franklin's or Henry's speech below. Then decide whether the portion was written to persuade hostile audience members or friendly audience members. Explain your choice.*

(Patrick Henry) Should I keep back my opinions at such a time, though fear of giving offense, I should consider myself as guilty of treason toward my country, and of an act of disloyalty toward the Majesty of Heaven, which I revere above all earthly kings.

1. _____

_____

(Benjamin Franklin) Sir, to find this system [document] approaching so near to perfection as it does; and I think it will astonish our enemies, who are waiting with confidence to hear, that our councils are confounded . . . that our States are on the point of separation, only to meet hereafter for the purpose of cutting one another's throats.

2. _____

_____

(Patrick Henry) They [the British] tell us, sir, that we are weak – unable to cope with so formidable an adversary. But when shall we be stronger? Will it be the next week, or the next year? Will it be when we are totally disarmed, and when a British guard shall be stationed in every house?

3. _____

_____

"Speech in the Virginia Convention" by Patrick Henry
"Speech in the Convention" by Benjamin Franklin
Vocabulary Builder

Related Words

A. DIRECTIONS: *Many related words in the English language were taken from words in Latin and Greek. The Greek word* despotes *means "master." The Latin words* privus *and* legis *mean "individual" and "law." Answer the questions below using the following words:*

despot   despotism   privilege   privileged

1. Which word names a special right granted to only one person? _____

2. Which word names a system of rule by one master or tyrant? _____

3. Which word names an absolute ruler? _____

4. Which word describes someone having rights that others do not have? _____

Using the Word List

despotism   insidious   privileges   salutary   unanimity   vigilant

B. *Use a word from the Word List to answer each question about word origins.*

1. Which word comes from the Latin *unus*, meaning "one," and *animus*, meaning "mind," and means the state of having complete agreement? _____
_____

2. Which word comes from the Latin *vigilia*, meaning "watchful," and means being wide awake and on the alert? _____
_____

3. Which word comes from the Latin *salus*, meaning "health," and means "beneficial"? _____
_____

4. Which word comes from the Latin *privus* and *legis*, and means special rights for individuals? _____
_____

5. Which word comes from the Greek *despotes*, meaning "master," and means a system of tyranny? _____
_____

6. Which word comes from the Latin *insidere*, meaning "to lie in wait for," and means "deceitful" or "treacherous"? _____
_____

"**Speech in the Virginia Convention**" by Patrick Henry

"**Speech in the Convention**" by Benjamin Franklin

Integrated Language Skills: Support for Writing: Compare-and-Contrast Essay

As you prepare to write a **compare-and-contrast-essay** for the two speeches by Patrick Henry and Benjamin Franklin, enter information into the graphic organizer below. Be sure to provide at least one example from each speech to support each idea in the graphic organizer.

Speech in the Virginia Convention Patrick Henry	Examples from Henry Speech
When does Henry think one should compromise? When does Henry think one should lead?	

Speech in the Convention Benjamin Franklin	Examples from Franklin Speech
When does Franklin think one should compromise? When does Franklin think one should lead?	

On a separate page, write the first draft of your compare-and-contrast essay. When you revise your draft, clarify your points to be sure a reader understands how the speeches are alike and how they are different.

The Declaration of Independence by Thomas Jefferson
from **The Crisis, Number 1** by Thomas Paine
Literary Analysis: Persuasion

Persuasion is writing that attempts to convince readers to accept a specific viewpoint about an issue and to take a particular action. A good persuasive writer generally uses a combination of logical and emotional appeals, involving the audience both intellectually and emotionally in order to persuade them thoroughly.

A **logical appeal** uses a chain of reasoning to establish the validity of a proposed argument. Whether reasoning from particular examples to a general conclusion or from the general to the specific, writers use evidence to persuade their audiences intellectually. Notice how Paine moves from specific evidence to more general remarks in the chain of reasoning he presents here.

> Britain, with an army to enforce her tyranny, has declared that she has a right *(not only* to TAX) but "*to* BIND *us in* ALL CASES WHATSOEVER," and if being *bound in that manner,* is not slavery, then is there not such a thing as slavery upon earth.

An **emotional appeal** seeks to stir the reader's feelings. It relies not so much on reasoned arguments as on charged words and symbols that evoke sympathy or distaste. Among the strongest emotional appeals are anecdotes or examples that dramatize a situation. For instance, Paine's story of the Tory tavernkeeper and his nine-year-old child makes a strong appeal to the human desire to ensure a good future for one's children.

DIRECTIONS: *For each of these passages, clarify the type or types of appeal that Paine uses and the effect he hopes to have on the audience.*

1. Tyranny, like hell, is not easily conquered; yet we have this consolation with us, that the harder the conflict, the more glorious the triumph. What we obtain too cheap, we esteem too lightly; 'tis dearness only that gives everything its value.

   _____

   _____

   _____

2. I turn with the warm ardor of a friend to those who have nobly stood, and are yet determined to stand the matter out: I call not upon a few, but upon all; not on *this* state or *that* state, but on *every* state.

   _____

   _____

3. Not all the treasurers of the world, so far as I believe, could have induced me to support an offensive war, for I think it murder; but if a thief breaks into my house, burns and destroys my property, and kills or threatens to kill me, or those that are in it, and to "*bind me in all cases whatsoever,*" to his absolute will, am I to suffer it? . . . If we reason to the root of things we shall find no difference; neither can any just cause be assigned why we should punish in the one case and pardon in the other.

   _____

   _____

   _____

The Declaration of Independence by Thomas Jefferson
from The Crisis, Number 1 by Thomas Paine
Reading Strategy: Recognizing Charged Words

Charged words evoke an emotional response that can make writing more memorable. Charged words are especially useful in making persuasive writing more forceful. In *The Crisis*, for example, Thomas Paine uses many negatively charged words to attack the British monarchy:

I cannot see on what grounds the king of Britain can look up to heaven for help against us: a *common murderer*, a *highwayman*, or a *housebreaker*, has as good a pretense as he.

DIRECTIONS: *Underline the charged words in these sentences. Then, on the lines provided, briefly explain the emotional response each word evokes.*

1. "But when a long train of abuses and usurpations, pursuing invariably the same object, evinces a design to reduce them under absolute despotism. . . . "

_____

_____

_____

2. "He has refused his assent to laws the most wholesome and necessary for the public good."

_____

_____

_____

3. "In every stage of these oppressions we have petitioned for redress in the most humble terms."

_____

_____

_____

4. "Tyranny, like hell, is not easily conquered."

_____

_____

_____

5. "I turn with the warm ardor of a friend to those who had nobly stood, and are yet determined to stand the matter out."

_____

_____

_____

The Declaration of Independence by Thomas Jefferson
from **The Crisis, Number 1** by Thomas Paine
Vocabulary Builder

Using the Latin Word Parts *-rect-* and *-tude*

A. DIRECTIONS: *The Latin root* -rect- *means "straight" or "right." The Latin suffix* -tude *means "having or possessing _____." The word* rectitude *means "having moral rightness." Use the words below to answer the questions that follow*

erect   fortitude   rectify   solitude

1. Which word comes from *-rect-*, meaning "right" and the suffix *-ify*, meaning "to make or cause" and means to set right"? _____

2. Which word comes from the root *-fort-*, meaning "strength," and the suffix *-tude*, and meaning courage"? _____

3. Which word comes from the prefix *-e*, meaning "up," and the word part *-rect-*, meaning "upright"? _____

4. Which word comes from the Latin *solus*, meaning "alone," and the suffix *-tude* meaning "the state of being alone"? _____

Using the Word List

acquiesce   assent   candid   harass
prudent   rectitude   redress   tyranny

B. DIRECTIONS: *Answer each of the questions below about the italicized words from the Word List.*

1. If you are *candid* with someone, are you <u>honest</u> or <u>dishonest</u>? _____

2. If you *acquiesce* to someone's request, do you say <u>yes</u> or <u>no</u>? _____

3. Is a person who is *prudent* someone who takes <u>risks</u> or someone who is <u>cautious</u>? _____

4. Is a person seeking *redress* looking for new <u>clothing</u> or looking for <u>justice</u>? _____

5. If you move your head to *assent* to a question, do you <u>nod</u> or <u>shake</u> your head? _____

6. If a person acts with rectitude, does he or she act with <u>honor</u> or <u>dishonor</u>? _____

7. If you *harass* people, do you <u>welcome</u> them or <u>bother</u> them?_____

8. Is a *tyranny* a form of government run by a <u>parliament</u> or an <u>absolute ruler</u>? _____

The Declaration of Independence by Thomas Jefferson
from **The Crisis, Number 1** by Thomas Paine

Integrated Language Skills: Support for Writing

Jefferson and Paine wrote to persuade their listeners. Think of a situation in your school that you believe should be changed. To prepare for writing a **persuasive editorial** to your school newspaper that will identify the problem and present a solution, collect your ideas in the graphic organizer below.

Proposal to Change _____

Problem: Main Statement

Problem: Details (use negative language)

Solution: Main Statement

Solution: Details (use positive language)

On a separate page, draft a persuasive editorial to your school newspaper defining the problem and outlining your solution. When you revise your draft, be sure to use language with negative and positive connotations, just as Jefferson and Paine did.

"To His Excellency, General Washington"
by Phillis Wheatley

Literary Analysis: Heroic Couplets and Archetypal References

Heroic couplets are an important element of poetry. A heroic couplet is a rhyming pair of lines using iambic pentameter—five pairs of syllables, the first one unstressed and the second one stressed. An example from "To His Excellency, General Washington," is this pair of lines:

"Celestial choir! Enthron'd in realms of light,

Columbia's scenes of glorious toils I write."

Just as heroic couplets associate Wheatley's poem with greatness, so too do the many references to archetypal figures from classical mythology. Wheatley even creates a new goddess, Columbia, to represent America.

A. DIRECTIONS: *On the lines after each quotation from "To His Excellency, General Washington," explain the reference to a god or goddess and the characteristics or qualities it stresses.*

1. "See mother earth her offspring's fate bemoan."

   _____

   _____

   _____

   _____

2. "Columbia's scenes of glorious toils I write."

   _____

   _____

   _____

   _____

3. "As when Eolus heaven's fair face deforms."

   _____

   _____

   _____

   _____

B. DIRECTIONS: *Read the heroic couplet from "To His Excellency, General Washington" below. Then, rewrite it on the lines and insert the markings above the syllables for stressed and unstressed syllables.*

A crown, a mansion, and a throne that shine,
With gold unfading, WASHINGTON! be thine.

_____

_____

"To His Excellency, General Washington"
by Phillis Wheatley

Reading Strategy: Reread to Clarify Meaning

All writing is easier to understand if you reread difficult passages, and look up the definitions of unfamiliar words. In addition, poetry is often clearer if you rearrange the words into more familiar grammatical structures. For example, instead of using regular subject-verb order, poetry often inverts the order by placing the subject after the verb. Consider this line: *Columbia's scenes of glorious toils I write.* Rearranging the words into a more usual order can help you understand the line's meaning: *I write of Columbia's scenes of glorious struggles.*

A. DIRECTIONS: *Clarify the meaning of these lines from "To His Excellency, General Washington" by rewriting them in a more normal word order. Also, substitute a simpler or more modern word or phrase for each word in italics. Use the context or a dictionary to help you define the italicized words.*

1. While freedom's cause her anxious breast *alarms*

   _____

2. See mother earth her *offspring's* fate *bemoan,*

   _____

3. Where high *unfurl'd* the *ensign* waves in air

   _____

4. Shall I to Washington their praise *recite?*

   _____

5. Hear every tongue thy *guardian* aid *implore!*

   _____

6. When *Gallic* powers *Columbia's* fury found;

   _____

7. While *round increase* the rising hills of dead.

   _____

8. And through the air their *mingled* music floats.

   _____

"To His Excellency, General Washington"
by Phillis Wheatley
Vocabulary Builder

Using the Word List

implore   lament   martial   pensive   propitious   tempest

A. DIRECTIONS: *After each line from the poem, two possible definitions are given in parentheses for the word in italics. Underline the correct definition.*

1. Muse! Bow *propitious* while my pen relates. (rude, favorable)

2. Enwrapp'd in *tempest* and a night of storms; (calm, disturbance)

3. The grace and glory of thy *martial* band. (military, dance)

4. Hear every tongue thy guardian aid *implore*! (reject, beg)

5. *Lament* thy thirst of boundless power too late. (celebrate, mourn)

6. Anon Britannia droops the *pensive* head. (lighthearted, thoughtful

B. DIRECTIONS: *Answer each question below based on the meaning of the italicized word.*

1. Are you more likely to be *pensive* before going to a picnic or before taking a test?

   _____

2. Would you *lament* a loss by your school team or an award for your science project?

   _____

3. Which would you call a *tempest*, a hurricane or a rainstorm?

   _____

4. Which kind of clothing is *martial*, a doctor's scrubs or a general's uniform?

   _____

5. What kind of weather is *propitious* for skiing, a rainstorm or a snowstorm?

   _____

6. Would you *implore* a dentist for a filling or a friend to borrow a DVD?

   _____

Name _____ Date _____

"To His Excellency, General Washington"
by Phillis Wheatley

Integrated Language Skills: Support for Writing: Position Statement

To organize your information for the **position statement** you are to write, gather information about Washington from the poem. Fill in each box below with quotes and details from the poem. Also, add your own brief opinion about the question in each box.

What are Washington's characteristics as a general?

What are Washington's characteristics as a potential political leader?

Should Phillis Wheatley's poem be used in the presidential campaign of George Washington?

What are Phillis Wheatley's skills as a poet?

How well does Wheatley's poem capture the image of Washington that would be used in the campaign?

Now, use your organizer notes to write a position statement to argue whether or not you think Phillis Wheatley's poem should be used in the campaign to elect George Washington the first president of the United States.

Benjamin Franklin: Author in Depth

Read some more about Benjamin Franklin's "firsts." Then, choose the aphorism under each paragraph that best matches the "first" described. Write the letter of the correct aphorism on the line.

Scurvy, a disease caused by the lack of vitamin C, was common in Franklin's time. He recommended eating citrus and other fruits to keep healthy gums and skin, even before vitamin C was discovered.

____ 1. A. Hunger is the best pickle.

B. An apple a day keeps the doctor away.

C. The rotten apple spoils his companions.

In the days before electric lighting, people could work well only during the daylight hours. Franklin developed the idea of daylight savings time as a way to give people more working hours during the long-sunlit days of summer.

____ 2. A. If your head is wax, don't walk in the sun.

B. There will be sleeping enough in the grave.

C. Dost thou love life? Then do not squander time; for that's the stuff life is made of.

As a statesman, Franklin traveled across the Atlantic often. He learned about the workings of ships. He began to suggest that Americans use the Chinese model of dividing ships' underwater portions into watertight compartments. Thus, a leak in one compartment would not cause the sinking of the whole ship. This was not one of Franklin's inventions, but a suggestion as a result of his intense study.

____ 3. A. God helps those who help themselves.

B. Great estates may venture more, but little boats should keep near shore.

C. A small leak will sink a great ship.

Ben invented the Franklin stove, which allowed people to heat their homes more safely than burning wood in a fireplace. His stove was made of iron and used less wood. Franklin also set up the first fire-fighting company as well as the first fire insurance company to protect people against losses due to fires.

____ 4. A. An ounce of prevention is worth a pound of cure.

B. Tis easier to build two chimneys than to keep one in fuel.

C. When the well's dry, they know the worth of water.

Despite his impressive list of inventions, and despite his many aphorisms about making money, Franklin never patented his inventions. He believed people should serve the community.

____ 5. A. A slip of the foot you may soon recover, but a slip of the tongue you may never get over.

B. The noblest question in the world is, what good may I do in it?

C. Genius without education is like silver in the mine.

from **The Autobiography** and *from* **Poor Richard's Almanack** by Benjamin Franklin
Literary Analysis: Autobiography

An **autobiography** is a person's written account of his or her own life. Though by its nature subjective, it nevertheless offers valuable insight into the author's personality, thoughts, and feelings.

DIRECTIONS: *Read these passages from* The Autobiography. *Then, on the lines provided, sum up what they reveal about Franklin's attitudes and personality.*

1. "As I knew, or thought I knew, what was right or wrong, I did not see why I might not always do the one and avoid the other."

   _____

   _____

2. "While my care was employed in guarding against one fault, I was often surprised by another."

   _____

   _____

3. "I determined to give a week's strict attention to each of the virtues successively."

   _____

   _____

4. "I was surprised to find myself so much fuller of faults than I imagined."

   _____

   _____

5. "The man came every now and then from the wheel to see how the work went on, and at length would take his ax as it was, without further grinding. 'No,' said the smith, 'turn on, turn on; we shall have it bright by and by; as yet, it is only speckled.' 'Yes,' said the man, 'but I think I like a speckled ax best.'"

   _____

   _____

6. ". . . a perfect character might be attended with the inconvenience of being envied and hated; and that a benevolent man should allow a few faults in himself, to keep his friends in countenance."

   _____

   _____

from The Autobiography and **from Poor Richard's Almanack** by Benjamin Franklin
Literary Analysis: Aphorisms

The **aphorisms**—short sayings with a message—that Franklin wrote for *Poor Richard's Almanack* also tell readers about the writer's personality.

DIRECTIONS: *Read these aphorisms from* Poor Richard's Almanack. *Then, on the lines provided, sum up what each means.*

1. Have you something to do tomorrow, do it today.

   _____

2. Write injuries in dust, benefits in marble.

   _____

3. The doors of wisdom are never shut.

   _____

4. Three may keep a secret if two of them are dead.

   _____

5. Well done is better than well said.

   _____

6. No gains without pains.

   _____

7. A true friend is the best possession.

   _____

8. A slip of the foot you may soon recover, but a slip of the tongue you may never get over.

   _____

Name _____   Date _____

from **The Autobiography** and *from* **Poor Richard's Almanack** by Benjamin Franklin
Reading Strategy: Cause-and-Effect Relationships

A good way to understand a writer's selection is to look for **cause-and-effect relationships**. What event causes another event to happen? What emotion by the writer leads to what behavior? Read the following examples from Franklin's *The Autobiography*:

> As I knew, or thought I knew, what was right and wrong, I did not see why I might not always do the one and avoid the other.

The cause-and-effect relationship here can be summed up easily: **CAUSE: Know what's right; EFFECT: Do what's right.**

DIRECTIONS: Read each passage below, from either *The Autobiograpy* or *Poor Richard's Almanack*, and sum up the cause-and-effect relationship for each by using CAUSE: and EFFECT: and short statements.

> I proposed to myself, for the sake of clearness, to use rather more names [virtues], with fewer ideas annexed to each, than a few names [virtues] with more ideas; . . .

1. CAUSE: _____

   EFFECT: _____

> This article [Order], therefore, cost me so much painful attention, . . . and [I] had such frequent relapses, that I was almost ready to give up the attempt, . . .

2. CAUSE: _____

   EFFECT: _____

> . . . that a perfect character might be attended with the inconvenience of being envied and hated [by one's friends] . . .

3. CAUSE: _____

   EFFECT: _____

> No gains without pains.

4. CAUSE: _____

   EFFECT: _____

> Haste makes waste.

5. CAUSE: _____

   EFFECT: _____

from The Autobiography and **from Poor Richard's Almanack** by Benjamin Franklin
Vocabulary Builder

Using the Root -vigil-

A. DIRECTIONS: *The word root -vigil- can mean "remaining awake to watch or observe." The suffix -ance means "the state of"; -ant means "being in the state of." The prefix* hyper- *means "excessively; overly; too." Write a probable definition for each term.*

1. vigilant _____

2. hypervigilance _____

Using the Word List

   arduous   avarice   incorrigible   posterity   squander   vigilance

B. DIRECTIONS: *Match each word on the left with its definition on the right. Write the letter of each definition in the blank next to the word it defines.*

___ 1. arduous   A. alertness

___ 2. avarice   B. difficult

___ 3. posterity   C. waste

___ 4. squander   D. descendants

___ 5. vigilance   E. greed

___ 6. incorrigible   F. badly behaved

C. DIRECTIONS: *Circle the letter of the word or phrase that best defines the italicized word in each sentence.*

1. The men were so *incorrigible* they had to be released from the team.
   A. unskilled   B. poorly behaved   C. insincere   D. unhappy

2. Our baby sitter cared for her charges with *vigilance*.
   A. candy   B. stories   C. watchfulness   D. boredom

3. The famous author left her fortune to her *posterity*.
   A. descendants   B. church   C. publisher   D. charities

from **The Autobiography and** *from* **Poor Richard's Almanack** by Benjamin Franklin
Grammar and Style: Subordinating Conjunctions

A **subordinating conjunction** introduces a dependent clause and joins it to the independent or main clause in a sentence. A dependent clause has a subject and a verb, but it needs the independent clause to make sense. See this example from Franklin's *The Autobiography*:

> *As* I knew, . . . what was right and wrong, I did not see why I might not always do the one and avoid the others.

The subordinating conjunction above is *as*. It introduces the dependent clause "As I knew what was right and wrong," which, when connected with the independent clause, becomes a complete sentence.

Common subordinating conjunctions are *as, if, because, since, after, until,* and *before.*

DIRECTIONS: *Read each of the sentences below. Then, circle the subordinating conjunction, and write the dependent clause on the line.*

1. Before he started his project, Franklin made a list of virtues.

   _____

2. Franklin almost gave up his project because he had so much trouble with the virtue of Order.

   _____

3. As Franklin discovered a fault in himself, he marked it in his book.

   _____

4. Franklin hoped to work on his habits until he had achieved perfection.

   _____

5. Since his scraping put holes in his books, he had to replace them regularly.

   _____

6. Which of these aphorisms from *Poor Richard's Almanack* contains a subordinating conjunction? Write the aphorism on the line, and circle the subordinating conjunction.

   A true friend is the best possession.

   If your head is wax, don't walk in the sun.

   A small leak will sink a great ship.

   _____

Name _____   Date _____

from **The Autobiography** and *from* **Poor Richard's Almanack** by Benjamin Franklin
Integrated Language Skills: Support for Writing:
Analytical Cause-and-Effect Essay

To prepare to write your **analytical cause-and-effect essay**, gather information in the graphic organizer below. First, choose a subject for your essay. Your essay may be humorous, serious, persuasive, or informative. The subject can be an event in which you were involved, a cause about which you feel strongly, or any other subject. Next, list at least three causes and effects that you will use in your essay. Remember, one cause might have more than one effect. For example, if you break your leg on a hike, this cause might lead to these effects: a trip to the hospital, having your leg splinted, staying in bed for a week, and so forth. Also, several causes might lead to one effect.

CAUSE-and-EFFECT ESSAY

Subject of Essay	First cause-and-effect relationship
Second cause-and-effect relationship	**Third cause-and-effect relationship**

On a separate page, use the information in your graphic organizer to write a draft of your cause-and-effect essay. When you revise your draft, be sure to use transition words to make you cause-and-effect relationships clear.

Name _____   Date _____

from The Autobiography by Benjamin Franklin and **"Straw Into Gold"** by Sandra Cisneros
Literary Analysis: Comparing Autobiographies

Autobiographies tell us about the life and times of the writer—his or her character, what he or she values, what his or her goals are, and so forth. Though the autobiographical selections by Benjamin Franklin and Sandra Cisneros are set in very different times and see life through the eyes of vastly different people, they have some similarities. Both talk about wanting to do something and do it well, and both relate the results of their attempts.

DIRECTIONS: *Read each pair of passages below, from the selections by Franklin and Cisneros. On the lines, use brief phrases to tell how each pair of selections are similar and how they are different. Be sure to consider the style of writing when you compare and contrast.*

Benjamin Franklin – *The Autobiography*

But, on the whole, though I never arrived at the perfection I had been so ambitious of obtaining, but fell far short of it, yet I was, by the endeavor, a better and a happier man than I otherwise should have been if I had not attempted it;

Sandra Cisneros – "Straw into Gold"

I've managed to do a lot of things in my life I didn't think I was capable of and which many others didn't think me capable of either. . . . Sitting at my favorite people-watching spot, the snaky Woolworth's counter across the street from the Alamo, I can't think of anything else I'd rather be than a writer

1. Similar _____

_____

Different_____

_____

Benjamin Franklin–*The Autobiography*

I concluded, at length, that the mere speculative conviction that it was our interest to be completely virtuous was not sufficient to prevent our slipping; and that the contrary habits must be broken, and good ones acquired and established, before we can have any dependence on a steady, uniform rectitude of conduct. For this purpose I therefore contrived the following method.

Sandra Cisneros–"Straw into Gold"

I had the same sick feeling when I was required to write my critical essay for my MFA exam – the only piece of noncreative writing necessary in order to get my graduate degree. How was I to start? There were rules involved here, unlike writing a poem or story, which I did intuitively. There was a step-by-step process needed and I had better know it.

2. Similar _____

_____

Different _____

_____

Comparing Literary Works

from **The Autobiography** by Benjamin Franklin and **"Straw Into Gold"** by Sandra Cisneros

Vocabulary Builder

Using the Word List

capable   flourished   intuitively   nostalgia   taboo

A. DIRECTIONS: *Answer each question below about the italicized word from the Word List.*

1. If your personality tends toward *nostalgia*, do you like listening to old music or listening only to new music?

   _____

2. If a specific behavior is *taboo*, is it encouraged or forbidden? _____

   _____

3. If someone chooses an answer on a math test *intuitively*, does this mean he or she works out the answer, or quickly sees it in his or her head?

   _____

4. If your aunt's garden *flourished* last summer, did it grow well or dry up in the drought?

   _____

5. If you want to hire a *capable* employee, do you want someone who is high-priced, or efficient?

   _____

B. DIRECTIONS: *Choose the word that is the synonym for each word in capital letters. Write the letter of your choice in the blank.*

____ 1. TABOO:
   A. banned   **B.** permitted   **C.** marked

____ 2. NOSTALGIA:
   A. nausea   **B.** longing   **C.** excitement

____ 3. CAPABLE:
   A. reasonable   **B.** demanding   **C.** competent

____ 4. FLOURISHED:
   A. granted   **B.** thrived   **C.** disappeared

____ 5. INTUITIVELY:
   A. responsibly   **B.** reasonably   **C.** instinctively

Integrated Language Skills: Support for Writing: Compare Literary Works

Before you begin to write your essay to compare Benjamin Franklin's *The Autobiography* with Sandra Cisneros's "Straw Into Gold," gather your information into the graphic organizer below. Look through the selections for main ideas and details to enter into the organizer.

A Comparison of the Selections of Benjamin Franklin and Sandra Cisneros

What challenges do Franklin and Cisneros describe?	**Franklin**
	Cisneros
To what extent does each writer succeed?	**Franklin**
	Cisneros
How does each writer define success?	**Franklin**
	Cisneros

Now, write a draft of your essay that compares the work of Benjamin Franklin and Sandra Cisneros. When you revise your draft, be sure you have made clear how the works are alike and how they are different.

Name _____ Date _____

DIRECTIONS: *Use the space provided to answer the questions.*

1. At the beginning of his commentary, what surprising fact does the writer single out about the Middle Passage? How does this fact enhance the importance of Olaudah Equiano's narrative?

   _____

   _____

   _____

   _____

2. According to Andrews, why must it have been difficult for Equiano to compose his narrative?

   _____

   _____

3. What is the first stop on Equiano's "virtual tour" of the slave ship? What details does Equiano use to describe the scene on the ship's deck?

   _____

   _____

   _____

   _____

4. According to Andrews, with whom do readers of Equiano's narrative sympathize? From whom are readers alienated?

   _____

   _____

5. What does Andrews claim is the significance of Equiano's peek through the ship's quadrant? Does this claim sound justified, in your opinion? Briefly explain your answer.

   _____

   _____

   _____

   _____

   _____

   _____

William L. Andrews
Listening and Viewing

Segment 1: Meet William L. Andrews
- How did William L. Andrews first become interested in studying African American history and culture?
- How does Andrews act as a middle man between today's readers and nineteenth-century writers?

_____

_____

_____

_____

Segment 2: William L. Andrews Introduces Olaudah Equiano
- Why is Olaudah Equiano an important historical figure?
- What are slave narratives, and why do you think they are important to society?

_____

_____

_____

_____

Segment 3: The Writing Process
- Why does William L. Andrews want to know what primary sources say about the people he writes about?
- How would this information be helpful when reading a slave narrative?

_____

_____

_____

_____

Segment 4: The Rewards of Writing
- How can reading slave narratives have relevance to your life?
- What can today's reader learn by reading autobiographies such as Equiano's?

_____

_____

_____

_____

from **The Interesting Narrative of the Life of Olaudah Equiano** by Olaudah Equiano
Literary Analysis: Slave Narratives

A **slave narrative** is an autobiographical account of life as a slave. Often written to expose the horrors of human bondage, it documents a slave's experiences from his or her own point of view. The selection from Equiano's narrative provides an especially grim description of the long voyage from Africa to Barbados that Equiano was forced to endure when he was only eleven years old.

In addition to being a form of autobiography, slave narratives had both a political and social aim—to expose the evils of slavery, in the service of ending it, and to document the horrors of the slave trade. The descriptions of what slaves endured inspired readers to action and were used by slaves, abolitionists, and others who fought slavery in their campaign to end this evil practice.

DIRECTIONS: *Read the excerpts from Equiano's account of his trip across the Atlantic. Then, answer the questions.*

> The closeness of the place [ship's hold], and the heat of the climate, added to the number in the ship, which was so crowded that each had scarcely room to turn himself, almost suffocated us. This produced [much] perspirations, so that the air soon became unfit for respiration, . . . and brought on a sickness among the slaves, of which many died – thus falling victims to the [shortsighted greed], as I may call it, of their purchasers. . . .The shrieks of the women, and the groans of the dying, rendered the whole a scene of horror almost inconceivable.

1. How might this passage have affected readers emotionally? _____

_____

_____

2. Why would the slavers have filled the ship's hold with so many more people than would comfortably fit into it? _____

_____

3. What does Olaudah mean by calling the deaths of slaves from sickness an example of [shortsighted greed] on the part of their purchasers?

_____

> We were not many days in the merchant's custody, before we were sold after their usual manner, which is this: On a signal given (as the beat of a drum), the buyers rush at once into the yard where the slaves are confined, and make choice of that parcel they like best. . .

4. Which words and phrase in this excerpt reinforce in the reader's mind that slavery was a form of business for slaveowners? _____

_____

5. As an abolitionist reading these excerpts, how would you have used them in your struggle against the crime of slavery? Focus on how you would make use of the descriptive language and the reality that selling human beings was a "business."

_____

_____

from The Interesting Narrative of the Life of Olaudah Equiano by Olaudah Equiano
Reading Strategy: Summarizing

When you **summarize** a passage or a selection, you state briefly in your own words its main ideas and most important details. A good way of checking your understanding of a text, summarizing is especially helpful when you read material written in another time period or in an unfamiliar style.

A. DIRECTIONS: *As you read or reread the selection by Olaudah Equiano, fill out this chart to help you keep track of the main ideas and key details you need to include in your summary. One sample entry has been done for you.*

Main Ideas	Details
The slaves on the ship were kept in close confinement under terrible conditions.	terrible stench; crowded; filthy; shrieks and groans; many perish; Equiano thinks death would be a relief

B. DIRECTIONS: *Use the chart you completed to write a summary of the selection on the lines provided.*

_____

_____

_____

_____

_____

_____

_____

_____

from **The Interesting Narrative of the Life of Olaudah Equiano** by Olaudah Equiano
Vocabulary Builder

Using the Root *-ject-*

A. DIRECTIONS: *The word root* -ject- *comes from the Latin* jacere, *meaning "to throw." In this selection, Equiano describes a dejected slave who throws himself into the ocean. Dejected means "discouraged" and comes from the prefix* de-, *meaning "down," and* -ject-, *meaning "throw." On the lines provided, write the word below that completes each sentence.*

ejected   inject   project   rejected

1. The speaker hoped he could _____ some common sense into the discussion.

2. After the altercation, the umpire _____ the pitcher from the game.

3. To be a good actor, you must learn to _____ your voice to be heard throughout the theater.

4. The writer's story was _____ by three magazines before someone accepted it.

Using the Word List

copious   heightened   inseparable   pacify   wretched

B. DIRECTIONS: *On the line, write the letter of the definition before the word it defines.*

___ 1. copious   A. calm
___ 2. wretched   B. abundant
___ 3. heightened   C. became higher or stronger
___ 4. inseparable   D. miserable
___ 5. pacify   E. constantly together

C. DIRECTIONS: *On the lines provided, write whether each pair of words are synonyms or antonyms.*

1. heightened/lessened _____

2. copious/scarce _____

3. pacify/subdue _____

4. wretched/dejected _____

5. inseparable/separated _____

6. dejected/joyful _____

from **The Interesting Narrative of the Life of Olaudah Equiano** by Olaudah Equiano

Integrated Language Skills: Support for Writing: Museum Placard

Before you write your **museum placard,** take notes in the graphic organizer below of the important things that happened to Olaudah Equiano and that he observed on his journey across the Atlantic. Put these events in the form of main ideas and details. How was the slave ship arranged? How did the slaves act? How did the crew act? What did Equiano learn (even positive events such as his learning how to use the ship's quadrant)?

Ideas and Details from *The Interesting Narrative of the Life Of Olaudah Equiano*

How was the slave ship arranged?

How did his fellow slaves act?

How did the slaver crew act?

What sights and sounds did Equiano experience?

What positive experiences did Equiano have?

Now, check reliable references to see how widespread Equiano's experiences were and to find more general information to include on your placard. Then draft your placard, keeping your audience in mind. Revise to make sure the information is accurate, clear, and concise.

"Letter to His Wife" by John Adams
"Letter to Her Daughter from the New White House" by Abigail Adams
Primary Source: Letters

Primary sources are central to an understanding of historical events. They are written in a specific period by people who are living then. They reveal the writers' attitudes and feelings, political and social background, and much more about people and places. These two letters, written by a husband to his wife and his wife to their daughter, reveal specific information about the lives of John and Abigail Adams as they moved into their new home in Washington.

DIRECTIONS: *Read each passage from the primary sources, and then answer the questions.*

from John Adams to his Wife, November 2, 1800

. . . The Building is in a State to be habitable. . . . I shall not attempt a description of it. You will form the best Idea of it from Inspection.

from Abigail Adams to her daughter, November 21, 1800

. . . You must keep all this [her criticism of the White House] to yourself, and, when asked how I like it, say that I write you the situation is beautiful, which is true. The house is made habitable, but there is not a single apartment finished. . . We have not the least fence, yard, or other convenience without [outside]. . . The principal stairs are not up, and will not be this winter.

1. What is the main difference between the two letters in terms of the description of the White House? Why do you think this difference exists? Keep in mind the role of women in this period of history.

   _____

   _____

2. Why do you think John Adams doesn't "attempt a description of [the house]"?

   _____

3. Both writers use the word *habitable* in their descriptions of the White House. Reread these portions. Given the meaning of habitable as "fit to live in" do these statements strike you as humorous, when taken together? Why or why not?

   _____

   _____

from Abigail Adams to her daughter

. . . bells [to signal from one room to another] are wholly wanting, not one single one through the whole house, . . . This is so great an inconvenience, that I know not what to do or how to do. . . But . . . if they will put me up some bells and let me have firewood enough to keep fires, I design to be pleased. I could content myself almost anywhere [for] three months; . . .

4. Abigail Adams moves from being sorely disappointed in the White House to telling her daughter that she can be content anywhere for a short time. What does this letter tell you about the character of the first First Lady of the United States?

   _____

   _____

"Letter to His Wife" by John Adams
"Letter to Her Daughter from the New White House" by Abigail Adams
Vocabulary Builder

Using the Word List

commissioners	contract	establishment	inspection	interspersed
procure	recourse	scale	unabated	

A. DIRECTIONS: *Determine which word choice is the synonym of each capitalized word below. Circle the letter of the correct choice.*

1. CONTRACT: A. introduction   B. agreement   C. signature   D. mortgage
2. INSPECTION: A. alignment   B. declaration   C. assessment   D. retraction
3. UNABATED: A. unpainted   B. undiminished C. immoral   D. unhappy
4. RECOURSE: A. answer   B. evil   C. influence   D. remedy
5. ESTABLISHMENT: A. enterprise   B. rooftop   C. insurance   D. conveyance
6. INTERSPERSED: A. unhinged   B. recalcitrant C. scattered   D. refurbished
7. COMMISSIONERS: A. waiters   B. officials   C. competitors D. convicts
8. PROCURE: A. parade   B. insist   C. rejoice   D. obtain
9. SCALE: A. size   B. weight   C. color   D. texture

B. DIRECTIONS: *Write the word from the Word List that best completes each sentence. You will not use all of the words*

1. The tulips were _____ with daffodils in the garden.

2. If the storm had remained _____ for much longer, we would have had to leave our home.

3. We could hardly imagine the _____ of the mountains that rose up ahead of us.

4. The spy's only _____ to being found out was to leap from the window and flee.

5. As soon as we sign the _____, work on the new park can begin.

6. This restaurant is the finest _____ on this short block.

Name _____ Date _____

Essential Questions Workshop—Unit 1

In their stories, poems, and nonfiction, the writers in Unit One express ideas that relate to the three Essential Questions framing this book. Review the literature in the unit. Then, for each Essential Question, choose an author and at least one passage from his or her writing that expresses a related idea. Use this chart to complete your work.

Essential Question	Author/Selection	Literary Passage
How does literature shape or reflect society?		
What is the relationship between place and literature?		
What makes American literature American?		

Unit 2 Introduction
Names and Terms to Know

A. DIRECTIONS: *Write a brief sentence explaining each of the following names and terms. You will find all of the information you need in the Unit 2 Introduction in your textbook.*

1. Louisiana Purchase: _____
   _____

2. Andrew Jackson: _____
   _____

3. Trail of Tears: _____
   _____

4. Henry Wadsworth Longfellow: _____
   _____

5. "barbaric yawp": _____
   _____

6. Seneca Falls Convention _____
   _____

B. DIRECTIONS: *Use the hints below to help you answer each question.*

1. How did new technology change life in the United States during the American Renaissance?
   [Hints: What types of new technology developed during the 19th century? How did this new technology improve American life?]

   _____

   _____

   _____

2. What was the relationship between geographic expansion and Indian removal?
   [Hints: What did easterners do as the United States acquired more western territory? How did this activity affect the Indian peoples? What was Indian removal?]

   _____

   _____

   _____

3. How did Transcendentalism figure in the American Renaissance?
   [Hints: Who were the Transcendentalists? What ideals did they express?]

   _____

   _____

   _____

Unit 2 Introduction

Essential Question 1: What is the relationship between place and literature?

A. DIRECTIONS: *Answer the questions about the first Essential Question in the Introduction about the relationship between place and literature. All the information you need is in the Unit 2 Introduction in your textbook.*

1. *Discoveries Through Exploration*

    a. As they moved westward, Americans were impressed with _____
_____

    b. What were some examples of natural wonders found by American settlers?
_____

2. *Attitudes Toward the Land*

    a. What opportunities did American settlers find as they moved to new parts of the country? _____
_____

    b. What nonmaterial feelings did the American landscape inspire? _____
_____

3. *Attitudes Toward Nature Expressed in the Literature*

    a. Describe the settings for the "new American mythology." _____
_____

    b. American masters of literature during this period included _____
_____

    c. Give examples of other artists who reflected Americans' appreciation of nature.
_____

B. DIRECTIONS: *Answer the questions that include the Essential Question Vocabulary words.*

    1. Name a person who inspires you with *awe.* _____
_____

    2. What kind of language would you expect to hear from someone with a sense of *grandeur*?
_____

    3. Would a company's board be pleased to learn that there had been an *expansion* in the market for their product? Explain.
_____

Unit 2 Introduction

Essential Question 2: How does literature shape or reflect society?

A. DIRECTIONS: *On the lines provided, answer the questions about the second Essential Question in the Introduction about the relationship between the writer and society. All the information you need is in the Unit 2 Introduction in your textbook.*

1. *Social and Political Forces of the Period*

   a. Give examples of new technology in 19th-century America. _____
   _____

   b. The effects of the new technology were _____
   _____

   c. What is an example of the growth of democracy during this time? _____
   _____

   d. The spread of democracy did not include these groups: _____
   e. Slavery divided the country because _____
   _____

2. *What Americans Read*

   a. Popular writings in this period included _____
   _____

   b. What two British writers were extremely popular during this time?
   _____

3. *What American Writers Wanted to Achieve*

   a. Describe the "social vision" expressed by American writers of this period. _____
   _____

   b. Which American writers expressed a "romantic vision"? _____
   _____

   c. The "transcendental vision" argued that _____
   _____

B. DIRECTIONS: *Complete the sentence stems based on the Essential Question Vocabulary words.*

1. A *personal* narrative is one that reveals _____.
2. The vacation was *fantastic* because _____.
3. When someone is *self-reliant*, he or she handles problems _____.

Unit 2 Introduction

Essential Question 3: What makes American literature American?

A. DIRECTIONS: *On the lines provided, answer the questions about the third Essential Question in the Introduction about what makes American literature American. All the information you need is in the Unit 2 Introduction in your textbook.*

1. *American Styles of Speaking and Writing*

   a. American English was characterized by _____
   _____

   b. Give examples of colloquial expressions. _____
   _____

   c. In what way did Walt Whitman represent the American voice? _____
   _____

2. *American Literary Character Types*

   a. Examples of the "frontiersman" character can be found in _____
   _____

   b. Examples of the "romantic hero" in American Renaissance writing include
   _____

   c. Describe the "Transcendental seeker." _____
   _____

3. *American Literary Themes*

   a. What does "Westering" mean? _____
   b. What feelings did "bright Romanticism" express? _____
   _____

   c. Writing that exemplifies "dark Romanticism" had a different viewpoint, which was that
   _____

   d. Why was self-reliance an important value during the American Renaissance? _____
   _____

B. DIRECTIONS: *Answer the following questions based on the Essential Question Vocabulary words.*

   1. How does *technology* bring people together? _____
   _____

   2. Name one of the basic *rights* protected by the Constitution. _____
   _____

   3. What attitude are most people likely to have during periods of *prosperity*? _____
   _____

Name _____ Date _____

Unit 2 Introduction
Following-Through Activities

A. CHECK YOUR COMPREHENSION *Use this chart to complete the Check Your Comprehension activity in the Unit 2 Introduction. In the middle column, fill in two key concepts related to each Essential Question. In the right column, list a key author connected with each concept. One concept-author pairing has been done for Place and Literature.*

ESSENTIAL QUESTION	KEY CONCEPT	KEY AUTHOR
Place and Literature	kinship with nature _____	Thoreau 2._____
American Literature	1. _____ 2. _____	1._____ 2._____
Writer and Society	1. _____ 2. _____	1._____ 2._____

B. EXTEND YOUR LEARNING: *Use this graphic organizer to help plan your research for the Extend Your Learning activity.*

What invention are you researching?	_____
What aspects of American life did the invention change?	_____ _____ _____
What ripple effects did the invention cause?	_____ _____ _____
Whom did the invention benefit most?	_____ _____ _____
Whom did the invention harm?	_____ _____ _____
Technical/scientific vocabulary to use:	_____ _____ _____

Name _____ Date _____

"The Devil and Tom Walker" by Washington Irving
Literary Analysis: Characterization

Characterization is the way a writer reveals and develops characters. With **direct characterization,** the writer makes explicit statements about a character. With **indirect characterization,** the writer makes statements that allow the reader to make inferences about a character.

Examples: Tom Walker was a miserly fellow. (direct characterization)

Tom Walker fed his horse the bare minimum. (indirect characterization)

DIRECTIONS: *The numbered items are examples of indirect characterization. The lettered items are examples of direct characterization. On the line, write the letter of the item that has the same meaning.*

_____1. Passersby often heard her voice raised in arguments with her husband.

_____2. Tom sat down and had a comfortable conversation with Old Scratch.

_____3. The one thing Tom would not do was to become a slave-trader.

_____4. Tom refused to allow his debtor any more time, foreclosing on the home.

_____5. Seeing Old Scratch outside, Tom turned pale and his knees shook.

_____6. Tom's wife urged him to do whatever he had to do in exchange for wealth.

_____7. Tom began to go to church every Sunday, praying loudly and strenuously.

_____8. Tom had his horse buried with his feet uppermost, so he would be ready for riding on the last day, when the world would be turned upside down.

a. Tom was not afraid of the Devil.

b. Tom was a heartless money-lender.

c. Tom was afraid of the Devil.

d. Tom was outwardly religious.

e. Tom's wife loved money more than she loved her husband.

f. Tom was not completely bad.

g. Tom was superstitious.

h. Tom's wife was a quarrelsome woman.

"The Devil and Tom Walker" by Washington Irving

Reading Strategy: Evaluate Social Influences of the Historical Period

The characters in "The Devil and Tom Walker" are American colonists living in New England in the late 1720s and early 1730s. The dialogue, the narrator's comments about the characters, and the events that the characters experience help the reader to recognize and **evaluate the social influences of the period.** Of course, some of these influences and attitudes are often exaggerated in Irving's satirical story. Nevertheless, readers do get a picture of colonial life in the New England of Tom Walker's day.

DIRECTIONS: *On the basis of each passage that follows, evaluate the social influences of New Englanders, or American colonists in general, in the 1720s and 1730s. Write your evaluation on the lines provided.*

1. Tom Walker . . . had a wife as miserly as himself: they were so miserly that they even conspired to cheat each other . . . many and fierce were the conflicts that took place about what ought to have been common property.

   _____

   _____

   _____

2. "I [the Devil] amuse myself by presiding at the persecutions of Quakers and Anabaptists; I am the great patron and prompter of slave dealers, and the grandmaster of the Salem witches."

   _____

   _____

   _____

3. About the year 1727, just at the time that earthquakes were prevalent in New England, and shook many tall sinners down upon their knees. . . .

   _____

   _____

   _____

4. Such was the end of Tom Walker and his ill-gotten wealth. Let all griping money brokers lay this story to heart.

   _____

   _____

   _____

"The Devil and Tom Walker" by Washington Irving
Vocabulary Builder

Using the Latin Prefix *ex-*

A. DIRECTIONS: *The prefix* ex- *often means "out." To extort is "to twist out of, or force to give away." Complete each sentence with a word from the list below.*

exhale   export   extrovert   exoskeleton

1. If you ship a product out of the country, you _____ it.
2. An _____ is an outgoing person.
3. When you breathe out, you _____.
4. An insect's outer shell is called an _____.

Using the Word List

discord   extort   ostentation   parsimony   prevalant   treacherous

B. DIRECTIONS: *The following sentences are missing two words. On the line before each number, write the letter of the pair of terms that best completes each sentence.*

____ 1. He was a(n) _____ who tried to _____ money.
    A. criminal—extort
    B. ostentation—acquire
    C. discord—steal
    D. parsimony—save

____ 2. The house was _____, a monument to _____.
    A. treacherous—loyalty
    B. bright—parsimony
    C. extorted—love
    D. lavish—ostentation

____ 3. The _____ was evidence of her _____.
    A. discord—calm
    B. extortion—generosity
    C. small portion—parsimony
    D. tasteful decor—ostentation

____ 4. Because of the _____ mood of joy, everyone was _____.
    A. ostentatious—crying
    B. prevalent—smiling
    C. preferred—parsimonious
    D. fleeting—treacherous

____ 5. The man's _____ deed was motivated by his _____.
    A. parsimonious—courage
    B. treacherous—greed
    C. upsetting—discord
    D. ostentatious—stinginess

____ 6. Their constant _____ reflected the _____ in their marriage.
    A. bickering—discord
    B. treachery—excitement
    C. cheerfulness—parsimony
    D. ostentation—gloom

Name _____ Date _____

"The Devil and Tom Walker" by Washington Irving
Support for Writing

As you prepare to write an updated **retelling** of "The Devil and Tom Walker," enter information in the chart below. Remember that you want to communicate the same message but with different plot elements and details about the characters. Also remember to use modern examples of food, clothing, and current events.

Modern Retelling of "The Devil and Tom Walker"	
New title:	
Characters with new details: Tom Tom's wife The Devil	
New plot elements: Where Tom and Wife live Where they meet Devil What happens with characters How story ends	
Modern day references: Clothing Food Current events	

On a separate page, write a draft of your updated version of the Irving tale. When you revise your draft, be sure you have updated the elements of the nineteenth-century story to reflect today's world.

Name _____ Date _____

"**Crossing the Great Divide**" by Meriwether Lewis
"**Commission of Meriwether Lewis**" by Thomas Jefferson
Primary Sources Worksheet

The two documents in this selection are concerned with the exploration of the Louisiana Purchase. Thomas Jefferson's memorandum outlines what Meriwether Lewis is expected to do and learn. Meriwether Lewis's journal describes his experiences as he follows Jefferson's suggestions.

DIRECTIONS: *Use the table below to compare Lewis's experiences with what Jefferson expects of him.*

What Lewis Says or Does	How This Fulfills Jefferson's Orders
1.	
2.	
3.	
4.	

"Crossing the Great Divide" by Meriwether Lewis
"Commission of Meriwether Lewis" by Thomas Jefferson
Vocabulary Builder

Using the Root -spec-

A. DIRECTIONS: *The Latin root -spec- means "to look" or "to see." Keep that in mind as you write on the line the letter of the choice that best completes each sentence.*

1. A *spectator* is someone who _____ a game.
   A. participates in
   B. watches
   C. referees
   D. scores

2. A health *inspector* comes to a restaurant in order to _____.
   A. eat dinner
   B. criticize the food
   C. see if food is being properly handled
   D. entertain clients

3. You wear *spectacles* _____.
   A. to see better
   B. to protect against the rain
   C. to change your appearance
   D. to keep warm

Using the Word List

celestial	conciliatory	conspicuous	discretion	dispatched
latitude	longitude	membrane	practicable	prospect

B. DIRECTIONS: *Write the vocabulary word or words that best complete the sentence.*

1. It did not seem _____ to carry heavy equipment over the mountains.

2. The explorers noted their _____ and _____ in their report about their location.

3. The explorers were told to use their own _____ about when to return home.

4. The scouts were _____ down the river to gather information about the surroundings.

5. Not wishing to surprise the natives, the explorers tried to be as _____ as possible.

6. The _____ of a hostile reception was always on the explorers' minds.

7. The explorers made _____ gestures toward the natives, in an attempt to win their trust.

8. The natives used the _____ of certain trees to line their canoes.

9. The explorers sometimes depended on _____ navigation to determine their positions.

from **"The Song of Hiawatha"** and **"The Tide Rises, The Tide Falls"**
by Henry Wadsworth Longfellow
"Thanatopsis" by William Cullen Bryant
"Old Ironsides" by Oliver Wendell Holmes

Literary Analysis: Meter

The **meter** of a poem is the rhythmic pattern created by the arrangement of stressed and unstressed syllables. The basic unit of meter is the **foot**, which usually consists of one stressed syllable and one or more unstressed syllables. The most common foot in English-language poetry is the **iamb**, an unstressed syllable followed by a stressed syllable, as in the word *today*.

The type and number of feet per line determine the poem's meter. For example, a pattern of three iambs per line is called **iambic trimeter**; four iambs per line, **iambic tetrameter**; five iambs per line, **iambic pentameter**. The process of analyzing a poem's meter is called **scansion**, or **scanning** the poem. Here are examples of scanned lines.

| Iambic tetrameter: | Beneath it rung the battle shout |
| Iambic pentameter: | To him who in the love of Nature holds |

DIRECTIONS: *Scan the following stanza of "Old Ironsides" by marking the stressed and unstressed syllables. Then, describe the metrical pattern of the poem on these lines:*

_____

_____

Oh, better that her shattered hulk

    Should sink beneath the wave;

Her thunders shook the mighty deep,

    And there should be her grave;

Nail to the mast her holy flag,

    Set every threadbare sail,

And give her to the god of storms,

    The lightning and the gale!

from **"The Song of Hiawatha"** and **"The Tide Rises, The Tide Falls"**
by Henry Wadsworth Longfellow
"Thanatopsis" by William Cullen Bryant
"Old Ironsides" by Oliver Wendell Holmes

Reading Strategy: Summarizing to Repair Comprehension

Summarizing is a valuable way to check and **repair your reading comprehension.** When you summarize something, you briefly state its main points and key details in your own words.

DIRECTIONS: *Summarize each stanza below on the lines provided.*

1. "Thanatopsis":

    Yet not to thine eternal resting place
Shalt thou retire alone, nor couldst thou wish
Couch more magnificent. Thou shalt lie down
With patriarchs of the infant world—with kings,
The powerful of the earth—the wise, the good,
Fair forms, and hoary seers of ages past,
All in one mighty sepulcher.

_____

_____

_____

2. "Old Ironsides":

    Oh, better that her shattered hulk
      Should sink beneath the wave;
Her thunders shook the mighty deep,
      And there should be her grave;
Nail to the mast her holy flag.
      Set every threadbare sail,
And give her to the god of storms,
      The lightning and the gale!

_____

_____

_____

from "The Song of Hiawatha" and **"The Tide Rises, The Tide Falls"**
by Henry Wadsworth Longfellow
"Thanatopsis" by William Cullen Bryant
"Old Ironsides" by Oliver Wendell Holmes

Vocabulary Builder

Using the Latin Root *-fac-*

A. DIRECTIONS: *One of the meanings of the word root -fac- is "the face," or, by extension, "outward appearance." Keeping that in mind, write on the line the letter of the choice that best completes each item.*

_____ 1. If you make a *facsimile* of a document, what will it look like?
    A. a different color from the original   C. identical to the original
    B. a reverse image of the original   D. smaller or larger than the original

_____ 2. The *façade* of a building is its
    A. front.   C. back.
    B. courtyard.   D. interior.

_____ 3. A *facet* of a gemstone is one of
    A. the ways it might be set.
    B. its small, polished surfaces.   C. the imperfections inside it.
    D. the places where it is found in nature.

Using the Word List

eloquence   efface   pensive   venerable

B. DIRECTIONS: *On the lines provided, rewrite each sentence, substituting the correct word from the Word List in place of its italicized definition.*

1. The valleys were blanketed in a *thoughtful* quietness.

   _____

2. The old man was knowledgeable and *worthy of respect*.

   _____

3. The ravages of time will soon *erase* the letters on the monument.

   _____

4. The speaker's *skillful use of language* moved the audience to tears.

   _____

Name _____ Date _____

from **"The Song of Hiawatha"** and **"The Tide Rises, The Tide Falls"**
by Henry Wadsworth Longfellow
"Thanatopsis" by William Cullen Bryant
"Old Ironsides" by Oliver Wendell Holmes

Support for Writing

Use this chart to prepare for writing your **compare-and-contrast** essay. First, choose one five-to ten-line passage each from two poems in this grouping (Longfellow's poems, "Thanatopsis," "Old Ironsides"). Then, list the stylistic devices that help create the mood of each passage.

Poem:	Lines: Mood:
Subject	
Meter	
Images	
Word Choice	
Other Details That Affect Mood	

Poem:	Lines: Mood:
Subject	
Meter	
Images	
Word Choice	
Other Details That Affect Mood	

On a separate page, draft your essay, incorporating these details to support the mood you identify for each passage. When you revise, be sure, that your details from the poems are accurate.

"The Minister's Black Veil" by Nathaniel Hawthorne

Literary Analysis: Parable and Symbol

A **parable** teaches a moral lesson through a simple story about humans. Often a parable leaves out specific details about characters or about the location of the story. Parables also often use **symbols** to suggest universal truths. These techniques make the story more applicable to all readers. For example, in "The Minister's Black Veil," Hawthorne does not reveal the reason Parson Hooper is wearing the veil because the people's reaction to the veil and what it may symbolize is the critical part of the parable.

Hawthorne calls "The Minister's Black Veil" a parable because he feels strongly about the moral lesson of the story.

DIRECTIONS: *Look at each of the following excerpts. Then, in the space provided, write how you think the language reinforces the message of the parable for all readers.*

Excerpt	How the Language Conveys the Parable
1. Children, with bright faces, tripped merrily beside their parents, or mimicked a graver gait, in the conscious dignity of their Sunday clothes. Spruce bachelors looked sidelong at the pretty maidens, and fancied that the Sabbath sunshine made them prettier than on weekdays.	
2. At its conclusion, the bell tolled for the funeral of a young lady. The relatives and friends were assembled in the house, and the more distant acquaintances stood about the door, speaking of the good qualities of the deceased . . .	
3. When Mr. Hooper came, the first thing that their eyes rested on was the same horrible black veil, which had added deeper gloom to the funeral, and could portend nothing but evil to the wedding.	

"The Minister's Black Veil" by Nathaniel Hawthorne

Reading Strategy: Draw Inferences to Determine Essential Meaning

When you **draw an inference** in reading a story, you use the surrounding details to make a reasonable guess about the essential meaning of the story. To draw thoughtful inferences, look carefully at the writer's description of events and characters and use of literary devices. For example, note Hawthorne's detail as he describes Mr. Hooper's black veil on the Sunday he appears in church.

> Swathed about his forehead, and hanging down over his face, so low as to be shaken by his breath, Mr. Hooper had on a black veil. On a nearer view it seemed to consist of two folds of crape . . . With this gloomy shade before him, good Mr. Hooper walked onward, at a slow and quiet pace, stooping somewhat, and looking on the ground . . .

Based on Hawthorne's description, you might infer that something bad has happened to someone close to Hooper.

DIRECTIONS: *Read the details from "The Minister's Black Veil" in the following chart. Write down what you know from the story and from your own life. Write what you think the author means.*

Details	What I Know	Inference
1. That mysterious emblem was never once withdrawn. It shook with his measured breath . . . it threw its obscurity between him and the holy page . . . and while he prayed, the veil lay heavily upon his uplifted countenance.		
2. It was remarkable that of all the busybodies and impertinent people in the parish, not one ventured to put the plain question to Mr. Hooper . . . Hitherto whenever there appeared the slightest call for such interference, he had never lacked advisers . . .		

Name _____ Date _____

"The Minister's Black Veil" by Nathaniel Hawthorne
Vocabulary Builder

Using the Root -path-

A. DIRECTIONS: *The word root -path- means "feeling, suffering, or disease." Keep that in mind as you answer the following questions on the lines provided.*

1. *Pathology* is a branch of medicine. With what issues in medicine do you think it is concerned?

   _____

2. The prefix *anti-* means "against." If you felt extreme *antipathy* toward another person, would you want that person to be your friend? Explain.

   _____

3. The prefix *sym-* means "with." If your friend suffered a terrible disappointment, how would you show that you were *sympathetic*?

   _____

Using the Word List

imperceptible   impertinent   inanimate   obstinacy   pathos   venerable

B. DIRECTIONS: *Revise each sentence so that the underlined vocabulary word is used in a logical way. Be sure to keep the vocabulary word in your revision.*

Example: The <u>starving</u> animal just picked at the food that was offered.

Revision: The <u>starving</u> animal gobbled up the food that was offered.

1. Because of Megan's <u>obstinacy</u>, she was always willing to change her mind for good reasons.

   _____

2. No one had any respect for the <u>venerable</u> old man.

   _____

3. The <u>inanimate</u> object jumped all over the room.

   _____

4. The audience laughed uproariously at the <u>pathos</u> in the play.

   _____

5. The <u>impertinent</u> child showed great respect to his elders.

   _____

6. The sound of the lion's roar was <u>imperceptible</u> from twenty feet away.

   _____

"**The Minister's Black Veil**" by Nathaniel Hawthorne
Grammar and Style: Using Adjective and Adverb Clauses

An **adjective clause** is a subordinate clause that modifies a noun or pronoun by telling *what kind* or *which one*. An **adverb clause** is a subordinate clause that modifies a verb, adjective, adverb, or verbal by telling *where, when, in what way, to what extent, under what condition,* or *why*.

Example: The veil <u>that Mr. Hooper wore</u> was disturbing to the congregation. (adjective clause modifying the noun *veil*)

<u>When Mr. Hooper started wearing the veil</u>, everyone wondered why. (adverb clause modifying the verb *wondered*)

A. PRACTICE: *Underline the adjective or adverb clause in each sentence. On the line, identify it as an adjective clause or adverb clause, and indicate which word it modifies.*

1. As the people approached the meetinghouse, the sexton tolled the bell.

   _____

2. Mr. Hooper, who walked slowly toward the meetinghouse, was wearing a veil.

   _____

3. Mr. Hooper gave a powerful sermon while the parishioners wondered about the veil.

   _____

4. The veil, which was made of black crape, covered most of Mr. Hooper's face.

   _____

5. After he performed the wedding ceremony, Mr. Hooper raised a glass to his lips.

   _____

B. Writing Application: *Use each subordinate clause in a sentence. Tell whether it is an adjective clause or an adverb clause, and tell which word it modifies.*

1. when the visitors were seated in Mr. Hooper's home

   _____

2. who had been engaged to him for some time

   _____

3. as she hinted at the rumors surrounding the veil

   _____

4. that Mr. Hooper suffered

   _____

5. which he refused to remove

   _____

"The Minister's Black Veil" by Nathaniel Hawthorne
Support for Writing

As you gather information for your **interpretive essay about ambiguity,** use this organizer to record details related to the veil. List descriptions of the veil, dialogue about the veil, and characters' actions relating to the veil.

Details in "The Minister's Black Veil"	
Descriptions of the veil	
Dialogue about the veil	
Characters' actions	

On a separate page, write a draft of your interpretive essay. When you go back to revise your work, be sure that you have supported your interpretation with evidence from the story.

"The Fall of the House of Usher" and **"The Raven"** by Edgar Allan Poe
Edgar Allan Poe: Biography

The sad, colorful life of Edgar Allan Poe made him America's first tormented genius. A writer of haunting poetry, brilliant detective fiction and thrilling horror stories, and insightful literary criticism, Poe unfortunately knew only limited success in his lifetime. Yet he eventually became one of the most popular American writers, largely due to his ability to call up the dark, unknown side of human experience.

A. DIRECTIONS: *Edgar Allan Poe has been the subject of many plays, films, and other works. Imagine that you are helping to create a documentary about Poe's life and career. Write a brief summary of each part of Poe's life. Then, suggest a visual or two to use to illustrate each part.*

Part I (childhood): "Orphan Raised Overseas"—**Summary:** _____
_____

Suggested visual(s): _____

Part II (military): "The Poet in the Army"—**Summary:** _____
_____

Suggested visual(s): _____

Part III (literary career): "Turning to Fiction and Criticism"—**Summary:**
_____

Suggested visual(s): _____

Part IV (last years): "A Sad End"—**Summary:** _____
_____

Suggested visual(s): _____

B. DIRECTIONS: *Imagine that you are Edgar Allan Poe being interviewed. Give his responses to the following questions.*

Interviewer: You were raised in England and spent time in the army when you started your writing career. What experiences in your life influenced your work?

Poe: _____
_____

Interviewer: Mr. Poe, what sort of reader do you think will be drawn to your stories and poems?

Poe: _____
_____

Interviewer: Finally, Mr. Poe, what qualities do *you* think are distinctly American? How do you show these qualities in your writings?

Poe: _____
_____

"The Fall of the House of Usher" and "The Raven" by Edgar Allan Poe
Literary Analysis: Single Effect

Edgar Allan Poe said that a short story should be written to create a **single effect.** Every character, detail, and incident, from the first sentence on, should contribute to this effect. This same principle can be applied to **narrative poems**, poems that tell a story.

DIRECTIONS: *Following are settings and characters described in "The Fall of the House of Usher." On the lines below each setting or character, list three specific details about that setting or character that you feel contribute to the single effect of Roderick's terror and mounting dread.*

1. *Setting:* The room in which Usher spends his days

   A. _____

   B. _____

   C. _____

2. *Setting:* Madeline's tomb

   A. _____

   B. _____

   C. _____

3. *Setting:* The house at the end of the story

   A. _____

   B. _____

   C. _____

4. *Character:* Roderick Usher

   A. _____

   B. _____

   C. _____

5. *Character:* Madeline Usher

   A. _____

   B. _____

   C. _____

"The Fall of the House of Usher" and **"The Raven"** by Edgar Allan Poe
Literary Analysis: Gothic Style

The gothic style has several well-known characteristics that have made it popular for centuries among writers and other artists. To concoct a gothic style, a writer would use several distinct ingredients and techniques:

Recipe for Gothic Style

- Take one bleak and remote setting.
- Fold in a character who suffers physical and/or psychological torment.
- Mix with events of a macabre or violent nature.
- Add supernatural or otherworldly elements (optional).
- Stir using vivid language with dark and dangerous meanings.

DIRECTIONS: *Now supply your own examples of gothic ingredients in this recipe card:*

My Own Gothic Mix

- Take this setting: _____
- Fold in this character: _____
- Mix with these events: _____
  _____
- Add this otherworldly element: _____
  _____
- Stir with phrases like this: _____
  _____

DIRECTIONS: *For each gothic element listed below, add another example from "The Fall of the House of Usher" or "The Raven," as indicated.*

1. Bleak setting in "The Fall of the House of Usher": <u>Fungus covers the House of Usher.</u>

   Another example: _____

2. Bleak, remote setting in "The Raven": <u>"midnight dreary"</u>

   Another example: _____

3. Characters' torments in "The Fall of the House of Usher": <u>Roderick's acute illness</u>

   Another example: _____

4. Narrator's torments in "The Raven": <u>The narrator is "weak and weary."</u>

   Another example: _____

"The Fall of the House of Usher" and **"The Raven"** by Edgar Allan Poe
Reading Strategy: Break Down Long Sentences

When an author writes a long, complicated sentence, you can clarify the meaning by breaking it down into its logical parts. Look especially for the subject and predicate at its core. After you have identified them, state the core in your own words.

Poe's sentence: A cadaverousness of complexion; an eye large, liquid, and luminous beyond comparison; lips somewhat thin and very pallid, but of a surpassingly beautiful curve; a nose of a delicate Hebrew model, but with a breath of nostril unusual in similar formations; a finely molded chin, speaking, in its want of prominence, of a want of moral energy; hair of a more than weblike softness and tenuity—these features, with an inordinate expansion above the region of the temple, made up altogether a countenance not easily to be forgotten.

Core sentence: These features made up a countenance not easily forgotten.

Own words: He had a memorable face.

DIRECTIONS: *Underline the core of the following sentences from "The Fall of the House of Usher." Then restate the core in your own words.*

1. During the whole of a dull, dark, and soundless day in the autumn of that year, when the clouds hung oppressively low in the heavens, I had been passing alone, on horseback, through a singularly dreary tract of country, and at length found myself, as the shades of evening drew on, within view of the melancholy House of Usher.

   _____

2. I reined my horse to the precipitous brink of a black and lurid tarn that lay in unruffled luster by the dwelling, and gazed down—but with a shudder even more thrilling than before—upon the remodeled and inverted images of the gray sedge, and the ghastly tree stems, and the vacant and eyelike windows.

   _____

3. He admitted, however, although with hesitation, that much of the peculiar gloom which thus afflicted him could be traced to a more natural and far more palpable origin—to the severe and long-continued illness—indeed to the evidently approaching dissolution of a tenderly beloved sister, his sole companion for long years, his last and only relative on earth.

   _____

4. Our books—the books which, for years, had formed no small portion of the mental existence of the invalid—were, as might be supposed, in strict keeping with this character of phantasm.

   _____

"The Fall of the House of Usher" and **"The Raven"** by Edgar Allan Poe
Vocabulary Builder

Using the Latin Root -voc-

A. DIRECTIONS: *The root -voc- comes from the Latin* vox, *meaning "voice." On the lines provided, explain how the root -voc- influences the meaning of each of the italicized words.*

1. The environmental board in our town *advocates* passage of a strong law against dumping waste in Lake Jasper.

   _____

2. Studying the works of Poe will probably improve your *vocabulary*.

   _____

3. The cottage was *evocative* of happy childhood memories.

   _____

Using the Word List

anomalous   equivocal   importunate
munificent   sentience   specious

B. DIRECTIONS: *For each item, write on the line the letter of the pair of words that expresses a relationship most like the pair in capital letters.*

____ 1. FALSE : SPECIOUS ::
   A. beautiful : ugly   B. violent : wicked   C. plentiful : abundant

____ 2. NORMAL : ANOMALOUS ::
   A. valuable : worthless   B. blue : color   C. sleepy : tired

____ 3. EQUIVOCAL : SURE ::
   A. physician : disease   B. vocal : talkative   C. vague : clear

____ 4. SENTIENCE : FEELING ::
   A. capable: skill   B. visible : darkness   C. worth : value

____ 5. BENEFACTOR : MUNIFICENT ::
   A. donor : charity   B. giver : taker   C. philanthropist : generous

____ 6. IMPORTUNATE : INSIST ::
   A. unlucky : luck   B. talkative : chat   C. create : thought

"The Fall of the House of Usher" and **"The Raven"** by Edgar Allan Poe

Grammar and Style: Comparative and Superlative Adjectives and Adverbs

Adjectives and adverbs have **comparative** and **superlative** forms.

- When two things are being compared, we use the comparative form. Most comparatives are formed by adding the suffix -er: *smaller, lower, younger.* Some comparatives are formed by using the word *more* or *less: more unusual, more quickly, less expensive.*

- When three or more things are being compared, we use the superlative form. Most superlatives are formed by adding the suffix -est: *smallest, lowest, youngest.* Some superlatives are formed by using the word *most* or *least: most unusual, most quickly, least expensive.*

A. PRACTICE: *Identify the italicized adjective or adverb as a comparative or superlative form. Write* comparative *or* superlative *on the line.*

1. Sandra wore her *most ostentatious* hat in the parade. _____

2. Jan's *prettiest* skirt has ruffles along the hem. _____

3. Jason learned the game *more easily* than he had expected. _____

4. Milo was two inches *taller* than his brother. _____

B. Writing Application: *Write the correct form of the adjective or adverb on the line.*

1. (difficult) Of the two poems, this one is _____ to understand.

2. (surprising) The _____ scene in the whole story was when Madeline Usher got out of the coffin.

3. (dreary) The narrator thought the area was the _____ place he had ever seen.

4. (cheerful) Roderick Usher thought he would become _____ if his friend came for a visit.

5. (peculiar) The _____ thing about Roderick Usher was his tendency to be very reserved.

6. (bleak) The raven tapped at the door on the _____ night in December.

7. (loudly) As the night went on, the raven tapped _____ than before.

8. (ominously) The raven said "Nevermore" _____ the sixth time.

9. (frightening) Which do you think is the _____ stanza in this poem?

10. (effective) Of the two works of literature, which do you think is _____ as an exercise in terror?

Name _____ Date _____

Support for Writing

As you prepare to write a **critical essay** supporting one of the two critics' views of "The Fall of the House of Usher," first reread the story and decide which of the following views you share. Enter details supporting that view on the chart below.

- The narrator and the other two characters are all insane. (Davidson)
- Each character represents part of a single person; for example the conscious mind, the unconscious mind, and the soul. (Lovecraft)
- The house itself is eerily connected to the inhabitants and cannot continue standing after they are dead (Lovecraft)

Critical Appraisal of "The Fall of the House of Usher"	
Main idea about what is going on in story	Expansion of main idea
Support from first part of story	
Support from middle of story	
Support from end of story	

Draft your essay on a separate page. Indicate the critic with whom you agree as you state the main idea you share. Then incorporate details supporting that idea. When you revise, be sure that the main idea is clear and that you give enough details from the story to support it.

"The Fall of the House of Usher" by Edgar Allan Poe

"Where *Is* Here?" by Joyce Carol Oates

Literary Analysis: Comparing Gothic Literature

Gothic literature, whether traditional or modern, has as its chief characteristic an air of mystery, magic, and the supernatural. Elements of horror are rampant; the reader can expect the sense of impending doom to culminate in some horrific or violent incident. The setting in a work of gothic literature is often a bleak or remote setting that contributes to the gloomy atmosphere.

DIRECTIONS: *Read these passages from the selections. Then, on the lines below, comment on the similarities and differences between them.*

. . . I scanned more narrowly the real aspect of the building. Its principal feature seemed to be that of an excessive antiquity. The discoloration of ages had been great. Minute fungi overspread the whole exterior, hanging in a fine tangled web-work from the eaves. Yet all this was apart from any extraordinary dilapidation. No portion of the masonry had fallen; and their appeared to be a wild inconsistency between its still perfect adaptation of parts, and the crumbling condition of the individual stones. (from "The Fall of the House of Usher")

The father had moved to another window and stood quietly watching, his cheek pressed against the glass. "He's gone down to the old swings. I hope he won't sit in one of them, for memory's sake, and try to swing—the posts are rotted almost through." The mother drew breath to speak but sighed instead, as if a powerful current of feeling had surged through her. The father was saying, "Is it possible he remembers those swings from his childhood? I can't believe they're actually that old." The mother said vaguely, "They were old when we bought the house." (from "Where *Is* Here?")

_____

_____

_____

_____

_____

_____

_____

_____

_____

_____

_____

_____

_____

_____

"The Fall of the House of Usher" by Edgar Allan Poe
"Where *Is* Here?" by Joyce Carol Oates
Vocabulary Builder

Using the Latin Root *-pul-*

A. DIRECTIONS: *The root* -pul- *means "to push into motion." Using that information, write on the line the letter of the choice that best completes each sentence.*

_____1. If Linda has the *compulsion* to keep her room tidy,
   A. she never tidies her room.
   B. she keeps her room tidy all the time.
   C. she does not care at all about her room.

_____2. A company that specializes in jet *propulsion* is concerned with
   A. building jets.
   B. recycling jet parts.
   C. making jets go.

_____3. *Expulsion* is a penalty principals use when
   A. they want to get a student out of the school.
   B. they want to include a student in the school.
   C. they want to make class sizes equal.

_____4. If attendance at a school event is *compulsory*,
   A. students can choose to go or not.
   B. everyone must attend.
   C. the event will take place after school.

Using the Word List

   cavernous   exasperation   fastidious   impulsively   stealthily

B. DIRECTIONS: *On the line, write the letter of the pair of words that expresses a relationship most like the pair in capital letters.*

_____1. STEALTHILY : SNEAKY : :
   A. spy : patriot
   B. slyly : secretive
   C. happily : gladly
   D. sad : unhappy

_____2. FASTIDIOUS : SLOPPY : :
   A. neat : clean
   B. careful : meticulous
   C. tidy : messy
   D. dust : vacuum

_____3. EXASPERATION : ANNOYANCE : :
   A. temper : shouting
   B. ant : picnic
   C. anger : calm
   D. vexation : irritant

_____4. IMPULSIVELY : HESITATE : :
   A. reflectively : think
   B. painstakingly : plod
   C. quickly : fast
   D. generously : hoard

_____5. CAVERNOUS : VAST : :
   A. miniature : tiny
   B. beauteous : ugly
   C. enormous : elephant
   D. cave : rock

"The Fall of the House of Usher" by Edgar Allan Poe
"Where *Is* Here?" by Joyce Carol Oates

Support for Writing

As you gather information about the settings for your **compare-and-contrast essay,** keep track of details on this Venn diagram.

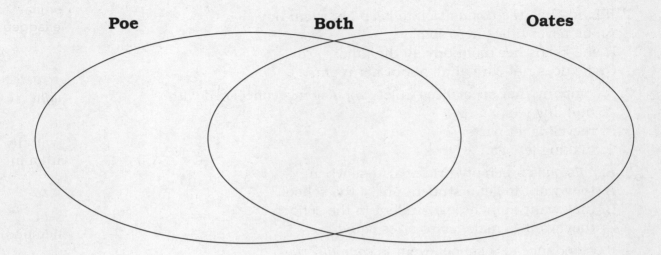

Poe **Both** **Oates**

Below or on a separate page, write a draft of your comparison-and-contrast essay. When you revise your work, be sure that you support your points with evidence from the stories.

from **Moby-Dick** by Herman Melville
Literary Analysis: Symbol

In *Moby-Dick*, many elements take on symbolic meanings as the novel progresses. A **symbol** is a person, place, action, or thing that also represents an abstract meaning beyond itself. In the following passage, for example, the sharks may be symbols of Ahab's destructive behavior or the destructive response of nature to Ahab's mad pursuit of the whale.

> And still as Ahab glided over the waves the unpitying sharks accompanied him; and so pertinaciously stuck to the boat; and so continually bit at the plying oars, that the blades became jagged and crunched, and left small splinters in the sea, at almost every dip.

DIRECTIONS: *Read the following passages from* Moby-Dick. *On the lines provided after each passage, identify one symbol that the passage contains and explain what the symbol might represent.*

1. "I came here to hunt whales, not my commander's vengeance. How many barrels will thy vengeance yield thee even if thou gettest it, Captain Ahab? It will not fetch thee much in our Nantucket market."

   "Nantucket market! hoot! But come closer, Starbuck. . . ."

   "Vengeance on a dumb brute!" cried Starbuck, "that simply smote thee from blindest instinct! Madness! To be enraged with a dumb thing, Captain Ahab, seems blasphemous."

   _____

   _____

   _____

2. "The ship? Great God, where is the ship?". . . Concentric circles seized the lone boat itself, and all its crew, and each floating oar. and every lance pole, and spinning, animate and inanimate, all round and round in one vortex, carried the smallest chip of the *Pequod* out of sight.

   _____

   _____

   _____

3. A sky hawk that tauntingly had followed the main-truck downwards from its natural home among the stars, . . . this bird now chanced to intercept its broad fluttering wing between the hammer and the wood: and simultaneously feeling that ethereal thrill, the submerged savage beneath, in his deathgrasp, kept his hammer frozen there: and so the bird of heaven, with archangelic shrieks, and his imperial beak thrust upwards, and his whole captive form folded in the flag of Ahab, went down with his ship, which like Satan, would not sink to hell till she had dragged a living part of heaven along with her.

   _____

   _____

   _____

from **Moby-Dick** by Herman Melville

Reading Strategy: Identify Relevant Details

To recognize and understand the symbols and theme of a work of literature, **identify the relevant details** that the author uses. Such details can lead you to the essential message or main idea of the work. Consider, for example, the following passage:

> "Give way!" cried Ahab to the oarsmen, and the boats darted forward to the attack; but maddened by yesterday's fresh irons that corroded in him, Moby-Dick seemed combinedly possessed by all the angels that fell from heaven.

Here Melville connects Moby-Dick to a larger idea by comparing him to "all the angels that fell from heaven," or devils. This detail suggests that Moby-Dick might be a symbol of evil or of the darker side of human nature.

DIRECTIONS: *Read the following passage, which opens your textbook selection from* Moby-Dick. *Then, on the lines provided, answer the questions about the passage.*

> One morning shortly after breakfast, Ahab, as was his wont, ascended the cabin gangway to the deck. There most sea captains usually walk at that hour, as country gentlemen, after the same meal, take a few turns in the garden.
>
> Soon his steady, ivory stride was heard, as to and fro he paced his old rounds, upon planks so familiar to his tread, that they were all over dented, like geological stones, with the peculiar mark of his walk. Did you fixedly gaze, too, upon that ribbed and dented brow; there also, you would see still stranger footprints—the footprints of his one unsleeping, ever-pacing thought.
>
> But on the occasion in question, those dents looked deeper, even as his nervous step that morning left a deeper mark. And, so full of his thought was Ahab, that at every uniform turn that he made, now at the mainmast and now at the binnacle, you could almost see that thought turn in him as he turned, and pace in him as he paced; so completely possessing him, indeed, that it all but seemed the inward mold of every outer movement.

1. Which details suggest that Ahab is a symbol?

   _____

   _____

2. With what abstract idea or ideas does Melville seem to connect him here?

   _____

   _____

3. Identify one more detail in the passage that might have symbolic significance.

   _____

   _____

4. Which details suggest that it is a symbol?

   _____

5. What abstract idea or ideas does it seem to symbolize?

   _____

   _____

from **Moby-Dick** by Herman Melville

Vocabulary Builder

Using the Prefix *mal-*

A. DIRECTIONS: *The prefix* mal- *means "bad." The word* maledictions *combines the prefix* mal- *with the root* -dict-, *which means "speak." Keep that in mind as you write on the line the letter of the choice that best completes each of these sentences.*

1. _____ is often described as malodorous.
   A. Cinnamon   C. A squirrel
   B. A rose   D. A skunk

2. A *malnourished* child most likely eats _____ meals.
   A. well-balanced   C. hearty
   B. skimpy   D. tasty

3. A *malcontent* probably _____ his or her job.
   A. loves   C. is puzzled by
   B. hates   D. never complains about

4. A man with a *malady* has _____.
   A. a disease   C. happiness
   B. great wealth   D. an aristocratic wife

5. A woman might be called a *malefactor* if she _____.
   A. gives to charity   C. commits a crime
   B. teaches math   D. loves her husband

Using the Word List

impulsive   inarticulate   inscrutable   maledictions   pedestrian   prescient

B. DIRECTIONS: *On the line before each word in the left column, write the letter of its definition in the right column.*

___ 1. inscrutable   A. having foreknowledge
___ 2. maledictions   B. not able to speak
___ 3. prescient   C. curses
___ 4. inarticulate   D. not able to be easily understood
___ 5. impulsive   E. ordinary; commonplace
___ 6. pedestrian   F. acting suddenly and without careful
                               thought

Name _____ Date _____

from **Moby-Dick** by Herman Melville
Grammar and Style: Using Participles, Gerunds, and Infinitives

A **participle** is a verb form, typically ending in *-ed* or *-ing*, used as a modifier, either alone or in a phrase.

Examples: The *astonished* sailors listened as Ahab raged about the whale.

Starbuck, *worried* about the captain, remained silent.

A **gerund** is a verb form, typically ending in *-ing* or *-ed*, used as a noun, either alone or in a phrase.

Examples: *Pacing* the deck was Ahab's morning activity.

Ahab was obsessed with *avenging* himself on the whale.

An **infinitive** is the form of the verb with *to*. It can function as a noun, an adjective, or an adverb, either alone or in a phrase.

Examples: Ahab was determined to *destroy* the white whale.

The crew had many tasks *to accomplish*.

A. PRACTICE: *In each of the following sentences, identify the underlined phrase as a gerund, infinitive, or participial phrase.*

1. To encourage the crew, Ahab offered a reward. _____

2. The dolphins, breaking the surface of the ocean, were beautiful. _____

3. The team of harpooners selected by the captain did excellent work. _____

4. After assembling on the deck, the crew listened to the captain. _____

5. To keep the ship running smoothly, the crew performs various duties. _____

6. The vortex seized the *Pequod*, carrying the ship out of sight. _____

B. Writing Application: *Write three sentences, using a gerund, infinitive, or participial phrase. Use each type of phrase at least once, and label each one.*

1. _____

_____

2. _____

_____

3. _____

_____

Name _____ Date _____

from Moby-Dick by Herman Melville
Support for Writing

As you think about writing a **character study**, think about why Captain Ahab seems to you either mad or great. Also, think about the main events of the selection and what they reveal about Ahab. Enter the information into the chart below.

Ahab's Character	
Main Events First Part of Selection	
Main Events Middle Part of Selection	
Main Events End of Selection	
My Opinion of Ahab/ Reasons for My Opinion	

On a separate page, write a draft that gives your opinion about whether Ahab is mad or great. Explain why you drew these conclusions or made these judgements about Ahab. When you revise your work, be sure you have justified your opinion with examples from the selection.

Name _____ Date _____

from **Nature**, from **Self-Reliance**, and "**Concord Hymn**"
by Ralph Waldo Emerson

Literary Analysis: Figurative Language

Emerson uses various types of **figurative language** to express his meaning and make his abstract ideas seem more concrete. Figurative language is language that is used imaginatively rather than literally. Here are some types of figurative language:

- **imagery**, or word pictures that appeal to the senses
- **metaphor**, or a comparison between two or more unlike things without the use of the word *like* or *as*
- **description**, or a detailed portrayal of something in words
- **synecdoche**, or the use of one part of something to stand for the whole

When Emerson uses these tools in his writing, he clarifies his ideas and makes them easier for the reader to understand.

DIRECTIONS: *Read these passages from Emerson's work. Then, on the lines provided, identify the underlined sections as imagery, metaphor, description, or synecdoche.*

1. In good health, <u>the air is a cordial of incredible virtue.</u> _____

   _____

2. I become <u>a transparent eyeball</u>. _____

   _____

3. For nature is not always tricked in holiday attire, but the same scene which yesterday <u>breathed perfume and glittered</u> as for the frolic of the nymphs is overspread with melancholy today. _____

   _____

4. <u>Society is a joint-stock company</u> in which the members agree for the better securing of his bread to each shareholder. _____

   _____

5. He who would gather <u>immortal palms</u> must not be hindered by the name of goodness.

   _____

6. He may as well concern himself with <u>his shadow on the wall</u>. _____

   _____

7. Here once the embattled farmers stood / And fired <u>the shot heard round the world</u>.

   _____

8. Down <u>the dark stream which seaward creeps</u>. _____

   _____

Name _____ Date _____

from **Nature**, *from* **Self-Reliance**, and "Concord Hymn"
by Ralph Waldo Emerson

Reading Strategy: Challenging, or Questioning, the Text

One way to gain more understanding of a work is to **challenge the text**, or **question** the author's assertions. Here are some guidelines:

- Identify the author's opinions and restate them in your own words.
- Evaluate the examples, reasons, or other evidence the author provides to support his or her opinions.
- Consider other evidence that supports or refutes the author's opinions.
- On the basis of the evidence, decide if you agree or disagree with the author.

DIRECTIONS: *Read the following passage from* Self-Reliance. *Then challenge the text by performing the numbered activities below. Write your responses on the lines provided.*

Society everywhere is in conspiracy against the manhood of every one of its members. Society is a joint-stock company in which the members agree for the better securing of his bread to each shareholder, to surrender the liberty and culture of the eater. The virtue in most request is conformity. Self-reliance is its aversion. It loves not realities and creators, but names and customs.

1. Restate Emerson's basic opinion about society.

_____

_____

2. Identify and evaluate the evidence Emerson uses to support that opinion.

_____

_____

_____

3. Provide examples from everyday life to support and refute Emerson's opinion of society.

Support: _____

_____

_____

Refute: _____

_____

_____

from **Nature,** *from* **Self-Reliance,** and **"Concord Hymn"**
by Ralph Waldo Emerson
Vocabulary Builder

Using the Latin Prefix *ab-*

A. DIRECTIONS: *The Latin prefix* ab- *means "away" or "from." Absolve means "to free from guilt or blame, or from having to fulfill a duty or a promise." On the line after each sentence below, explain how the italicized word reflects the meaning of the prefix* ab-.

1. That idea is *absurd*—please come up with a less ridiculous suggestion.

   _____

2. It is usually pleasant this time of year, but today was *abnormally* hot.

   _____

3. Poetry uses images to make *abstract* ideas or emotions more concrete.

   _____

4. Unwilling to decide about the issue, Senator Díaz *abstained* from voting.

   _____

5. Most of the class came to school today, but two students were *absent*.

   _____

Using the Word List

absolve   aversion   chaos   conviction   decorum   perpetual   tranquil

B. DIRECTIONS: *On the line, write the letter of the word that is most nearly the same in meaning as the word in capitals.*

____	1. CHAOS:	A. joy	B. pain	C. confusion	D. silence
____	2. AVERSION:	A. attraction	B. distaste	C. discrepancy	D. revision
____	3. PERPETUAL:	A. passive	B. weak	C. constant	D. fussy
____	4. DECORUM:	A. decoration	B. rudeness	C. quota	D. rightness
____	5. CONVICTION:	A. wish	B. dream	C. belief	D. promise
____	6. ABSOLVE:	A. pardon	B. worry	C. insult	D. harm
____	7. TRANQUIL:	A. peaceful	B. excited	C. full	D. wistful

from Nature, *from* Self-Reliance, and "Concord Hymn"
by Ralph Waldo Emerson
Support for Writing

To gather material for your critical evaluation of the selection from *Self-Reliance*, enter key points into the chart below.

My Critique of *Self-Reliance*	
Main Ideas of Essay/Beginning	
Main Ideas of Essay/Middle	
Main Ideas of Essay/End	
Emerson's Argument/Summary Statement	
My Opinion/Support from Text	

On a separate page, write a first draft of your critical evaluation. When you revise your work, be sure you have made your critical opinion of the essay clear and have supported it with examples from the selection.

Name _____ Date _____

Contemporary Commentary
Gretel Ehrlich Introduces from *Walden* by Henry David Thoreau

DIRECTIONS: *Use the space provided to answer the questions.*

1. At first, why was Thoreau's landscape at Walden Pond unfamiliar to Ehrlich?

   _____

   _____

2. What examples from *Walden* does Ehrlich use to support her assertion that the heart of an essay is "an attempt to understand the nature of things"?

   _____

   _____

   _____

3. **A.** In her commentary, Ehrlich stresses Thoreau's philosophical idea that "life is change." What details does Ehrlich cite to support this idea?

   _____

   _____

   B. Do you agree with the claim that "life is change"? Briefly explain why or why not.

   _____

   _____

4. According to Ehrlich, how would Thoreau advise us to cope with the speed and complexity of modern life?

   _____

   _____

5. Explain what Thoreau means by the "auroral character."

   _____

   _____

6. Do you believe that Thoreau was right in encouraging us to "march to a different drummer" if that's where our destiny takes us? Briefly explain your opinion.

   _____

   _____

   _____

7. What questions about Thoreau's *Walden* does Ehrlich's commentary raise in your mind at this point?

   _____

   _____

Gretel Ehrlich
Listening and Viewing

Segment 1: Meet Gretel Ehrlich
• Why does Gretel Ehrlich recommend traveling to other countries?
• What have you learned from either moving to or visiting a place different from your hometown?

_____

_____

_____

_____

Segment 2: Gretel Ehrlich Introduces *Walden* by Henry David Thoreau
• How has Gretel Ehrlich's writing been influenced by Thoreau?

_____

_____

_____

_____

Segment 3: The Writing Process
• Why does Gretel Ehrlich believe it is important to constantly record one's observations and thoughts by taking notes?
• What method of collecting information do you rely on when writing?

_____

_____

_____

_____

Segment 4: The Rewards of Writing
• What does Gretel Ehrlich believe is the obligation of a writer?
• What insights about humanity do you think you could gain by reading books about other cultures?

_____

_____

_____

_____

Name _____ Date _____

from **Walden** and *from* **Civil Disobedience** by Henry David Thoreau
Literary Analysis: Style

Readers should look not only at what a writer has to say but also at how the writer says it. The way a writer puts thoughts into words is called **style.** Following are some important elements of style and some questions useful in analyzing a writer's style.

- **Choice of words:** Does the writer choose simple and direct words or words that are more complex and formal?
- **Length of sentences:** Does the writer make frequent use of long or short sentences? Does the sentence length vary?
- **Type and structure of sentences:** Does the writer use a fair amount of questions or commands? Many simple sentences, or compound-complex sentences? Does the writer always open with the subject of a sentence or vary sentence beginnings?
- **Rhythm:** Does the writer create an internal rhythm by repeating words or ideas from sentence to sentence?
- **Use of literary devices:** Does the writer use vivid imagery and strong similes, metaphors, and other figures of speech?

DIRECTIONS: *Read this passage from* Walden. *Then, on the lines below the passage, analyze the different elements of Thoreau's style.*

To my imagination it retained throughout the day more or less of this auroral character, reminding me of a certain house on a mountain which I had visited the year before. This was an airy and unplastered cabin, fit to entertain a traveling god, and where a goddess might trail her garments. The winds which passed over my dwelling were such as sweep over the ridges of mountains, bearing the broken strains, or celestial parts only, of terrestrial music.

1. Word choice: _____

_____

2. Sentence length: _____

_____

3. Sentence type/structure: _____

_____

_____

4. Rhythm: _____

_____

5. Literary devices: _____

_____

_____

Name _____ Date _____

Reading Strategy: Analyze the Author's Implicit and Explicit Philosophical Assumptions

In both *Walden* and **Civil Disobedience,** Thoreau expresses his **philosophical assumptions,** the system of belief and values that guided his life and actions. He expresses these ideas both **implicitly,** merely suggesting them, and **explicitly,** stating them directly. As you read, analyze Thoreau's philosophy. To do this, note his main ideas and the evidence he uses to support these ideas. Then compare his ideas and evidence by comparing them with your own life experiences. Organize your notes in the following chart.

Thoreau's Main Ideas	
Thoreau's Evidence	
My Experiences	
Analysis	

Name _____ Date _____

from **Walden** and *from* **Civil Disobedience** by Henry David Thoreau
Vocabulary Builder

Using the Root -*flu*-

A. DIRECTIONS: *The root -flu- means "flow." Using that information, write on the line the letter of the choice that best completes each sentence.*

____ 1. If Laura shows *fluency* in Russian,
    A. she has little knowledge of Russian.
    B. she has studied Russian but cannot master it.
    C. she speaks it easily.

____ 2. In an *affluent* society,
    A. many people have and spend money.
    B. most people are very poor.
    C. most people earn good money but refuse to spend it.

Using the Word List

| alacrity | dilapidated | expedient | magnanimity | sublime | superfluous |

B. DIRECTIONS: *Circle the letter of the choice that best completes each sentence.*

1. The building was so dilapidated that the city wanted to have it
    A. demolished.   B. publicized.   C. photographed.

2. Her novels include a fair amount of superfluous information, making them rather
    A. easy to read.   B. time consuming.   C. melancholy.

3. The city's architecture was absolutely sublime, so viewing it usually inspired
    A. disgust.   B. indifference.   C. awe.

4. When Jill accepted with alacrity the difficult task he gave her, her boss was
    A. annoyed.   B. impressed.   C. furious.

5. When Thoreau calls government an expedient, he means it is a
    A. tool.   B. useless enterprise.   C. bureaucracy.

6. People display magnanimity when they
    A. hold a grudge.   B. give to charity.   C. perform tasks efficiently.

Name _____ Date _____

from **Walden** and *from* **Civil Disobedience** by Henry David Thoreau
Support for Writing

As you prepare to write your editorial about the relevance of Thoreau's ideas today, reread the selections. Decide whether you support or reject Thoreau's ideas. Make entries into the chart below that strengthen your position.

Editorial on Simplicity
Why I support or reject Thoreau's ideas of simplicity: _____
Examples from today's world to support my opinion: _____   _____
Examples from Thoreau's world to support my opinion: _____   _____
Direct quotes from Thoreau that strengthen my position: _____   _____

On a separate page, write a draft of your editorial. Then revise it, and be sure to justify the choice you have made with examples from Thoreau or with examples from today's world. Submit your editorial to the school newspaper.

Emily Dickinson's Poetry
Literary Analysis: Rhyme and Paradox

Emily Dickinson plays with rhyme in her poetry, using several different types. She uses **exact rhyme,** in which two or more words have the identical vowel and final consonant sounds in their last stressed syllables. For example, *pound* and *sound* rhyme exactly, as do *brain* and *contain.* She also uses **slant rhyme,** in which the final sounds are similar but not identical. For example, *pond* and *sound* are slant rhymes, as are *brain* and *frame.* In addition, Dickinson uses **internal rhyme,** in which words within a single line of poetry rhyme with each other.

Another technique that Dickinson uses to keep her poetry interesting is **paradox,** or seemingly contradictory statements that actually present a truth. For example, when she says "The Brain—is wider than the Sky," it seems impossible. However, when you realize the capacity of the brain, you can see the truth in the statement.

A. DIRECTIONS: *On the lines after each passage from Dickinson's poetry, identify the words that rhyme, and indicate whether the rhymes are exact slant, or internal.*

1. My life closed twice before its close—
   It yet remains to see
   If Immortality unveil
   A third event to me.

   _____

2. Or rather—He passed Us—
   The Dews grew quivering and chill—
   For only Gossamer, my Gown—
   My Tippet—only Tulle—

   _____

3. None may teach it—Any—
   'Tis the Seal Despair—
   An imperial affliction
   Sent us of the Air—

   _____

4. I heard a Fly buzz—when I died—

   _____

B. DIRECTIONS: *Explain the paradox in this passage:*

   My life closed twice before its close—

   _____

   _____

Emily Dickinson's Poetry

Reading Strategy: Rereading to Monitor and Repair Comprehension

Emily Dickinson's poetry can sometimes be confusing because she often omits words that are expected to be understood. She also sometimes inverts the usual word order of a sentence. A good way to **monitor and repair your comprehension** of confusing passages is to **reread** the material. As you do so, mentally fill in the words that seem to be missing, or put the words in their usual order. This can lead you to the probable meaning of the passage.

DIRECTIONS: *Complete this chart by writing your interpretation of each passage. The first one is done for you.*

Original Line	Probable Meaning
1. For only Gossamer, my Gown	My gown was made of only gossamer
2. Since then—'tis Centuries—and yet / Feels shorter than the Day / I first surmised the Horses Heads / Were toward Eternity—	
3. The Brain is deeper than the sea— / For—hold them—Blue to Blue—The one the other will absorb / As Sponges—Buckets do—	
4. There is a solitude of space / A solitude of sea / A solitude of death, but these / Society shall be	

Emily Dickinson's Poetry
Vocabulary Builder

Using the Root *-finis-*

A. DIRECTIONS: *The root -finis-, often shortened to -fin-, means "end" or "limit." On the lines provided, explain how the meaning of the word is conveyed in each of the following words.*

1. define _____

_____

2. refinish _____

_____

3. finale _____

_____

Using the Word List

affliction   ample   eternity   finite   infinity   interposed   surmised

B. DIRECTIONS: *On the line provided, write the word from the Word List that best completes each sentence.*

1. From her expression, I _____ that she was not happy to see me.
2. There had to be an end to the tunnel, but it seemed to stretch into _____.
3. An immortal god or goddess lives for all _____.
4. Only a _____ number of ways existed to solve the problem.
5. After cooking all day, Sophie had _____ amounts of food for her many guests.
6. Don developed asthma at a young age, and this _____ limited his activities.
7. A moth _____ between my eyes and the computer screen.

C. DIRECTIONS: *On the line, write the letter of the pair of words that expresses a relationship most like the pair in capital letters.*

___ 1. FINITE : INFINITY ::
    A. fatal : fate
    B. endless : eternity
    C. mortal : immortality
    D. significant : importance

___ 2. AMPLE : PLENTIFUL ::
    A. much : little
    B. enough : inadequate
    C. food : drink
    D. slight : scarce

___ 3. SURMISED : SPECULATION ::
    A. anticipated : compliment
    B. forewarned : prediction
    C. flattered : insult
    D. pampered : aid

___ 4. AFFLICTION : PNEUMONIA ::
    A. thoughtful : serious
    B. symptom : cough
    C. ancient : old
    D. depressed : jolly

Emily Dickinson's Poetry
Support for Writing

As you search Emily Dickinson's poetry for references to boundlessness, the infinite, and things without limit, keep track of your findings in the chart below.

Name of Poem	Detail referring to boundlessness, the infinite, or things without limit

On the lines below, write a general statement about Dickinson's views about the infinite. Put a check next to the details in your chart that best support this statement. Then, on a separate page, write a draft of your blog entry. Begin with your general statement, and support that statement with details from the poems. Be sure to punctuate each direct quotation correctly, and cite the poem in which it appears.

_____

_____

Walt Whitman's Poetry

Literary Analysis: American Epic Poetry

Walt Whitman is the inventor of a new brand of poetry: **American epic poetry.** Unlike traditional epic poetry, which features an ambitious and untouchable hero, Whitman's brand celebrates the common person and acknowledges that all human beings have a spiritual kinship with one another. Rather than focusing on the story of a single hero's quest, Whitman focuses on the interconnectedness of all humanity.

DIRECTIONS: *For each of the following passages from Whitman's poetry, explain how it exemplifies American epic poetry.*

1. And what I assume you shall assume, / For every atom belonging to me as good belongs to you. _____

   _____

   _____

2. My tongue, every atom of my blood, formed from this soil, this air, / Born here of parents born here from parents the same, and their parents the same. _____

   _____

   _____

3. I am enamor'd of . . . the builders and steerers of ships and the wielders of axes and mauls, and the drivers of horses, / I can eat and sleep with them week in and week out.

   _____

   _____

4. By the bivouac's fitful flame, / A procession winding around me, solemn and sweet and slow—but first I note, / The tents of the sleeping army _____

   _____

   _____

5. I hear America singing, the varied carols I hear. / Those of mechanics . . . / The carpenter . . . / The mason . . . / The boatman . . . / The shoemaker . . . / The wood-cutter's song . . ."

   _____

   _____

Walt Whitman's Poetry
Reading Strategy: Adjust Reading Rate

Good readers know that they should **adjust** their **reading rate,** depending on the difficulty level of the material they are reading. They slow down when they come to more difficult passages, and they speed up when they come to easier ones. How can you tell when you should slow down? If the lines are long and dense and the vocabulary is relatively abstract, the passage will probably require more study. If the lines are short and the vocabulary is relatively concrete, the passage will probably require less study.

DIRECTIONS: *On the chart below, note three passages from Whitman's poetry that you read slowly. Explain why you slowed down when you came to these passages. Then, explain the meaning of the passage.*

Passage	Why I Slowed Down	Meaning of Passage

Walt Whitman's Poetry
Vocabulary Builder

Multiple Meaning Words

A. DIRECTIONS: *On the line, write the letter of the choice that best defines the underlined word.*

_____1. The stirring bees flitted from flower to flower, gathering pollen.
A. mixing with a spoon
B. emotional
C. busy
D. waking up slowly

_____2. The horses ran freely, without check, across the prairie.
A. restraint
B. one's bill at a restaurant
C. a mark of approval
D. to examine for accuracy

_____3. After adding the figures in each column, Alex determined the grand total.
A. diagrams
B. numbers
C. shapes
D. illustrations

_____4. The soldiers note the positions of the enemy camps.
A. a musical tone
B. a promise to pay
C. a short letter
D. observe

Using the Word List

abeyance   bequeath   effuse   robust   stealthily   stirring

B. DIRECTIONS: *On the lines provided, rewrite each sentence by replacing the italicized word with a simpler word that means the same thing.*

1. I depart as air, I shake my white locks at the runaway sun, I *effuse* my flesh in eddies, and drift it in lacy jags.

_____

2. Creeds and school in *abeyance*, retiring back a while sufficed at what they are, but never forgotten.

_____

3. In the history of earth hitherto the largest and most *stirring* appear tame and orderly to their ampler largeness and stir.

_____

4. I *bequeath* myself to the dirt to grow from the grass I love . . .

_____

5. . . . as I lift my eyes they seem to be *stealthily* watching me.

_____

6. . . . at night the party of young fellows, *robust*, friendly, Singing with open mouths their strong melodious songs.

_____

Name _____ Date _____

Walt Whitman's Poetry
Support for Writing

To organize your material to write a Whitman-esque poem (a poem in Whitman's style), enter information in the chart below.

Poem in Imitation of Walt Whitman	
Poem Topic	
Sensory images and details	
arrangement of lines	
Catalogs (long lists)	
anaphora (repetition of phrases or sentences with similar structure or meanings)	
onomatopoeia (worda that sound like their meaning)	

On a separate page, write a draft of your poem. When you revise, be sure you have used a variety of line lengths, sensory images, catalogs, anaphora, onomatopoeia, and lots of enthusiasm.

Essential Questions Workshop—Unit 2

In their stories, poems, and nonfiction, the writers in Unit Two express ideas that relate to the three Essential Questions framing this book. Review the literature in the unit. Then, for each Essential Question, choose an author and at least one passage from his or her writing that expresses a related idea. Use this chart to complete your work.

Essential Question	Author/Selection	Literary Passage
How does literature shape or reflect society?		
What is the relationship between place and literature?		
What makes American literature American?		

Name _____ Date _____

Names and Terms to Know

A. DIRECTIONS: *Write a brief sentence explaining each of the following names and terms. You will find all of the information you need in the Unit Introduction in your textbook*

1. Fort Sumter: _____

2. Homestead Act: _____

_____

3. The Gilded Age: _____

_____

4. Horatio Alger: _____

5. Muckrakers: _____

6. Local color: _____

_____

B. DIRECTIONS: *Use the hints below to help you answer each question.*

1. How did the Civil War change American life?
   [Hints: How long did the Civil War last, and how many soldiers died in its battles? How did the war change the North? How did it change the South?]

_____

_____

2. How did the "Age of Electricity" make the lives of Americans both better and worse?
   [Hints: What were some of the inventions and other technological developments of the last half of the 19th century? In what way did these developments make life easier? What negative things did these developments bring about?]

_____

_____

3. Explain how the American frontier vanished a few decades after the Civil War.
   [Hints: What was the effect of the Homestead Act? What did the improved methods of transportation make possible? What replaced the American wilderness? What happened to the Native Americans?]

_____

_____

_____

Unit 3 Introduction

Essential Question 1: How does literature shape or reflect society?

A. DIRECTIONS: *Answer the questions about the first Essential Question in the Introduction, about the relationship between the writer and society. All the information you need is in the Unit 3 Introduction in your textbook.*

1. *Literary Forms for Expressing Social and Political Issues*

   a. What were spirituals and what did they communicate? _____
   _____

   b. Give examples of autobiographical writings of the period. _____
   _____

   c. Muckrakers focused on revealing _____
   _____

2. *Popular Literature*

   a. What do "rags-to riches" stories tell about? _____
   _____

   b. The surprise ends of O. Henry's short stories stress_____
   _____

   c. Give two examples of popular "escapist" writers. _____
   _____

3. *Realism, Naturalism, and the Social and Political Issues*

   a. How did the Civil War change American optimism? _____
   _____

   b. The fiction of Realism depicted _____
   _____

   c. Two poets who wrote of ordinary people were _____
   _____

   d. Writers of the Naturalist movement took Realism a step further by _____
   _____

B. DIRECTIONS: *Answer the questions that include the Essential Question Vocabulary words.*

1. What did spirituals like "Go Down, Moses" *lament* in society? _____
   _____

2. As *industry* grew, how did industrial-age American society feel about the western frontier?
   _____

3. What level of society would Mark Twain's realistic *vernacular* dialogue portray? _____
   _____

Unit 3 Introduction

Essential Question 2: What is the relationship between place and literature?

A. DIRECTIONS: *On the lines provided, answer the questions about the second Essential Question in the Introduction, about the relationship between place and literature. All the information you need is in the Unit 3 Introduction in your textbook.*

1. *Northern Writers and the Physical Environment*

   a. Technological advances in the North encouraged people to _____
   _____

   b. What issues caused by urban growth did Civil-War-era writers focus on? _____
   _____

2. *Southern Writers and the Physical Environment*

   a. How did the Civil War change the physical environment in the South? _____
   _____

   b. In contrast to Northern writers, Southern writers focused more on _____
   _____

3. *Expressions of Place in Civil-War-Era Writing*

   a. "Local color" writing featured _____
   _____

   b. Give examples of local color writers. _____
   _____

   c. Give examples of writers who used urban settings. _____
   _____

B. DIRECTIONS: *Complete the sentence stems based on the Essential Question Vocabulary words.*

   1. Mining California's *resources*, Bret Harte wrote _____
   _____

   2. Edith Wharton wrote *urban* novels about _____
   _____

   3. Two *regional* writers exploring Midwestern rural society were _____
   _____

Unit 3 Introduction

Essential Question 3: What makes American literature American?

A. DIRECTIONS: *On the lines provided, answer the questions about the third Essential Question in the Introduction, about what makes American literature American. All the information you need is in the Unit 3 Introduction in your textbook.*

1. *Literary Elements Contributing to the American Style*

   a. Give examples of the types of settings to be found in American literature at this time.
   _____

   b. What two types of speech were typical of American writing? _____

   c. In American writing, humor often served the purpose of _____
   _____

2. *Roles of Civil-War Era Writers*

   a. In contrast to Romantic writers, Realistic writers _____
   _____

   b. What did writers who specialized in local color depict, and how? _____
   _____

   c. What were some European influences on Naturalistic American writers? _____
   _____

   d. Naturalistic writers believed that human behavior was controlled by _____
   _____

3. *Turn-of-the-Century America as Portrayed in Literature*

   a. The Romantic beliefs of the American Renaissance had given way to _____
   _____

   b. What view of war replaced the idealism of "Old Ironsides"? _____
   _____

   c. Emerson's self-reliance was succeeded by _____

   d. Exceptional heroes were being replaced by _____

   e. What attitude toward science is revealed in the millions visiting the 1893 World's Fair in Chicago? _____

B. DIRECTIONS: *Complete the sentence stems based on the Essential Question Vocabulary words.*

   1. Expressing *pessimism* about self-reliance were _____

   2. American writing grew more *realistic* after _____

   3. Americans sought a *fortune* of gold in _____

Name _____ Date _____

Following-Through Activities

A. CHECK YOUR COMPREHENSION: *Use this chart to complete the Check Your Comprehension activity in the Unit 3 Introduction. In the middle column, fill in two key concepts related to each Essential Question. In the right column, list a major author connected with each concept.*

ESSENTIAL QUESTION	Key Concepts	Major Author
Writer and Society	1. 2.	1. 2.
Place and Literature	1. 2.	1. 2.
American Identity	1. 2.	1. 2.

B. EXTEND YOUR LEARNING: *Use this graphic organizer to help plan your research for the Extend Your Learning activity.*

Speaker	
Speaker's Purpose(s)	
Speaker's Favorite Topics	
Elements of Speaker's Style	

Name _____ Date _____

"An Occurrence at Owl Creek Bridge" by Ambrose Bierce
Literary Analysis: Point of View

A writer's purpose helps determine the **point of view** from which a story is told. In "An Occurrence at Owl Creek Bridge," for example, Ambrose Bierce reveals the tragically ironic nature of war through the events surrounding one person—Peyton Farquhar. Limited third-person narration allows Bierce to explore Farquhar's thoughts and feelings while preserving the objective distance needed for the story's ironic ending. As the plot develops in this story, Bierce uses **stream-of-consciousness** writing to help readers see the quick, moment-by-moment working of Farquhar's mind.

DIRECTIONS: *Rewrite the following passages of "An Occurrence at Owl Creek Bridge" from the point of view indicated. Be prepared to explain how each point of view changes the story.*

1. A man stood upon a railroad bridge in northern Alabama, looking down into the swift water twenty feet below. The man's hands were behind his back, the wrists bound with a cord. A rope closely encircled his neck.

First-person point of view, stream of consciousness _____

_____

_____

_____

_____

_____

_____

_____

2. As Peyton Farquhar fell straight downward through the bridge he lost consciousness and was as one already dead. From this state he was awakened—ages later, it seemed to him—by the pain of a sharp pressure upon his throat, followed by a sense of suffocation.

Third-person omniscient point of view _____

_____

_____

_____

_____

_____

_____

_____

_____

_____

Name _____ Date _____

"An Occurrence at Owl Creek Bridge" by Ambrose Bierce
Reading Strategy: Identify Chronological Order

To make their stories interesting, writers often begin with an especially dramatic event and then flash backward in time to supply the reader with necessary information. In "An Occurrence at Owl Creek Bridge," the author begins with Peyton Farquhar standing on the railroad bridge about to be hanged. Then he follows with a flashback to tell how Peyton Farquhar got into that situation. In addition, Bierce flashes forward to show events leaping forward in time.

As you read stories like this one, it is a good strategy to keep the **chronological order** clear in your mind.

DIRECTIONS: *In the "mental" flashforward, Ambrose Bierce gives the reader many clues that the events are taking place in an imaginary future rather than in an actual present. Below are excerpts from the story. In the space provided, explain how each excerpt provides a clue to the nature of the flashforward.*

1. He was now in full possession of his physical senses. They were, indeed, preternaturally keen and alert. Something in the awful disturbance of his organic system had so exalted and refined them that they made record of things never before perceived. He felt the ripples upon his face and heard their separate sounds as they struck.

   _____

   _____

   _____

   _____

2. Suddenly he felt himself whirled around and round—spinning like a top. The water, the banks, the forests, the now distant bridge, fort and men—all were commingled and blurred.

   _____

   _____

   _____

   _____

3. At last he found a road which led him in what he knew to be the right direction. It was as wide and straight as a city street, yet it seemed untraveled. No fields bordered it, no dwelling anywhere. Not so much as the barking of a dog suggested human habitation.

   _____

   _____

   _____

   _____

"An Occurrence at Owl Creek Bridge" by Ambrose Bierce
Vocabulary Builder

Using the Latin Root -dict-

A. DIRECTIONS: *The word root -dict- is Latin in origin and means "word; saying; expression."*
On the lines below, explain how each word reflects the meaning of the root -dict-.

1. contradict (*contra-* means "opposite"): _____

2. dictionary (*-ary* means "thing connected with"): _____

3. predict (*pre-* means "before"): _____

4. *verdict* (*-ver-* means "true"): _____

Using the Word List

    apprised   deference   dictum   etiquette   ineffable   summarily

B. DIRECTIONS: *Replace the underlined word or phrase with a synonym from the Word List.*

1. Any citizen caught . . . will be <u>immediately</u> hanged.

   _____

2. According to military <u>policy</u>, it was necessary to execute the spy.

   _____

3. Farquhar felt <u>unutterable</u> joy.

   _____

4. in the code of military <u>behavior</u>

   _____

5. Silence and fixity are forms of <u>courtesy.</u>

   _____

6. A sharp pain in his wrist <u>informed</u> him.

   _____

Name _____   Date _____

"An Occurrence at Owl Creek Bridge" by Ambrose Bierce
Support for Writing

To organize your information to write a **critical essay** about the story you have just read, enter examples of Bierce's stream of consciousness into the chart below.

Stream of Consciousness in "An Occurrence at Owl Creek Bridge"

Example 1 of stream of consciousness from story	How it reveals character's thoughts
_____ _____ _____	_____ _____ _____
Example 2 of stream of consciousness from story _____ _____ _____	**How it reveals character's thoughts** _____ _____ _____
Example 3 of stream of consciousness from story _____ _____ _____	**How it reveals character's thoughts** _____ _____ _____

On a separate page, write your first draft, showing how each example of stream of consciousness contributes to the dramatic impact of the story. As you revise, add direct quotes from the story to support your opinions.

from **Mary Chesnut's Civil War** by Mary Chesnut
"Recollections of a Private" by Warren Lee Goss
"A Confederate Account of the Battle of Gettysburg" by Randolph McKim
Primary Sources: War Correspondence

A. DIRECTIONS: *Read each passage from one of the selections. Then, generate two questions that arise from the quotation.*

Today at dinner there was no allusion to things as they stand in Charleston Harbor. There was an undercurrent of intense excitement. There could not have been a more brilliant circle. . . . These men all talked so delightfully. For once in my life I listened.

—*Mary Chesnut's Civil War*

1. _____

2. _____

"Cold chills" ran up and down my back as I got out of bed after the sleepless night, and shaved preparatory to other desperate deeds of valor. I was twenty years of age, and when anything unusual was to be done, like fighting or courting, I shaved.

—*"Recollections of a Private"*

3. _____

4. _____

The first day I went out to drill, getting tired of doing the same things over and over, I said to the drill sergeant: "Let's stop this fooling and go over to the grocery." His only reply was addressed to a corporal: "Corporal, take this man out and drill him"; and the corporal did! I found that suggestions were not so well appreciated in the army as in private life, and that no wisdom was equal to a drillmaster's "Right face," "Left wheel," and "Right, oblique, march."

—*"Recollections of a Private"*

5. _____

6. _____

Then came General Ewell's order to assume the offensive and assail the crest of Culp's Hill, on our right. . . . The works to be stormed ran almost at right angles to those we occupied. Moreover, there was a double line of entrenchments, one above the other, and each filled with troops. In moving to the attack we were exposed to enfilading fire from the woods on our left flank, besides the double line of fire which we had to face in front, and a battery of artillery posted on a hill to our left rear opened upon us at short range. . . .

—*"A Confederate Account of the Battle of Gettysburg"*

7. _____

8. _____

from **Mary Chesnut's Civil War** by Mary Chesnut
"Recollections of a Private" by Warren Lee Goss
"A Confederate Account of the Battle of Gettysburg" by Randolph McKim

Vocabulary Builder

Using the Word List

adjourned	brigade	convention	entrenchments	fluctuation
intercepted	obstinate	offensive	recruits	spectator

DIRECTIONS: *Rewrite each sentence below, replacing the italicized word or phrase with an appropriate word from the Word List.*

1. The *newly drafted soldiers* did not know how to march.

   _____

2. The enemy *seized* a letter that was being sent to headquarters.

   _____

3. The officers failed to make a decision, so they *closed for a time* the meeting.

   _____

4. The soldiers stayed in *long deep holes with steep sides* in order to avoid being shot.

   _____

5. The *unit of soldiers* prepared for battle.

   _____

6. The general was *stubborn* and wouldn't give up the fight.

   _____

7. A *person watching who wasn't involved in the fight* stood on the distant hill.

   _____

8. Citizens held a *meeting* to talk about ways they could help the wounded.

   _____

9. The battle showed a marked *change in intensity* throughout the day.

   _____

10. The commander told the officers to plan a *position of attack*.

    _____

"An Episode of War" by Stephen Crane
Literary Analysis: Realism and Naturalism

Realism is a type of literature that tries to show people and their lives as realistically as possible. Authors who write material within this literary movement focus on ordinary people rather than on exaggerated models of idealistic behavior. Often such writers emphasize the harsh realities of ordinary daily life, even though their characters are fictional.

Naturalism expands on the base begun by realism. Writers who create naturalistic literature follow the traits of realism, but they add the ideas that people and their lives are often deeply affected by natural forces such as heredity, environment, or even chance. People cannot control such forces, yet they must carry on the best way they can.

The main difference between the two movements is that naturalism emphasizes the lack of control its realistic characters have over the changes taking place in their lives. The influence of both literary movements can often be seen in the same piece of literature, such as "An Episode of War" by Stephen Crane.

DIRECTIONS: *Read the following passages from "An Episode of War." Tell whether you think each one reflects realism, naturalism, or both. Explain your answer.*

1. He was on the verge of a great triumph in mathematics, and the corporals were thronging forward, each to reap a little square [of coffee], when suddenly the lieutenant cried out and looked quickly at a man near him as if he suspected it was a case of personal assault. The others cried out also when they saw blood upon the lieutenant's sleeve.

   Realism, Naturalism, or both: _____

   Explain: _____

   _____

   _____

2. When he reached home, his sisters, his mother, his wife, sobbed for a long time at the sight of the flat sleeve. "Oh, well," he said, standing shamefaced amid these tears. "I don't suppose it matters so much as all that."

   Realism, Naturalism, or both: _____

   Explain: _____

   _____

Name _____ Date _____

"**An Episode of War**" by Stephen Crane
Reading Strategy: Clarify Historical Details

Your knowledge of the historical time period of a selection can help you make the most of a reading experience. Consider the historical, social, and political climate surrounding a piece of writing as part of its setting and context. For example, in "An Episode of War," the author writes, "His lips pursed as he drew with his sword various crevices in the heap. . . ." The detail about the sword helps you realize that the story did not happen recently—it happened in a time when swords were weapons of war.

Pay careful attention to **historical details** that make the story more vivid and meaningful.

DIRECTIONS: *Record some of your historical knowledge about the following issues during the American Civil War. Then write how the details affect your reading of the selections.*

Issues	Historical Knowledge	Effect on Reading
1. War tactics		
2. Medicine		
3. Communication		
4. Transportation		

"An Episode of War" by Stephen Crane
Vocabulary Builder

Using the Root -greg-

A. DIRECTIONS: *The word root -greg- means "herd or flock." On the line, write a word from the list that is suggested by the bracketed word or phrase.*

aggregation   congregation   egregious   gregarious

1. Marc is so [sociable] _____ that he always has a crowd of friends around him.
2. His mistake was so [conspiciously bad] _____, Eli asked if he could begin his audition again.
3. Lourdes' family has belonged to the same [church group] _____ for generations.
4. The students at Hoffman School are a(n) [collection] _____ of the city's diverse population.

Using the Word List

aggregation   commotion   disdainfully   precipitate   sinister

B. DIRECTIONS: *On the line, write the letter of the word or phrase that has the same meaning as the word in CAPITAL letters.*

____ 1. COMMOTION:
   A. bustle   B. action   C. delivery   D. restriction

____ 2. PRECIPITATE:
   A. prevent   B. dissuade   C. cause   D. expect

____ 3. DISDAINFULLY:
   A. loudly   B. contemptuously C. gladly   D. beautifully

____ 4. SINISTER:
   A. joyful   B. puzzling   C. righteous   D. threatening

C. DIRECTIONS: *Write the letter of the word or phrase that best completes each sentence.*

1. Laurel looked upon her brother disdainfully when he _____.
   A. spilled syrup on her skirt   C. helped her fix her car
   B. won the race   D. gave her the CD she'd wanted
2. Amelie was afraid that her grandmother's pneumonia might precipitate her _____.
   A. recovery   B. cough   C. death   D. lungs
3. The moving van was stuffed with an _____ of furniture, tools, and automobile parts.
   A. extravaganza B. aggregation   C. imbalance   D. offload

"An Episode of War" by Stephen Crane
Support for Writing

Use the chart to gather details for your **response to criticism.** List your responses to "An Episode of War" in the left column. In the right column, list quotations, incidents, examples, and other details that develop and support each response.

Main Idea	Quotations, examples, other details

On a separate page, write a draft of your **response to criticism,** using the details you have collected in the chart. When you revise your work, make sure you have supported each main idea with details. Recheck quotations to ensure that you have quoted the words accurately and enclosed them in quotation marks.

All-in-One Workbook
137

from **My Bondage and My Freedom** by Frederick Douglass
Literary Analysis: Autobiography and Tone

In his autobiography, Frederick Douglass provides his readers with a unique view of what it was like to be a slave. Douglass could have chosen to write a fictional work instead of an autobiography, but his purpose was to give readers a sense of the brutality of slavery, a goal that he could best convey through the power of real experiences. Notice how the tone of Douglass's autobiography complements his purpose and makes the experiences even more powerful.

DIRECTIONS: *Read the following passages from the selection. Describe the effect of each passage and tell how Douglass's tone and use of autobiography strengthens that effect.*

It was no easy matter to induce her to think and to feel that the curly-headed boy, . . . who was loved by little Tommy, and who loved little Tommy in turn; sustained to her only the relation of a chattel. I was *more* than that, and she felt me to be more than that. I could talk and sing; I could laugh and weep; I could reason and remember; I could love and hate.

_____

_____

_____

_____

I was no longer the light-hearted, gleesome boy, full of mirth and play, as when I landed first at Baltimore. Knowledge had come . . . This knowledge opened my eyes to the horrible pit, and revealed the teeth of the frightful dragon that was ready to pounce upon me, but it opened no way for my escape.

_____

_____

_____

_____

It was slavery—not its mere *incidents*—that I hated. I had been cheated. I saw through the attempt to keep me in ignorance . . . The feeding and clothing me well, could not atone for taking my liberty from me. The smiles of my mistress could not remove the deep sorrow that dwelt in my young bosom. Indeed, these, in time, came only to deepen my sorrow. She had changed; and the reader will see that I had changed, too. We were both victims to the same overshadowing evil—*she* as mistress, *I* as slave.

_____

_____

_____

_____

Name _____ Date _____

from **My Bondage and My Freedom** by Frederick Douglass
Reading Strategy: Establish a Purpose

Establishing a purpose for reading gives you an idea to focus on as you read. In reading the excerpt from *My Bondage and My Freedom,* one possible purpose is to evaluate the ethical influences of the period that shaped the characters and events of this period. As you read the selection, use this chart to record your conclusions.

Incident or character's behavior	Ethical influence of period

from **My Bondage and My Freedom** by Frederick Douglass
Vocabulary Builder

Using the Root *-bene-*

A. DIRECTIONS: *The root -bene- means "well" or "good" and is part of many words relating to goodness. Complete each sentence with one of these words:* beneficent, beneficial, beneficiary, benign.

1. As a _____, my mother received some money and jewelry after her aunt's death.

2. The petitioners were fortunate to have a judge with a _____ temperament.

3. Her work with the sick in Calcutta made Mother Teresa one of the most _____ people of our time.

4. The labor reforms of the nineteenth century were _____ to factory workers struggling for better working conditions.

Using the Word List

benevolent   consternation   deficient   fervent   intolerable   opposition

B. DIRECTIONS: *Match each word in the left column with its definition in the right column. Write the letter of the definition on the line next to the word it defines.*

___ 1. benevolent   A. passionate; zealous

___ 2. opposition   B. unbearable; unendurable

___ 3. consternation   C. kindly; charitable

___ 4. fervent   D. dismay; alarm

___ 5. intolerable   E. lacking; incomplete

___ 6. deficient   F. hostility; objection

from **My Bondage and My Freedom** by Frederick Douglass
Support for Writing

As you prepare to write a **college admission essay,** think about one experience that has shaped your life, just as Douglass describes how knowledge led to his freedom. Think about events that have made a difference in how you think or act today. Use the graphic organizer below to collect your information.

An Experience That Has Shaped My Life

My Experience (title): _____
_____

What happened first— How I felt or what kind of action I took	What happened next— How I felt or what kind of action I took	What happened finally— How I felt or what kind of action I took

On a separate page, write a first draft of the experience that helped shape who you are today. Put your events in chronological order. When you revise your work, be sure to make it clear to readers how this experience affected you.

Name _____ Date _____

Literary Analysis: Refrain, Allusion, and Allegory

A **refrain** is a word, phrase, line, or group of lines repeated at regular intervals. In spirituals, one of the main things a refrain does is emphasize the most important ideas. In "Go Down, Moses," for example, the refrain "Let my people go" is repeated seven times. The constant repetition serves to turn the cry for freedom into a demand for freedom.

These spirituals also rely upon **biblical allusions,** which are references to people, places, or events in the Bible. The allusion to Moses in "Go Down, Moses" refers to the biblical leader Moses, who led the Israelites out of Egypt.

Both spirituals include allegories. An **allegory** is a story that has two levels of meaning—one literal, the other symbolic. The symbolic meaning of "Swing Low, Sweet Chariot" refers to crossing the Ohio River to freedom for slaves.

DIRECTIONS: *Answering the following questions will help you understand how the use of refrains, biblical allusions, and allegory in "Go Down, Moses" and "Swing Low, Sweet Chariot" function to enrich the spirituals' meanings.*

1. Identify a refrain in "Swing Low, Sweet Chariot." _____

_____

_____

2. Identify and explain the allegory in "Go Down, Moses."

_____

_____

_____

3. What is the significance of the allusion to Jordan in "Swing Low, Sweet Chariot"?

_____

_____

4. In "Go Down, Moses," what emotional effect does the continual repetition of the refrains have? _____

_____

_____

5. Compare the refrains of "Go Down, Moses" and "Swing Low, Sweet Chariot." How are they alike and different? In your answer, consider what the refrains ask for or hope for and how those desires are conveyed in the two spirituals. _____

_____

_____

_____

_____

Name _____ Date _____

"Swing Low, Sweet Chariot" and "Go Down, Moses" Spirituals
Reading Strategy: Listen

DIRECTIONS: *Listen carefully to the sounds and rhythms of "Swing Low, Sweet Chariot" and "Go Down, Moses" as the two spirituals are read aloud. Pay particular attention to the rhymes and the sounds or phrases that are repeated. Often rhythm and repetition suggest a certain mood or attitude and contribute to the intensity of feeling generated by the song and its message. Fill in the two charts below to help you focus on your listening skills and identify the message presented in each spiritual.*

"Swing Low, Sweet Chariot"
Words that rhyme
Words or phrases that are repeated
Mood or attitude suggested by rhyme and repetition
Overall message of spiritual

"Go Down, Moses"
Words that rhyme
Words or phrases that are repeated
Mood or attitude suggested by rhyme and repetition
Overall message of spiritual

"Swing Low, Sweet Chariot" and "Go Down, Moses" Spirituals
Vocabulary Builder

Using the Root -press-

A. DIRECTIONS: *The root* -press- *means "push." In addition to being a complete word itself in English,* press *is also combined with many different prefixes and suffixes to form other words. Choose one of the words in the box to complete each sentence.*

depression   express   impression   press   pressurize   suppress

1. Barry tried hard to control himself, but he could not _____ his laughter.
2. In order to communicate with others, you must _____ your ideas clearly.
3. It is necessary to _____ an airplane's cabin so people can breathe at higher altitudes.
4. The dry cleaners will _____ the suit so it looks neat.
5. Anyone going on a job interview wants to make a good _____.
6. A person who feels sad all the time may be suffering from _____.

Using the Word List

oppressed   smite

B. DIRECTIONS: *Match each word in the left column with its definition in the right column. Write the letter of the definition on the line next to the word it defines.*

___ 1. oppressed   A. kill with a powerful blow
___ 2. smite   B. kept down by a cruel power or authority

C. DIRECTIONS: *On the line, write the letter of the pair of words that best expresses a relationship similar to that expressed in the pair in CAPITAL LETTERS.*

___ 1. SMITE: SLAP ::   ___ 2. OPPRESSED : FREE ::
    A. language : French   A. myth : legend
    B. seek : discover   B. waiter : restaurant
    C. costume : clothing   C. temporary : permanent
    D. happy : miserable   D. computer : monitor
    E. laugh : smile   E. scuff : scrape

"Swing Low, Sweet Chariot" and "Go Down, Moses" Spirituals
Support for Writing

Use the chart to gather background details for your **electronic slide presentation.** List the spirituals you will use in your presentation in the left column. In the right column, list three details about each spiritual. Details should focus on the historic context that influenced the writing of the spiritual and where, when, and why it was sung.

Spirituals	Background Notes
	1. _____ 2. _____ 3. _____
	1. _____ 2. _____ 3. _____
	1. _____ 2. _____ 3. _____
	1. _____ 2. _____ 3. _____

On a separate page, write a draft of the introductions you will use in **your electronic slide presentation,** using the background details you have recorded in the chart. When you revise your work, make sure that you have supported each main idea with details.

"The Gettysburg Address" by Abraham Lincoln
"Letter to His Son" by Robert E. Lee

Literary Analysis: Diction

Diction, or word choice, gives the writer's voice its unique quality. The writer's diction reflects the audience and purpose of the work. Consider how Lincoln, in "The Gettysburg Address," chooses words and constructs sentences to reflect the formal, austere occasion at which he spoke and to evoke feelings of dedication and patriotism in his audience. Lee's "Letter to His Son," in contrast, is more conversational, reflecting his familial relationship with his son, the informal occasion of a letter, and his desire to express his anguish over the impending war.

DIRECTIONS: *Read each question, and then circle the letter of the best answer.*

1. What was Lincoln's purpose in speaking at Gettysburg?
    A. to honor the dead and inspire listeners
    B. to display his oratorical powers

2. What was Lee's purpose in writing his letter to his son?
    A. to encourage his son to act with honor and to support the South
    B. to explain his position on the political situation and the actions he would take

3. Which sentence is better suited for a letter?
    A. As an American citizen, I take great pride in my country. . . .
    B. As a citizen of this great country, I take great pride in my nation. . . .

4. Which sentence is better suited for a speech?
    A. People will quickly forget what we have said here.
    B. The world will little note, nor long remember what we say here, . . .

5. Which phrase is better suited for a letter?
    A. Four score and seven years ago . . .
    B. Eighty-seven years ago . . .

6. Which phrase is better suited for a letter?
    A. . . . we are stuck between chaos and war.
    B. . . . we find ourselves entrapped between anarchy and civil war.

7. Which phrase is better suited for a letter?
    A. No one will remember or pay attention to today's speeches, . . .
    B. The world will little note, nor long remember what we say here, . . .

8. Which sentence is better suited for a public speech?
    A. We are met on a great battlefield of that war.
    B. Here we are at this great battlefield.

"The Gettysburg Address" by Abraham Lincoln
"Letter to His Son" by Robert E. Lee

Reading Strategy: Use Background Knowledge

Background knowledge may include information about the author, about the characters or subjects of the selection, or about the times and events discussed in the selection. Background knowledge can often include personal experiences of people and experiences similar to those in the selection. You learned that Robert E. Lee believed in the Union but opposed both slavery and secession. In this activity, you will learn more about Robert E. Lee to understand further the personal conflict he felt.

DIRECTIONS: *Read the information below. Then use the facts to explain your understanding of each excerpt from Lee's letter to his son.*

- Lee attended the United States Military Academy at West Point in 1825, graduating in 1829.
- In the late 1840s, Lee served in the Mexican War, where he was recognized for his skill and courage.
- Lee's family was a well-established, important family of Virginia. His father was a cavalry commander in the Revolutionary War and a friend of George Washington. Lee admired the first president and named one of his sons George Washington Custis Lee.
- Lee was an honorable and respected man who displayed kindness and humor, and who did not smoke, drink alcohol, or swear.
- Lee did not believe in slavery. Long before the Civil War broke out, he freed the slaves he had inherited.
- Lee felt that Virginia stood for George Washington's principles. He considered the Civil War as a second "Revolutionary War" for independence.

1. How [Washington's] spirit would be grieved could he see the wreck of his mighty labors!

   _____

   _____

2. I feel the aggression [of acts of the North] and am willing to take every proper step for redress. It is the principle I contend for, not individual or private benefit.

   _____

   _____

3. As an American citizen, I take great pride in my country, her prosperity and institutions, and would defend any state if her rights were invaded.

   _____

   _____

Name _____ Date _____

"The Gettysburg Address" by Abraham Lincoln
"Letter to His Son" by Robert E. Lee
Vocabulary Builder

Using the Word List

anarchy   consecrate   hallow   virtuous

A. DIRECTIONS: *Circle the synonym for the underlined word in each sentence or phrase.*

1. . . . we cannot <u>consecrate</u> (bless, profane)

2. . . . we cannot <u>hallow</u> (honor, haunt)

3. As far as I can judge by the papers, we are between a state of <u>anarchy</u> and civil war. (progress, chaos)

4. . . . his precious advice and <u>virtuous</u> example (moral, corrupt)

B. DIRECTIONS: *For each item, choose the word pair that best expresses a relationship similar to that expressed in the numbered pair. Circle the letter of your choice.*

___ 1. VIRTUOUS : PRINCIPLED ::
  A. isolated : incorporated
  B. abundant : void
  C. jubilant : blissful
  D. cleanse : soiled

___ 2. HALLOW : SACRED ::
  A. forget : remember
  B. defy : injustice
  C. revive : rejuvenation
  D. discover : learn

___ 3. ANARCHY : GOVERNMENT ::
  A. warfare : peace
  B. solution : answer
  C. commitment : promise
  D. excellence : success

___ 4. CONSECRATE : SANCTIFY ::
  A. initiate : commence
  B. identify : conceal
  C. fascinate : mystify
  D. innovate : perish

"The Gettysburg Address" by Abraham Lincoln
"Letter to His Son" by Robert E. Lee
Support for Writing

Use the chart to gather and organize ideas for your Compare-and-Contrast essay. Use the graphic organizer to compare and contrast the writers' historical perspective, affection for America, grief over the nation's crisis, and hopes for the future. In the right column, list quotations, incidents, examples, and other details that develop and support each response.

Abraham Lincoln	Robert E. Lee
Different:	**Different:**
Alike:	

On a separate page, write your Compare-and-Contrast essay about Lincoln's and Lee's historical perspective, affection for America, grief over the nation's crisis, and hopes for the future.

Name _____ Date _____

Contemporary Commentary

Nell Irvin Painter Introduces "An Account of an Experience with Discrimination" by Sojourner Truth

DIRECTIONS: *Use the space provided to answer the questions.*

1. According to Nell Irvin Painter, what kind of volunteer work did Sojourner Truth carry out in Washington, D.C., during the Civil War?

_____

_____

2. What were the events that Sojourner Truth dictated for publication in the antislavery press?

_____

_____

3. According to Painter, what are the "two American histories" to which Truth's experience of discrimination belongs?

_____

_____

_____

_____

4. Why was the war between black people and American railroads "national in scope"?

_____

_____

5. Identify three of the well-known African Americans named by Painter, and briefly describe how they suffered discrimination on railroad trains.

_____

_____

_____

_____

6. If you had a chance to interview Nell Irvin Painter, what are two questions you might ask her about how she performs historical research?

_____

_____

_____

_____

Nell Irvin Painter
Listening and Viewing

Segment 1: Meet Nell Irvin Painter
- How did Nell Irvin Painter first become interested in studying history?
- Why do you think historical writing is so important to society?

_____

_____

_____

Segment 2: Nell Irvin Painter Introduces Sojourner Truth
- Who was Sojourner Truth, and why was she an important historical figure during the Civil War?
- What two facts, which are often unknown, does Nell Irvin Painter want students to know?

_____

_____

_____

Segment 3: The Writing Process
- What is a primary source, and why are primary sources important to Nell Irvin Painter's historical narratives?

_____

_____

_____

Segment 4: The Rewards of Writing
- According to Nell Irvin Painter, why is it important that students view history critically?
- What do you think you can learn by reading historical narratives about people like Sojourner Truth?

_____

_____

_____

_____

Name _____ Date _____

"An Account of an Experience with Discrimination" by Sojourner Truth
Literary Analysis: Author's Purpose and Tone

An **author's purpose** is his or her reason for writing. For example, an author might write a letter to stay in touch with friends. Someone might write a journal entry to record feelings and details about an event in his or her life. An author's purpose helps shape his or her **tone,** which is the author's attitude toward the subject and audience. You may detect a tone of compassion, sorrow, anger, or pride, for example.

DIRECTIONS: *Complete each item using information from the selection and what you know about an author's purpose and tone.*

1. What is the author's purpose in these opening lines from "An Account of an Experience with Discrimination"? Explain your response.

   A few weeks ago I was in company with my friend Josephine S. Griffing, when the conductor of a streetcar refused to stop his car for me, although [I was] closely following Josephine and holding on to the iron rail.

   _____

   _____

   _____

2. What is Sojourner Truth's tone in these lines? How do you know?

   As I ascended the platform of the car, the conductor pushed me, saying "Go back—get off here." I told him I was not going off, then "I'll put you off" said he furiously, clenching my right arm with both hands, using such violence that he seemed about to succeed, when Mrs. Haviland told him he was not going to put me off.

   _____

   _____

   _____

3. Does the author's purpose or tone change in the course of this account? Explain.

   _____

   _____

   _____

Name _____ Date _____

"An Account of an Experience with Discrimination" by Sojourner Truth
Reading Strategy: Identify Relevant Details and Facts

To determine the **essential message** of a piece of writing, learn to **identify relevant facts and details.** Details and facts that are most relevant, or important, are those that are essential to understanding the main idea, characters, and setting. As you read, look for these relevant facts and details and how they are related.

DIRECTIONS: *Read the following excerpts from "An Account of an Experience with Discrimination." Each statement includes details and facts. Identify the two most relevant details and facts that will help you understand the selection.*

1. A few weeks ago I was in company with my friend Josephine S. Griffing, when the conductor of a streetcar refused to stop his car for me, although [I was] closely following Josephine and holding on to the iron rail.

   _____

   _____

2. She reported the conductor to the president of the City Railway, who dismissed him at once, and told me to take the number of the car whenever I was mistreated by a conductor or driver.

   _____

   _____

3. On the 13th I had occasion to go for necessities for the patients to the Freedmen's hospital where I have been doing and advising for a number of months. I thought now I would get a ride without trouble as I was in company with another friend, Laura S. Haviland of Michigan.

   _____

   _____

4. As I ascended the platform of the car, the conductor pushed me, saying "Go back—get off here."

   _____

   _____

5. "Does she belong to you?" said he in a hurried angry tone. "She replied, 'She does not belong to me, but she belongs to humanity.'

   _____

   _____

6. My shoulder was very lame and swollen, but is better. It is hard for the old slaveholding spirit to die. But die it must.

   _____

   _____

"An Account of an Experience with Discrimination" by Sojourner Truth
Vocabulary Builder

Using the Word List

ascended   assault

A. DIRECTIONS: *Rewrite each sentence, substituting a word from the Word List for each underlined word or phrase.*

1. Sojourner Truth <u>climbed up</u> the steps to enter the streetcar.

_____

2. The conductor denied that he had made a <u>violent attack</u> against Truth.

_____

B. DIRECTIONS: *For each item, choose the word pair that best expresses a relationship similar to that expressed in the numbered pair. Circle the letter of your choice.*

1. ASCENDED : MOUNTAIN ::
   A. swam : sea
   B. survived : continued
   C. enjoyed : responded
   D. relaxed : preference

2. ASSAULT : DEFEND ::
   A. souvenir : remember
   B. apology : forgive
   C. restraint : chain
   D. injustice : reform

Name _____ Date _____

"An Account of an Experience with Discrimination" by Sojourner Truth
Support for Writing

A newspaper reporter tries to answer the questions Who? What? When? Where? Why? and How? The most important information appears in the first paragraph so a reader can scan it and get an idea of what the story is about. Details to fill in the story are given in the following paragraphs.

Use the chart to gather and organize ideas for your **newspaper article** reporting on Sojourner Truth's experience with discrimination.

Questions	Answers (quotations, relevant facts, and details)
Who?	
What?	
When?	
Where?	
Why?	
How?	

On a separate page, write your newspaper article. Begin with a summary of the important facts of the incidents. Develop the story in the following paragraphs.

"The Boys' Ambition" *from* Life on the Mississippi and "The Notorious Jumping Frog of Calaveras County" by Mark Twain
Mark Twain: Biography

Mark Twain is one of America's greatest writers and humorists. His fiction incorporates lasting impressions of America in the late nineteenth century and insightful looks into human nature. He combines an examination of serious subjects with powerful and sometimes outrageous humor. Twain remains as important and delightful a literary figure today as in his heyday, more than a century ago.

A. DIRECTIONS: *Imagine that Mark Twain managed to find a way to travel forward in time, and he has agreed to appear before a contemporary American audience. You have been asked to introduce Mark Twain by giving a brief overview of his life. Identify three points you'll make for each segment of your talk. Suggest a photograph to illustrate each part.*

Life on the River (The early years) Key points: _____
_____

Photograph: _____
A Traveling Man (The middle years) Key points: _____
_____

Photograph: _____
A Restless Soul (The latter years) Key points: _____
_____

Photograph: _____

B. DIRECTIONS: *Imagine that you are Mark Twain, and you are appearing as a guest on a late-night TV show. Respond to these questions.*

Host: You once said that you would have been happier if you had been able to spend your entire life as a riverboat pilot rather than as a writer. You weren't serious, were you? What did you mean by that comment?

Twain: _____
_____

Host: You use humor very effectively in your writing. Explain to me how important you think humor is in the success of your writing.

Twain: _____
_____

Host: You have created some wonderful characters that are entirely American. In your opinion, how would you define a typical American?

Twain: _____
_____

"The Boys' Ambition" *from* **Life on the Mississippi** and **"The Notorious Jumping Frog of Calaveras County"** by Mark Twain

Literary Analysis: Humor

Humor in literature is writing that is intended to evoke laughter. American humorists use a variety of techniques to make their writing amusing. Mark Twain, for example, commonly uses hyperbole and regional dialect. He calls attention to human foibles and to incongruities between a speaker's tone and the events he describes and between logic and illogic. He points out the inability of people to control their surroundings

DIRECTIONS: *Decide whether the following passages are humorous because they contain hyperbole, regional dialect, incongruities, a sense of human foibles, or a combination of these elements. Write your answer on the lines following each passage.*

1. "He was the curiousest man about always betting on anything that turned up you ever see. . . ."

   _____

   _____

2. "If he even see a straddle bug start to go anywheres, he would bet you how long it would take him to get to . . . wherever . . . and if you took him up, he would foller that straddle bug to Mexico. . . ."

   _____

   _____

3. " . . . and *always* fetch up at the stand just about a neck ahead, as near as you could cipher it down."

   _____

   _____

4. 'He'd spring straight up and snake a fly off'n a counter there, and flop down on the floor ag'in as solid as a gob of mud."

   _____

   _____

5. He never smiled, he never frowned, he never changed his voice from the gentle-flowing key to which he tuned his initial sentence, he never betrayed the slightest suspicion of enthusiasm; but all through the interminable narrative there ran a vein of impressive earnestness and sincerity, which showed me plainly that, so far from his imagining that there was anything ridiculous or funny about his story, he regarded it as a really important matter, and admired its two heroes as men of transcendent genius in *finesse.*

   _____

   _____

"The Boys' Ambition" *from* **Life on the Mississippi** and **"The Notorious Jumping Frog of Calaveras County"** by Mark Twain

Reading Strategy: Understand Regional Dialect

Regional dialect is the informal language people use in everyday speech. Sometimes fiction writers use regional dialect to give readers a picture of certain characters. If you find it hard to understand this language when you're reading, try reading it aloud.

DIRECTIONS: *Read the following excerpts from "The Notorious Jumping Frog of Calaveras County." Write in your own words what you think each one means.*

1. ". . . he was the curiousest man about always betting on anything that turned up you ever see, if he could get anybody to bet on the other side; and if he couldn't he'd change sides."

   _____

   _____

   _____

2. "Thish-yer Smiley had a mare—the boys called her the fifteen-minute nag, but that was only in fun, you know, because of course she was faster than that—and he used to win money on that horse, for all she was so slow and always had the asthma, or the distemper, or the consumption, or something of that kind."

   _____

   _____

   _____

3. ". . . to look at him you'd think he warn't worth a cent but to set around and look ornery and lay for a chance to steal something. But as soon as money was up on him he was a different dog; his under-jaw'd begin to stick out like the fo'castle of a steamboat, and his teeth would uncover and shine like the furnaces."

   _____

   _____

   _____

4. ". . . all of a sudden he would grab that other dog jest by the j'int of his hind leg and freeze to it—not chaw, you understand, but only just grip and hang on till they throwed up the sponge, if it was a year."

   _____

   _____

   _____

Name _____ Date _____

"The Boys' Ambition" *from* Life on the Mississippi and "The Notorious Jumping Frog of Calaveras County" by Mark Twain
Vocabulary Builder

Using the Prefix *mono-*

A. DIRECTIONS: *The prefix* mono- *means "alone," "single," or "one." Use the clues given and what you know about the prefix* mono- *to figure out these word puzzles.*

1. knowing two languages = *bilingual;*

   knowing one language = _____

2. paralysis of one side of the body = *hemiplegia;*

   paralysis of a single limb = _____

3. a word with four or more syllables = *polysyllable*

   a word with one syllable = _____

4. having three of one type of chromosome = *trisomic*

   having a single chromosome = _____

Using the Word List

conjectured	eminence	garrulous	interminable
prodigious	monotonous	transient	

B. DIRECTIONS: *In the blank, write the letter of the Word List word that is closest in meaning to the numbered word.*

___ 1. guessed   A. transient

___ 2. celebrity   B. prodigious

___ 3. temporary   C. monotonous

___ 4. talkative   D. conjectured

___ 5. unvarying   E. interminable

___ 6. enormous   F. garrulous

___ 7. endless   G. eminence

"The Boys' Ambition" *from* **Life on the Mississippi** and **"The Notorious Jumping Frog of Calaveras County"** by Mark Twain

Grammar and Style: Fixing Misplaced and Dangling Modifiers

A **misplaced modifier** seems to modify the wrong word in a sentence because it is too far away from the word it really modifies. A **dangling modifier** seems to modify the wrong word—or no word at all—because the word it *should* modify isn't in the sentence. Misplaced and dangling modifiers can be single words, phrases, or clauses.

Misplaced:	*Sleepy*, the stores stood empty as the clerks nodded in their chairs.
Fixed:	The stores stood empty as the sleepy clerks nodded in their chairs.
Dangling:	*Turning upriver*, the next town was a few miles away.
Fixed:	Turning upriver, the steamboat headed toward the next town a few miles away.

A. PRACTICE: *Write a sentence using each phrase or word as a modifier. Then, circle the word or words that the phrase or clause modifies.*

1. that arrived at the landing

   _____

2. waiting his turn

   _____

3. lost in thought

   _____

4. looking carefully at his frog

   _____

5. who got the last laugh

   _____

B. Writing Application: *Decide whether the sentences below contain misplaced or dangling modifiers. If the sentence is written correctly, write "correct" on the line that follows it. If the sentence contains misplaced or dangling modifier, rewrite it correctly.*

1. Laughing heartily, the winning frog was cheered by the crowd.

   _____

2. Standing in the pilot house, he peered as far as he could see down the river.

   _____

3. Eager to see the steamboat arrive, the chores were left undone.

   _____

4. The passengers who left the steamboat wandered through the town.

   _____

5. Stories were often exaggerated while working as a reporter.

   _____

Name _____ Date _____

"The Boys' Ambition" *from* **Life on the Mississippi** and **"The Notorious Jumping Frog of Calaveras County"** by Mark Twain

Support for Writing

Think about Mark Twain's quote: "The humorous story may be spun out to great length, and may wander around as much as it pleases, and arrive nowhere in particular. . . . [It] is told gravely; the teller does his best to conceal the fact that he even dimly suspects there is anything funny about it." To gather information for your **analytical essay** about Twain's ideas of humor as they are reflected in "The Notorious Jumping Frog of Calaveras County," use the graphic organizer below.

Twain's Humor in "The Notorious Jumping Frog of Calaveras County"

Spins out at length (takes its time)	Arrives nowhere (doesn't have a point)	Is told gravely (with a serious tone)	Conceals humor (hides suggestions of humor)

On a separate page, draft your essay connecting each of Twain's points about humor with the example you have found in the story. When you revise, add examples to make your connections between Twain's comments and the story clearer.

from **The Life and Times of the Thunderbolt Kid** by Bill Bryson
Literary Analysis: Humor

Humor in literature is writing that is intended to make people laugh. American humorists use a variety of techniques to make their writing amusing. Bill Bryson, like Mark Twain, uses folk humor. Their techniques include use of **hyperbole, incongruity, regional** language and behavior, a focus on **human foibles,** and **comic characters.**

DIRECTIONS: *Decide whether the following passages are humorous because they contain hyperbole, incongruities, regional behavior or language, a display of human foibles, comic characters, or a combination of these elements. Write your answer on the lines following each passage.*

1. "The only downside of my mother's working was that it put a little pressure on her with regard to running the home and particularly with regard to dinner, which frankly was not her strong suit anyway."

   _____

2. "Like most people in Iowa in the 1950s, we were more cautious eaters in our house. On the rare occasions when we were presented with food with which we were not comfortable or familiar—on planes or trains or when invited to a meal cooked by someone who was not herself from Iowa—we tended to tilt it up carefully with a knife and examine it from every angle as if determining whether it might need to be defused."

   _____

3. "'It's a bit burned,' my mother would say apologetically at every meal, presenting you with a piece of meat that looked like something—a much-loved pet perhaps—salvaged from a tragic house fire."

   _____

4. "Hines's other proud boast was that he did not venture out of America until he was seventy years old, when he made a trip to Europe. He disliked much of what he found there, especially the food."

   _____

5. "All our meals consisted of leftovers. My mother had a seemingly inexhaustible supply of foods that had already been to the table, sometimes repeatedly."

   _____

Name _____ Date _____

from The Life and Times of the Thunderbolt Kid by Bill Bryson
Vocabulary Builder

Using the Word List

dubious   embark

A. DIRECTIONS: *Circle the synonym for the underlined word in each sentence or phrase.*

1. You soon learned to stand aside about ten to six every evening, for it was then that she would fly in the back door, throw something in the oven, and disappear into some other quarter of the house to <u>embark</u> on the thousand other household tasks that greeted her each evening. (commence, evaluate)

2. In our house we didn't eat . . . anything with <u>dubious</u> regional names like "pone" or "gumbo," or foods that had at any time been an esteemed staple of slaves or peasants.

   (humorous, questionable)

B. DIRECTIONS: *For each item, choose the word pair that best expresses a relationship similar to the one expressed in the numbered pair. Circle the letter of your choice.*

1. CERTAIN : DUBIOUS ::
   A. wishful : thoughtful
   B. threatened : endangered
   C. hungry : starving
   D. tasteless : delicious

2. TASK : EMBARK ::
   A. victim : rescue
   B. diet : hunger
   C. painter : create
   D. teacher : study

Name _____ Date _____

Support for Writing

Prepare to write your **essay** comparing character types in the selection from Bryson's *The Life and Times of the Thunderbolt Kid* and Twain's "The Notorious Jumping Frog of Calaveras County." Enter details from the selections in the chart below.

	Mother in *Thunderbolt Kid*	**Jim Smiley in "Jumping Frog"**
What makes the character funny?		
What makes the character sympathetic?		
How does the writer use the character to critique society or humanity?		

On a separate page, write a draft of your essay. Be sure to use transitions and an effective comparison-contrast organization to make your ideas clear. When you revise, make sure you have supported your main ideas with details from the selections.

Name _____ Date _____

"**To Build a Fire**" by Jack London

Literary Analysis: Conflict, Setting, Irony

Conflict is the struggle between two opposing forces or characters. An **internal conflict** is a struggle between conflicting thoughts and emotions within a character's mind. You face an internal conflict, for example, when you want to spend time studying for a test, yet you also want to go to a movie with your friends. An **external conflict** is a struggle between a character and an outside force, such as another character, society, nature, or fate. A pilot trying to land an airplane in strong winds is engaged in an external conflict—person against nature. In this last example, the **setting**—the place and time—serves as the source of the conflict. **Irony** is sometimes used to heighten the effect of the conflict by stressing a contradiction between what a character thinks and what the reader knows to be true.

DIRECTIONS: *Following are brief excerpts from "To Build a Fire." Identify the conflict in each as internal or external. Then identify the opposing forces and tell whether the setting is central to the conflict. Finally, identify any irony that may heighten the effect.*

1. "It was seventy-five below zero. Since the freezing point is thirty-two above zero, it meant that one hundred and seven degrees of frost obtained."

   _____

   _____

2. "He tried to keep this thought down, to forget it, to think of something else; he was aware of the panicky feeling that it caused, and he was afraid of the panic."

   _____

   _____

3. "He spoke to the dog . . . but in his voice was a strange note of fear that frightened the animal. . . . As it came within reaching distance, the man lost his control."

   _____

   _____

4. "High up in the tree one bough capsized its load of snow. . . . It grew like an avalanche, and it descended without warning upon the man and the fire, and the fire was blotted out!"

   _____

   _____

5. "He was very careful. He drove the thought of his freezing feet, and nose, and cheeks, out of his mind, devoting his whole soul to the matches."

   _____

   _____

6. ". . . it was a matter of life and death. This threw him into a panic, and he turned and ran up the creekbed along the old, dim trail."

   _____

   _____

7. "Well, he was bound to freeze anyway, and he might as well take it decently."

   _____

   _____

Name _____ Date _____

"**To Build a Fire**" by Jack London
Reading Strategy: Make Predictions

Making predictions about what you are reading based on clues in the text and on your previous experience can increase your enjoyment of a literary work and help you be a more effective reader. In "To Build a Fire," many of the clues come from the setting. The main character fails to recognize these clues, but as a reader, you can look for them and make predictions.

DIRECTIONS: *As you read "To Build a Fire," watch for clues from the setting that can help you predict what will happen next. In the chart below, list the clues, your predictions based on those clues, and the actual outcomes from the text.*

CLUES FROM SETTING	PREDICTION	OUTCOME

Name _____ Date _____

"To Build a Fire" by Jack London
Vocabulary Builder

Using the Latin Root -pend-

The Latin root -pend- means "to hang or extend" and appears in many English words.

A. DIRECTIONS: *Read the list of prefixes and their meanings. Then read each sentence and explain how the prefix and the root -pend- influence the meaning of the underlined word.*

de- = "down"
ap- = "near; toward"
sus- = "below; under"

1. Whether we head up to the cabin <u>depends</u> upon the weather.

_____

2. The definition of the new terms can be found in the <u>appendix</u> at the back of the book.

_____

3. Let's <u>suspend</u> the bird feeder from that branch.

_____

Using the Word List

    appendage   conflagration   conjectural   peremptorily   unwonted

B. DIRECTIONS: *Each question consists of a related pair of words in CAPITAL LETTERS, followed by four lettered pairs of words. Choose the lettered pair that best expresses a relationship similar to that expressed in the numbered pair and circle the letter of your choice.*

1. CAMPFIRE : CONFLAGRATION::
   A. car : truck
   B. spark : match
   C. flurry : blizzard
   D. sun : desert

2. CONJECTURAL : CERTAIN ::
   A. guess : fact
   B. generous : charitable
   C. delicious : tasty
   D. shifting : fixed

3. COMMANDS : PEREMPTORILY::
   A. awakes : retires
   B. sings : ballads
   C. moves : forward
   D. dances : gracefully

4. UNWONTED : SURPRISING ::
   A. undesired : hating
   B. cruel : frightening
   C. sparse : meager
   D. routine : unusual

5. APPENDAGE : LEG ::
   A. lost : found
   B. tree : branch
   C. fruit : apple
   D. result : cause

Name _____   Date _____

Grammar and Style: Using Introductory Phrases and Clauses

Using introductory phrases and clauses can help you vary your sentence structure and make your writing more interesting. A **phrase** is a group of words that acts as one part of speech but lacks a subject and a verb. A **clause** is a group of words that has a subject and a verb.

Subject First:	Old timers advised him not to set out.
Phrase First:	Knowing the danger of extreme cold, old timers advised him not to set out.
Subject First:	He set out despite the cold because he wanted to join his friends.
Clause First:	Because he wanted to join his friends, he set out despite the cold.

A. PRACTICE: *Use each phrase or clause to introduce a sentence.*

1. To build a fire in the snow and bitter cold

   _____

2. When he called to it

   _____

3. When he called to it

   _____

4. In the warm cabin

   _____

5. After his feet became soaked in the cold stream

   _____

B. Writing Application: *Rewrite each sentence, using a clause or phrase to begin your new sentence.*

1. The traveler relied upon his dog because he was alone in the wilderness.

   _____

2. Experienced Alaskans stayed inside on such bitter cold days.

   _____

3. He could not build a fire with his matches gone.

   _____

4. He nearly panicked when the snow put out the fire.

   _____

5. He walked quickly along the trail to keep warm.

   _____

Name _____ Date _____

"To Build a Fire" by Jack London
Support for Writing

Prepare to write your **literary analysis** of how the elements of "To Build a Fire" work together to communicate the story's message. Enter your thoughts and opinions in the chart below.

"To Build a Fire" — Analysis

Message of "To Build a Fire"	_____ _____ _____ _____
Setting : Details supporting message	_____ _____ _____ _____ _____
Characters: Details supporting message	_____ _____ _____ _____ _____
Plot: Details supporting message	_____ _____ _____ _____

On a separate page, write a draft of your literary analysis. State your thesis, as well as a main idea in each paragraph from your chart. When you revise, make sure you have supported your thesis, and add more details if you need to.

"Heading West" by Miriam Davis Colt
"I Will Fight No More Forever" by Chief Joseph
Primary Sources: Personal History and Speech

Documents such as memoirs and speeches that describe historical events from a personal point of view may contain opinions and beliefs as well as facts. Opinions and beliefs may depend upon **assumptions** by the writer. Often these are implied.

DIRECTIONS: *Read each passage from one of the two selections. Then, analyze and describe the assumption implied by the writer or speaker.*

1. **April 24th.** A hot summer day. The men in our company are out in the city, purchasing wagons and farming implements, to take along on the steamer up to Kansas City. —"Heading West"

   _____

   _____

2. **April 28th.** The steamer struck a "snag" last night. . . .

   April 30th. Here we are, at Kansas City, all safely again on terra firma. Hasten to the hotel—find it very much crowded. Go up, up, up, and upstairs to our lodging rooms. —"Heading West"

   _____

   _____

3. **May 3rd.** Father, it seems, fell back a little and found a place to camp in a tavern (not a hotel), where he fell in with the scores of Georgians who loaded a steamer and came up the river the same time that we did. He said he had to be very shrewd indeed not to have them find out that he was a "Free States" man.—"Heading West"

   _____

   _____

4. **May 12th**. . . . Look around and see the grounds all around the camp-fire are covered with tents, in which the families are staying. Not a house is to be seen. In the large tent here is a cook stove—they have supper prepared for us. . . .—"Heading West"

   _____

   _____

5. I want to have time to look for my children and see how many I can find. Maybe I shall find them among the dead.—"I Will Fight No More Forever"

   _____

   _____

"Heading West" by Miriam Davis Colt
"I Will Fight No More Forever" by Chief Joseph
Vocabulary Builder

A. DIRECTIONS: *Decide whether each statement below is true or false. Circle* **T** *or* **F**. *Then use the space provided to explain each of your answers.*

1. If you had *shares* in a piece of land you might enjoy owning it.
   T / F _____

2. If a *levee* lay between your home and a large river, you might have reason to worry about flooding during times of heavy rain.
   T / F _____

3. The native people feared that the new settlers were gaining a *foothold* on the land and would grow stronger and stronger.
   T / F _____

4. The heavily forested *prairie* seemed to stretch on for many miles.
   T / F _____

5. The wagons *forded* the river at a shallow place.
   T / F _____

Using the Word List

> emigrants   pervading   profusion   ravine

B. DIRECTIONS: *Rewrite each sentence below, replacing the italicized word or phrase with an appropriate word from the Word List.*

1. There were *people who moved* from many lands in the West.
   _____

2. As far as the eye could see, the prairie was covered by a *great abundance* of wild flowers.
   _____

3. The feeling *prevalent throughout* the Nez Perce camp was despair.
   _____

4. The people followed a *long, deep hollow in the ground* until they came to some water.
   _____

Name _____ Date _____

Literary Analysis: Irony

Irony is a contrast or a difference between what is stated and what is meant, or between what is expected to happen and what actually happens. **Situational irony** occurs when a result turns out differently than expected. For example, from the actions of Mrs. Mallard and her friends, readers expect that she will be overcome with grief at the news of her husband's death. Instead she exults in her freedom. **Dramatic irony** occurs when readers know something a character does not know. Readers know a few seconds before Mrs. Mallard, for example, that her husband is actually alive. Think of other stories you have read that use irony.

DIRECTIONS: *On the lines provided, identify stories you have read that use irony. Quote or summarize a passage that is an example of situational irony and one that is an example of dramatic irony. Then explain the irony in each passage.*

1. **Situational irony:**

   _____

   _____

   _____

   _____

   _____

   _____

   _____

   _____

   _____

   _____

2. **Dramatic irony:**

   _____

   _____

   _____

   _____

   _____

   _____

   _____

   _____

   _____

   _____

Name _____ Date _____

Reading Strategy: Analyze the Philosophical Argument

In their stories, authors sometimes express philosophical arguments in which they believe. When you **analyze the philosophical argument,** you examine details about the story's plot, characterization, or other story elements that illustrate or convey the argument.

DIRECTIONS: *On the chart below, list details about the plot and characters of Kate Chopin's story and explain how they illustrate or convey her philosophy.*

Details	How It Illustrates the Author's Philosophy

"The Story of an Hour" by Kate Chopin
Vocabulary Builder

Using the Word List

elusive   forestall   repression   tumultuously

A. DIRECTIONS: *Each question consists of a related pair of words in CAPITAL LETTERS, followed by four lettered pairs of words. Choose the lettered pair that best expresses a relationship similar to that expressed in the numbered pair. Circle the letter of your choice.*

___ 1. FORESTALL : DELAY ::
A. hurry : rush
B. worry : disregard
C. despair : believe
D. deserve : forgive

___ 2. SERENELY : TUMULTUOUSLY ::
A. precisely : accurately
B. possibly : remotely
C. recklessly : cautiously
D. strictly : resentfully

___ 3. DICTATOR : REPRESSION ::
A. dancer : music
B. judge : justice
C. actor : theater
D. student : school

___ 4. ELUSIVE : VAGUE ::
A. stout : harmless
B. sincere : delicate
C. resourceful : troubled
D. scholarly : studious

B. DIRECTIONS: *Select the Word List word that relates best to each situation, and write the word on the line.*

1. Mrs. Mallard's previous actions regarding her feelings about her marriage

_____

2. the way Mrs. Mallard's imaginings about the free days ahead of her went through her mind

_____

3. Richards's attempt to keep the shock of seeing her husband alive from Mrs. Mallard

_____

4. the mysterious, unsolvable nature of love

_____

"The Story of an Hour" by Kate Chopin
Support for Writing

Prepare to write a **reflective essay** about a time in which your life changed dramatically, such as a move from one home to another. Enter your memories and reflections on the event in the graphic organizer below.

Sometimes Life Changes Quickly

Event that changed my life:

_____

_____

_____

_____

_____

_____

Life before event:

_____

_____

_____

_____

_____

Life after event:

_____

_____

_____

_____

_____

My feelings about the change:

_____

_____

_____

_____

_____

On a separate page, write a draft of your reflective essay. Organize your thoughts either in chronological order or in their order of importance. When you revise your essay, be sure your thoughts and feelings about the dramatic event have been made clear to the reader. Add or eliminate information to strengthen the impression you wish to make.

"Douglass" and **"We Wear the Mask"** by Paul Laurence Dunbar
Literary Analysis: Formal Verse

Formal verse is poetry that follows a regular structure. Many formal poems follow a **rhyme scheme,** which is the regular pattern of rhyming words at the end of lines. One of the traditional forms of formal verse is the **sonnet,** which has fourteen lines that follow a specific rhyme scheme. Some sonnets consist of an eight-line octave followed by a six-line sestet. Some have three four-line quatrains and a final couplet.

DIRECTIONS: *Read the following lines from the poems. Identify the rhyme schemes.*

1.

Ah, Douglass, we have fall'n on evil days,

    Such days as thou, not even thou didst know,

    When thee, the eyes of that harsh long ago

Saw, salient, at the cross of devious ways,

And all the country heard thee with amaze.

    Not ended then, the passionate ebb and flow,

    The awful tide that battled to and fro;

We ride amid a tempest of dispraise.

Rhyme scheme: _____

2.

Now, when the waves of swift dissension swarm,

    And Honor, the strong pilot, lieth stark,

Oh, for thy voice high-sounding o'er the storm,

    For thy strong arm to guide the shivering bark,

The blast-defying power of thy form,

    To give us comfort through the lonely dark.

Rhyme scheme: _____

3.

We wear the mask that grins and lies,

It hides our cheeks and shades our eyes,

This debt we pay to human guile;

With torn and bleeding hearts we smile,

And mouth with myriad subtleties.

Rhyme scheme: _____

"Douglass" and "We Wear the Mask" by Paul Laurence Dunbar

Reading Strategy: Analyze the Effect of the Historical Period

When interpreting a poem, you sometimes need to **analyze the effects of the historical period** on lines. "Read between the lines"—carefully examining the words for what they say and imply about the period.

DIRECTIONS: *Answer these interpretive questions about the historical period of Dunbar's poetry. Refer to the selection if you need to.*

1. In "Douglass," who is the "we" in the excerpt "Ah, Douglass, we have fall'n on evil days"?

   _____

   _____

2. In "Douglass," what is the "awful tide that battled to and fro"?

   _____

   _____

   _____

3. In "Douglass," what does the "shivering bark" signify?

   _____

   _____

4. In "Douglass," what is the "lonely dark"?

   _____

   _____

5. Why does Dunbar address the poem "Douglass" to Frederick Douglass, an American abolitionist?

   _____

   _____

   _____

6. What is the mask hiding in "We Wear the Mask"?

   _____

   _____

7. Why does Dunbar want to "hide our cheeks" and "shade our eyes" in "We Wear the Mask"?

   _____

   _____

   _____

Name _____ Date _____

Vocabulary Builder

Related Words: Forms of *guile*

The word *guile* means "craftiness." The word *beguile* means "to mislead by craftiness or deceit." *Guile* and *beguile* are related words.

A. DIRECTIONS: *Form other words from* guile *and* beguile *by adding the suffixes listed. Write the meaning of each word on the lines.*

1. *beguile* + *-ed* _____

_____

2. *guile* + *-less* _____

_____

3. *beguile* + *-er* _____

_____

4. *beguile* + *-ing* _____

_____

Using the Word List

  guile   myriad   salient   stark   dissension

B. DIRECTIONS: *Circle the word that best completes each sentence.*

1. The error was salient and stood _____ all the rest.
   A. out from   B. below   C. by   D. to the right
2. Dissension over the final play of the game caused the players to become _____.
   A. joyful   B. timid   C. skeptical   D. upset
3. The stark trees stood out _____ against the rest of the landscape.
   A. boldly   B. subtly   C. darkly   D. colorfully
4. The guile shown by the con artist demonstrated her level of _____.
   A. brashness   B. trickiness   C. perkiness   D. voicelessness
5. The myriad colors made the room seem like a _____.
   A. paintbrush   B. airbrush   C. rainbow   D. gray color

Name _____ Date _____

"Douglass" and **"We Wear the Mask"** by Paul Laurence Dunbar
Support for Writing

Use library and Internet resources to find information on how critics responded to Dunbar's poetry. Record your findings on the chart below. Identify each source of your information.

Source	Details of Positive and Negative Reviews

On a separate page, write your report, summarizing your findings. Include examples, quotations, and other details to support your summary.

"Luke Havergal" and "Richard Cory" by Edwin Arlington Robinson
"Lucinda Matlock" and "Richard Bone" by Edgar Lee Masters
Literary Analysis: Speaker

Often, the **speaker** of a poem is the poet, but when the speaker is a fictional character, as in the poems by Edwin Arlington Robinson and Edgar Lee Masters, the poem may not only communicate a message, but also reveal the attitude of the speaker and possibly the development of his or her character. For example, in "Richard Cory," the speaker looks with envy and admiration on Cory for his wealth and breeding. This provides insight into the character speaking the poem—that he or she is not of the same economic or social class.

DIRECTIONS: *In some poems, the speaker's identity is obvious, but in other poems, such as "Luke Havergal," the speaker's identity and purpose are more mysterious. Read "Luke Havergal" again, and then answer the questions below. Cite examples from the poem to support your answers.*

1. What details from "Luke Havergal" provide clues to the speaker's identity?

   _____

   _____

2. Do you think the woman whom the speaker mentions is alive or dead? Why or why not?

   _____

   _____

   _____

   _____

3. Is the speaker of this poem providing advice about a physical journey or a supernatural one? How can you tell?

   _____

   _____

4. Does the speaker of this poem expect Luke Havergal to find happiness? How can you tell?

   _____

   _____

5. What do you think happened to Luke Havergal before the speaker began speaking?

   _____

   _____

"Luke Havergal" and **"Richard Cory"** by Edwin Arlington Robinson
"Lucinda Matlock" and **"Richard Bone"** by Edgar Lee Masters

Reading Strategy: Comparing and Contrasting

When you read poems by a single writer, on a similar theme, or dating from the same or even a different time period, it often helps you understand each poem if you apply the skill of **comparing and contrasting.** By comparing the poems' **formal elements, point of view,** and **theme,** you can gain insight into each poem as well as into the characteristics of the group.

DIRECTIONS: *Use this chart to help you compare and contrast the poems by Edwin Arlington Robinson and Edgar Lee Masters. For each poem, describe the characteristics at the top of each column. Use your finished chart to consider how they are alike and different.*

	Formal Elements	**Point of View**	**Theme**
"Luke Havergal"			
"Richard Cory"			
"Lucinda Matlock"			
"Richard Bone"			

"Luke Havergal" and "Richard Cory" by Edwin Arlington Robinson
"Lucinda Matlock" and "Richard Bone" by Edgar Lee Masters
Vocabulary Builder

Using the Latin Root -genus-

A. DIRECTIONS: *The Latin root -genus- means "birth, race, species, or kind." Define each underlined word below based on its use in the sentence and what you know about the word root -genus-.*

1. The physician explained that the disease was <u>congenital</u> and even the healthiest lifestyle would not have prevented its onslaught.

   _____

   _____

2. Poetry is one of the most intense, compact of all literary <u>genres.</u>

   _____

   _____

3. The beautiful stitching and vivid colors convinced her that the quilt was <u>genuine.</u>

   _____

   _____

4. Each <u>generation</u> of Americans has its own priorities and interests.

   _____

   _____

Using the Word List

> chronicles   degenerate   epitaph   repose

B. DIRECTIONS: *Above each underlined word in the following paragraph, write a synonym from the Word List.*

During her life, Arliss's accusers claimed she was a <u>corrupt</u> person, but when she died, the

community maintained a respectful silence as she was lowered into her final <u>rest</u>. The

headstone above her grave bore the <u>legend</u> "A loyal sister, a wise leader, loved by all." Still, the

<u>stories</u> of her many deceits and exploits persisted.

Name _____ Date _____

"Luke Havergal" and "Richard Cory" by Edwin Arlington Robinson
"Lucinda Matlock" and "Richard Bone" by Edgar Lee Masters
Support for Writing

Use the outline to organize ideas for your fictional narrative based on one of the poems in this grouping.

Poem: _____

I. Beginning: _____

    A. _____

        1. _____

        2. _____

    B. _____

        1. _____

        2. _____

I. Middle: _____

    A. _____

        1. _____

        2. _____

    B. _____

        1. _____

        2. _____

I. End: _____

    A. _____

        1. _____

        2. _____

    B. _____

        1. _____

        2. _____

Name _____ Date _____

"A Wagner Matinée" by Willa Cather
Literary Analysis: Characterization

Most readers enjoy a story more when they feel as if they know the characters as people. **Characterization** is the way in which a writer reveals a character's personality. A writer can make direct statements about a character, give a physical description, describe the character's actions, and/or tell the character's thoughts and comments.

DIRECTIONS: *Read each excerpt from the selection, and write down what each tells you about the character of Aunt Georgiana.*

1. "Whatever shock Mrs. Springer experienced at my aunt's appearance she considerately concealed."

   _____

   _____

2. ". . . a plain, angular, spectacled woman of thirty."

   _____

   _____

3. ". . . she eloped with him, eluding the reproaches of her family and the criticism of her friends by going with him to the Nebraska frontier."

   _____

   _____

4. ". . . in those days I owed to this woman most of the good that ever came my way, . . ."

   _____

   _____

5. "Don't love it so well, Clark, or it may be taken from you."

   _____

   _____

6. "When the violins drew out the first strain of the Pilgrims' chorus, my Aunt Georgiana clutched my coat sleeve."

   _____

   _____

7. "Poor old hands! They were stretched and pulled and twisted into mere tentacles to hold, and lift, and knead with; . . ."

   _____

   _____

8. "She burst into tears and sobbed pleadingly, 'I don't want to go, Clark, I don't want to go!'"

   _____

   _____

"**A Wagner Matinée**" by Willa Cather
Reading Strategy: Clarify

As you read, it is important to **clarify**, or check your understanding of, the details in what you read. You can clarify the details by reading a footnote, looking up a word in the dictionary, rereading a passage to refresh your memory, or reading ahead to find additional details.

DIRECTIONS: *Read each phrase from the selection. Answer the question using one clarifying strategy.*

1. ". . . the gangling farmer boy my aunt had known, scourged with chilblains . . ."
   What is a chilblain?

   _____

   _____

2. "[Aunt Georgiana] had come all the way in a day coach. . . ."
   What was the origin of Aunt Georgiana's trip, and what was her destination?

   _____

   _____

3. "One summer, which she had spent in the little village in the Green Mountains where her ancestors had dwelt for generations, . . ."
   Where are the Green Mountains?

   _____

   _____

4. "I suggested our visiting the Conservatory and the Common before lunch, . . ."
   Why would Aunt Georgiana be interested in the Conservatory?

   _____

   _____

5. ". . . with the bitter frenzy of the Venusberg theme and its ripping of strings, . . ."
   What is the significance of the term *Venusberg*?

   _____

   _____

6. "Soon after the tenor began the 'Prize Song,' I heard a quick-drawn breath, and turned to my aunt. Her eyes were closed, but the tears were glistening on her cheeks, . . ."
   Why did the "Prize Song" make Aunt Georgiana cry?

   _____

   _____

"A Wagner Matinée" by Willa Cather
Vocabulary Builder

Using Words From Music

Words from music can often have two meanings—one specific musical meaning and one for use in a nonmusical context.

A. DIRECTIONS: *Each sentence below contains a word from music. On the line below the sentence, write either* musical *or* nonmusical *to show how the word is used in the sentence.*

1. The team practiced as a <u>prelude</u> to the big game.

   _____

2. His <u>key</u> didn't fit in the new lock.

   _____

3. When we heard the <u>prelude</u>, we knew the performance had just started.

   _____

4. They played the song in a <u>minor</u> key.

   _____

Using the Word List

   inert   jocularity   prelude   reverential   tremulously

B. DIRECTIONS: *Each sentence includes a word or phrase that means about the same as one of the words in the Word List. Underline that word or phrase and write the Word List word in the blank.*

1. The orchestra began with the overture to the opera. _____

2. Aunt Georgiana was emotional and spoke with a quivering voice. _____

3. In the concert hall, she seemed somewhat less unable to move. _____

4. Clark's attempts at light-hearted joking seemed lost on Aunt Georgiana.

   _____

5. Clark had very respectful feelings for his aunt. _____

Name _____ Date _____

"**A Wagner Matinée**" by Willa Cather
Support for Writing

As you prepare to write an **editorial** on Willa Cather's portrayal of Nebraska, enter your arguments in the chart below. Keep in mind that you will be writing as though you are the editor of a Nebraska newspaper.

Why Willa Cather's "A Wagner Matinée" Is Fair/Not Fair to Nebraskans

Example from story: Why it supports my opinion
_____
_____
_____
_____
_____
_____
Example from story: Why it supports my opinion
_____
_____
_____
_____
_____
_____
Example from story: Why it supports my opinion
_____
_____
_____
_____
_____
_____

On a separate page, put your examples in order of importance and write a draft of your editorial. When you revise your work, make sure you have used persuasive language to make your point of view clear and powerful.

Essential Questions Workshop—Unit 3

In their stories, poems, and nonfiction, the writers in Unit Three express ideas that relate to the three Essential Questions framing this book. Review the literature in the unit. Then, for each Essential Question, choose an author and at least one passage from his or her writing that expresses a related idea. Use this chart to complete your work.

Essential Question	Author/Selection	Literary Passage
How does literature shape or reflect society?		
What is the relationship between place and literature?		
What makes American literature American?		

Unit 4 Introduction
Names and Terms to Know

A. DIRECTIONS: *Write a brief sentence explaining each of the following names and terms. You will find all of the information you need in the Unit 4 Introduction in your textbook.*

1. Woodrow Wilson: _____

2. female suffrage: _____
   _____

3. The New Deal: _____
   _____

4. Pearl Harbor: _____
   _____

5. *The Waste Land*: _____

6. The Harlem Renaissance: _____
   _____

B. DIRECTIONS: *Use the hints below to help you answer each question.*

1. How did World War I change Americans' spirit?
   [Hints: What spirit was associated with America before World War I? What were some of the most destructive aspects of World War I?]

   _____

   _____

   _____

2. How did Roosevelt's New Deal affect American society?
   [Hints: What was the Great Depression? What was the purpose of the New Deal, and what were some of its programs?]

   _____

   _____

   _____

3. How did World War II change America?
   [Hints: What is isolationism? Who were the U.S. allies in the war? What happened at Hiroshima and Nagasaki?]

   _____

   _____

   _____

Name _____ Date _____

Unit 4 Introduction

Essential Question 1: What is the relationship between place and literature?

A. DIRECTIONS: *Answer the questions about the first Essential Question in the Introduction, about the relationship between place and literature. All the information you need is in the Unit 4 Introduction in your textbook.*

1. *American Places Affecting American Life*

    a. What were the positive and negative aspects of the growth of many cities into metropolises? _____

_____

    b. During this period, towns became _____ and farms suffered from _____

2. *Non-American Places Affecting American Life*

    a. How did Americans feel as a result of World War I? _____

_____

    b. Parisian studios and cafes offered Americans _____

_____

3. *Impact on American Literature*

    a. Who were the "Lost Generation" and what did they do? _____

_____

    b. The emptiness and sterility of cities was portrayed in the works of such writers as

_____

    c. The Harlem Renaissance portrayed and celebrated _____

_____

B. DIRECTIONS: *Answer the questions that include the Essential Question Vocabulary words.*

    1. Would you expect to see open fields in a *metropolis*? Why or why not? _____

_____

    2. Why would someone who relocates feel like an *exile*? _____

_____

    3. Why might television be called a "*vast wasteland*"? _____

_____

Name _____ Date _____

Unit 4 Introduction

Essential Question 2: How did literature shape or reflect society?

A. DIRECTIONS: *On the lines provided, answer the questions about the second Essential Question in the Introduction, about the relationship between the writer and society. All the information you need is in the Unit 4 Introduction in your textbook.*

1. *Major Social and Political Events Affecting Americans*

    a. The devastation of World War I made it clear that _____
_____

    b. How did the Depression and the New Deal affect Americans?_____
_____

    c. What was the Dust Bowl, and when did it occur? _____
_____

    d. The horrors of World War II included _____

2. *Values, Attitudes, and Ideas*

    a. The values and beliefs of the nineteenth century were _____
_____

    b. Which groups in American society were affected by greater democratization?
_____

    c. The fragmentation of experience was _____

3. *Expressions in Literature*

    a. Give examples of traditional styles rejected by Modernists. _____
_____

    b. Name two Modernist female writers. _____

    c. Name a prominent Harlem Renaissance writer. _____

    d. What elements of Modernist style created discontinuity? _____
_____

    e. What areas of popular culture grew between 1914 and 1945? _____
_____

B. DIRECTIONS: *Answer the following questions that use the Essential Question Vocabulary words.*

1. When *disillusion* sets in, is it likely to make someone happier or not? Explain. _____
_____

2. Meals at our house are an exercise in *fragmentation* because _____
_____

3. My brother had trouble adjusting to the *transition* between _____
_____

Unit 4 Introduction

Essential Question 3: What makes American literature American?

A. DIRECTIONS: *On the lines provided, answer the questions about the third Essential Question in the Introduction, about what makes American literature American. All the information you need is in the Unit 4 Introduction in your textbook.*

1. *Modernist Changes*

   a. Give examples of how Modernists changed narrative conventions. _____
   _____
   _____

   b. What types of themes did Modernists explore? _____
   _____

   c. How is the Modernists' use of language different from that of earlier writers? _____
   _____

   d. What kinds of images and allusions did Modernists use? _____
   _____

2. *Relationship between Modernist Writers and the Public*

   a. At first the reading public turned away from Modernist writers because _____
   _____

   b. How and why did the attitude of the public to the Modernists change later on?
   _____

3. *American Identities in American Literature*

   a. How did the "denizen of the Waste Land" see the world? _____
   _____

   b. What qualities and writers are associated with the "Lost Generation"? _____
   _____

   c. Who is the "Triumphant Commoner," and what writers celebrated this person? _____
   _____

   d. What writers are associated with the "Poetic Maker"? _____
   _____

   e. Who are some African-American artists? _____

B. DIRECTIONS: *Answer the questions based on the Essential Question Vocabulary words.*

1. Would something that is *commonplace* be hard or easy to find? _____
2. Would *ambiguity* make something clearer or not? _____
3. Someone who uses *innovation* solves problems by _____

Unit 4 Introduction
Following-Through Activities

A. CHECK YOUR COMPREHENSION: *Use his chart to complete the Check Your Comprehension activity in the Unit 4 Introduction. In the left column, fill in two key concepts for each Essential Question, and then one author for each concept. One example for Literature and Society has already been done in your textbook.*

ESSENTIAL QUESTION	KEY CONCEPT	LITERARY CHANGES
Place and Literature	1. _____ 2. _____	1. _____ 2. _____
American Literature.	1. _____ 2. _____	1. _____ 2. _____
Literature and Society	1. _____ 2. _____	1. _____ 2. _____

B. EXTEND YOUR LEARNING: *Use this graphic organizer to help plan your research for the Extend Your Learning activity.*

Area of Popular Culture: _____

People
1. Who were some outstanding people in this field? _____
2. What did these individuals accomplish? _____
_____
_____

Works: Outstanding works and their special characteristics
_____
_____
_____

American Identity: What did these works say about Americans?
_____
_____
_____

Visual Support	**Audio Support**
_____ _____ _____ _____	_____ _____ _____ _____

"The Love Song of J. Alfred Prufrock" by T. S. Eliot
Literary Analysis: Dramatic Monologue

A **dramatic monologue** is a poem or speech in a play or novel in which a character speaks his or her thoughts aloud about a crucial event or feeling in the character's life. In "The Love Song of J. Alfred Prufrock," Prufrock is speaking to a silent companion—perhaps a part of himself. What Prufrock says reveals a deep split between what he desires and his ability to achieve his desires. Several times in the poem, Prufrock repeats these questions: "Do I dare?" and "How should I presume?" These repeated lines may suggest that Prufrock wishes to act but is deeply afraid of failure and rejection.

An **allusion** is a reference to a well-known person, place, event, literary work, or work of art. Eliot and other writers use allusions as a kind of shorthand to suggest complex ideas in just a few words. The allusions in "Prufrock" build a complex web of meaning.

DIRECTIONS: *Read the lines from the poem and answer the questions on another sheet of paper. Give examples from the poem as evidence to support your interpretation.*

1. In the following lines, what kind of women does Prufrock see? How does the allusion to Michelangelo contribute to your interpretation?

    In the room the women come and go / Talking of Michelangelo.

2. In the following lines, what might Prufrock wish he could dare to do?

    Time to turn back and descend the stair, / With a bald spot in the middle of my hair— / (They will say: "How his hair is growing thin!") / My morning coat, my collar mounting firmly to the chin, / My necktie rich and modest, but asserted by a simple pin— / (They will say: "But how his arms and legs are thin!") / Do I dare / Disturb the universe?

3. What could these lines show Prufrock is afraid of? To what does he compare himself? Why is this an apt comparison?

    And I have known the eyes already, known them all— / The eyes that fix you in a formulated phrase, / And when I am formulated, sprawling on a pin, / When I am pinned and wriggling on the wall, / Then how should I begin / To spit out all the butt-ends of my days and ways? / And how should I presume?

4. What might Prufrock want to do at this point? Why is he unable to do it?

    Shall I part my hair behind? Do I dare to eat a peach? / I shall wear white flannel trousers, and walk upon the beach. / I have heard the mermaids singing, each to each.

    I do not think that they will sing to me.

"The Love Song of J. Alfred Prufrock" by T. S. Eliot
Reading Strategy: Adjust Reading Rate

Adjust your reading rate in order to listen to the sound effects produced by the words and musical devices. Slow down or speed up and listen to the poem. **Listening** can be as important as the words themselves. Writers use sound effects and musical devices to enhance the poem's mood and meaning. One device they sometimes use is **alliteration,** which is the repetition of consonant sounds at the beginning of words or accented syllables. Other effects often used are repetition, rhyme, and rhythm. All of these devices are present in the following excerpt from "The Love Song of J. Alfred Prufrock."

> Time for you and time for me,/ And time yet for a hundred indecisions,/ And for a hundred visions and revisions./ Before the taking of a toast and tea.

Notice the repetition of the word *time.* It suggests that Prufrock is trying to convince himself that there is an abundance of time in which to be indecisive. The rhyming of *indecisions, visions,* and *revisions* gives the lines a fluid internal structure and a pleasing sound. The rhythm flows in beats, evoking the feeling of time passing. The excerpt ends with the alliteration of *t's* giving the line a sharp, prim and proper feel.

These musical qualities occur throughout "The Love Song of J. Alfred Prufrock," and to appreciate them, you must listen as you read.

DIRECTIONS: *Read each of the following excerpts aloud. On the lines following each one, note which musical devices are being used. Explain how they contribute to the musicality of the poem.*

1. "The yellow fog that rubs its back upon the window-panes, / The yellow smoke that rubs its muzzle on the window-panes."

_____

_____

_____

2. "And indeed there will be time/ To wonder, 'Do I dare?' And 'Do I dare?'/ Time to turn back and descend the stair,/ With a bald spot in the middle of my hair—"

_____

_____

_____

3. "I have seen the moment of my greatness flicker,/ And I have seen the eternal Footman hold my coat and snicker."

_____

_____

_____

All-in-One Workbook
195

"The Love Song of J. Alfred Prufrock" by T. S. Eliot
Vocabulary Builder

Using the Prefix *di-*

A. DIRECTIONS: *Each of the following sentences includes an italicized word that contains the prefix* di- *(or* dis-*), meaning "away" or "apart." Fill in the blank with a word or phrase that completes the sentence and reveals the meaning of the italicized word.*

1. When the botanist *dissected* the flower, she _____.
2. When an elected official is *divested* of his or her office, it is _____.
3. If a company produces a *diverse* line of products, each product is _____.
4. If I *divert* a child's attention from something, she will _____.
5. The protesters tried to *disrupt* the meeting, causing it to _____.

Using the Word List

digress   insidious   malingers   meticulous   obtuse   tedious

B. DIRECTIONS: *Replace each bracketed word or phrase with one of the words in the Word List.*

1. We suspect that the boy often [fakes illness] _____ when he claims he is too sick to go to school in the morning but feels well enough to go to a ball game in the afternoon.
2. Robert was such a [neat and careful] _____ cook that his kitchen was usually spotless.
3. Although Denise hinted that she would like to date him, Ramon seemed too [dense] _____ to understand.
4. The constant criticism and teasing that Laverne received from her older brother had a(n) [damaging] _____ effect on her self-confidence.
5. Pardon me if I [stray] _____ from the subject, but I have some interesting news.
6. Filing forms all day was such a [dull] _____ task that George nearly fell asleep.

"The Love Song of J. Alfred Prufrock" by T. S. Eliot
Support for Writing

To prepare to write a **character analysis** of J. Alfred Prufrock, enter information from the poem in the graphic organizer below. To respond to each heading, write examples from the poem.

The Character of J. Alfred Prufrock

What J. Alfred Prufrock does with his time	What J. Alfred Prufrock thinks/feels about love
What J. Alfred Prufrock thinks/ feels about himself	**What J. Alfred Prufrock thinks/ feels about other people**

What other people would say about J. Alfred Prufrock

On a separate page, write a draft of your character analysis, using evidence from the poem to support the statements you make about J. Alfred Prufrock. When you revise your work, be sure to replace vague language with more specific and descriptive words.

Ezra Pound, William Carlos Williams, H. D.
Literary Analysis: Imagist Poems

The imagists were American poets who became prominent between 1909 and 1918. The **imagist poems** they created evoke emotion and spark the imagination through **images**—words and phrases that appeal to the senses: sight, sound, touch, smell, and taste. The imagists limited the number of images they developed in a poem but developed them intricately in just a few words.

DIRECTIONS: *Read each poem or excerpt. Then answer the question.*

1. Name three concrete images in this poem.

   so much depends / upon / a red wheel / barrow / glazed with rain / water / beside the white / chickens.

   _____

   _____

   _____

2. List five words in this excerpt that can be seen as exact.

   Among the rain / and lights / I saw the figure 5 / in gold / on a red / fire truck

   _____

   _____

   _____

   _____

3. Which of the objectives of the Imagist poets do you think are achieved in this excerpt? Explain.

   I have eaten / the plums / that were in / the icebox / and which / you were probably / saving / for breakfast

   _____

   _____

   _____

   _____

   _____

   _____

   _____

   _____

   _____

   _____

Name _____ Date _____

Reading Stategy: Engage Your Senses

One way to enjoy, appreciate, and understand what you read is to engage your senses. Imagine yourself actually seeing, smelling, hearing, tasting, or touching the images presented by the writer. Put yourself at the scene mentally, and experience the images in your mind's eye.

DIRECTIONS: *Use this graphic organizer to help yourself engage your senses as you read these poems. From each poem, choose images that appeal to the senses. Write the image in the corresponding box or boxes. Remember that many images can be appreciated by more than one sense.*

	See	Hear	Touch	Smell	Taste
"In a Station of the Metro"					
"The Red Wheelbarrow"					
"The Great Figure"					
"This Is Just to Say"					
"Pear Tree"					

Ezra Pound, William Carlos Williams, H. D.
Vocabulary Builder

Forms of *appear*

The following words are based on the verb *appear,* meaning "to come into sight or into being" or "to become understood."

apparent   apparition   appearance

A. DIRECTIONS: *Rewrite each sentence by replacing the italicized word or words with one of the words above.*

1. The *seeming* cause of the accident was a drunk driver.

   _____

2. The *ghostly face* in the hallway mirror made the movie audience scream.

   _____

3. The glamorous young star knew that her *showing* at the charity event was important.

   _____

   _____

Using the Word List

apparition   dogma   voluminous

B. DIRECTIONS: *Fill in each blank with the word from the Word List that fits best.*

1. The professor carried on a(n) _____ correspondence with the author whose biography he was writing.

2. Don't accept as _____ the following rules about writing poetry; your own ideas may be just as good.

3. The grieving widow thought she saw a(n) _____ of her late husband standing in the moonlit garden.

Name _____ Date _____

Ezra Pound, William Carlos Williams, H. D.
Support for Writing

As you prepare to write a **review of a manuscript** by an Imagist poet, take notes on one of the poems in this selection. Use the graphic organizer to show why, as an editor, you will or will not accept the poem for publication.

Review of _____

What is strong in the poem	What is weak in the poem	Why I would/would not publish the poem

On a separate page, write your draft of a letter to the poet, telling him or her why you are or are not going to publish the poem. When you revise, replace vague words with specific descriptions.

Name _____ Date _____

"**Winter Dreams**" by F. Scott Fitzgerald
Literary Analysis: Characterization

Characterization is the revelation of characters' personalities throughout a story. Just like you, characters are partly shaped by the social influences of the historical period in which they live. Fitzgerald's characters reflect the post-World War I era in their perspectives on prosperity and personal freedom.

DIRECTIONS: *Read each excerpt from the selection and consider the effect that the social influences had on the character. Then, with this in mind, write down what you learn about each character.*

1. Dexter: "He wanted not association with glittering things and glittering people—he wanted the glittering things themselves."

   _____

   _____

2. Dexter: "All about him rich men's sons were peddling bonds precariously, or investing patrimonies precariously, or plodding through the two dozen volumes of the 'George Washington Commercial Course,' but Dexter borrowed a thousand dollars on his college degree and his confident mouth, and bought a partnership in a laundry."

   _____

   _____

3. Dexter: "So he signed his name one day on the register, and that afternoon played golf . . . He did not consider it necessary to remark that he had once carried Mr. Hart's bag over this same link, and that he knew every trap and gully with his eyes shut—but he found himself glancing at the four caddies who trailed them . . . "

   _____

   _____

4. Judy: "But I've just had a horrible afternoon. There was a man I cared about, and this afternoon he told me out of a clear sky that he was poor as a church mouse. He'd never hinted it before."

   _____

   _____

Name _____ Date _____

Reading Strategy: Draw Inferences to Determine Meaning

When you read a story, you can **draw inferences to determine meaning** by combining information from the story with your personal knowledge of human behavior. To draw inferences, you often need to read between the lines to infer emotions and motivations that are not directly stated.

DIRECTIONS: *Read each excerpt from "Winter Dreams." Then, answer the question that follows.*

1. As so frequently would be the case in the future, Dexter was unconsciously dictated to by his winter dreams.

   Does Dexter always plan his moves carefully and then follow them, or does he sometimes behave impetuously?

   _____

2. "You hit me in the stomach!" declared Mr. Hedrick wildly. / "Did I?" [Judy] approached the group of men. "I'm sorry. I yelled 'Fore!'" / ". . . Here I am! I'd have gone on the green except that I hit something."

   How does Judy probably feel about hitting Mr. Hedrick?

   _____

3. [Judy] wore a blue silk afternoon dress, and [Dexter] was disappointed at first that she had not put on something more elaborate.

   What does Judy's behavior toward Dexter on their first date reveal about her?

   _____

4. [Dexter] had been born in Keeble, a Minnesota village fifty miles farther north, and he always gave Keeble as his home instead of Black Bear Village. Country towns were well enough to come from if they weren't inconveniently in sight and used as footstools by fashionable lakes.

   How does Dexter probably feel about his background?

   _____

5. There was a pause. Then [Judy] smiled and the corners of her mouth drooped and an almost imperceptible sway brought her closer to [Dexter], looking up into his eyes.

   How does Judy use her physical attractiveness to her advantage?

   _____

Name _____ Date _____

"Winter Dreams" by F. Scott Fitzgerald
Vocabulary Builder

Using the Root -sed-

A. DIRECTIONS: *The following words contain the root -sed-, meaning "to sit." Look carefully at each word and its definition, then write a sentence in which you use the word. Pay close attention to the part of speech of each word.*

1. *subsidize, v.,* to help with costs

   _____

   _____

2. *sedentary, adj.* being seated much of the time

   _____

   _____

3. *resident, n.,* one who dwells in a place

   _____

   _____

4. *assiduous, adj.,* persistent; diligent in applying oneself

   _____

   _____

Using the Word List

fallowness	fortuitous	mundane	poignant	sediment	sinuous

B. DIRECTIONS: *In each blank, write the letter of the choice that is closest in meaning to the word in italics.*

___ 1. a *mundane* activity
   A. marvelous
   B. commonplace
   C. wavy
   D. sneaky

___ 2. the pond's *sediment*
   A. evaporation
   B. water
   C. current
   D. residue

___ 3. the field's *fallowness*
   A. inactivity
   B. foulness
   C. shallowness
   D. following

___ 4. a *poignant* moment
   A. picky
   B. painful
   C. poor
   D. wealthy

___ 5. a *fortuitous* event
   A. unlucky
   B. fifth
   C. chance
   D. lazy

___ 6. a *sinuous* turn
   A. wavy
   B. tough
   C. straight
   D. right

"Winter Dreams" by F. Scott Fitzgerald

Grammar and Style: Subject-Verb Agreement Problems

Subject-verb agreement means that the subject in a sentence must agree with the verb in number.

Example: *Seasons* that pass quickly *are* often the most precious.

Example: Either the *piano* or the *guitars are* out of tune.

Example: *Everyone* in the class *thinks* the poem is difficult.

A. PRACTICE: *Circle the correct verb to go with the subject in each sentence.*

1. Dexter (attend, attends) an expensive university back East.

2. The foursome (plan, plans) to play eighteen holes of golf.

3. The caddy that followed them (look, looks) bored.

4. A memory of long ago often (change, changes) our mood.

5. No one (is, are) more impatient than a young man who is in love.

B. Writing Application: *Read each sentence. If the subject agrees with the verb, write Correct; if it does not agree, write Incorrect. If the subject does not agree with the verb, rewrite the sentence correctly.*

1. First one caddy and then all the others asks to caddy for Mr. Hart.

   _____

   _____

2. Only four balls that were hit by the novice golfer was found.

   _____

   _____

3. Either the girl that plays golf is very good or she is very lucky.

   _____

   _____

4. There is many ways to succeed in life.

   _____

   _____

5. Dexter think too much before he makes a decision.

   _____

   _____

Name _____ Date _____

"Winter Dreams" by F. Scott Fitzgerald
Support for Writing

Use the chart to gather and organize ideas for your **literary criticism** of "Winter Dreams" as a commentary on the "American Dream." Use the graphic organizer to compare and contrast Dexter's desire for material success with his desire for Judy. Write quotations, details, and your own insights in the appropriate columns.

Desire for Material Success	Desire for Judy
Different:	Different:
Alike:	

On a separate page, write your literary criticism exploring Dexter's pursuit of the American Dream. Be sure to support each of your main ideas with quotations and other details from the story.

Name _____ Date _____

"The Turtle" *from* The Grapes of Wrath by John Steinbeck
Literary Analysis: Allegory and Theme

An **allegory** is a story with two or more levels of meaning—a literal level and one or more symbolic levels. The **theme** of a work of art is its central insight into life. In this story, the theme has both an allegorical, or symbolic, meaning and a literal meaning. The short glimpse into the life of the turtle represents the literal story. The allegorical meaning concerns survival and rebirth as symbolized by the turtle's slow but persistent efforts to continue and to survive.

DIRECTIONS: *Identify details in "The Turtle" that might be connected to the theme of survival. Explain how each detail relates to the story of the Joads or to the theme of survival in general.*

1. Story detail:

_____

_____

How it connects to theme:

_____

_____

_____

_____

2. Story detail:

_____

_____

How it connects to theme:

_____

_____

_____

_____

3. Story detail:

_____

_____

How it connects to theme:

_____

_____

_____

_____

"**The Turtle**" by John Steinbeck
Reading Strategy: Analyze Patterns of Symbolism

A **symbol** is anything that stands for or represents something else. The turtle's trials may symbolize life, for example. To understand the turtle, or any other element, as a symbol, look for patterns in its behavior and appearance. Begin by identifying and then analyzing the literal aspects of the event or thing and thinking how they may be interpreted symbolically.

DIRECTIONS: *As you read "The Turtle," look for elements that may be symbolic. Then analyze the literal aspects of these elements and summarize their symbolic meaning.*

Symbol	Literal Aspects of Event or Thing	Symbolic Meaning
Turtle		

"The Turtle" by John Steinbeck
Vocabulary Builder

Using the Prefix *pro-* and the Root *-trudere-*

The prefix *pro-* means "forward." The Latin root *-trudere-* means "to thrust."

A. DIRECTIONS: *Choose from the following words to complete the sentences. Use what you know about the prefix* pro- *and the Latin root* -trudere-.

protrude (L. *pro-* means "forward"; Latin *-trudere-* means "to thrust")
project (L. *jacere* means "to throw")
procrastinate (L. *cras* means "tomorrow.")
extrude (L. *ex-* means "out.")

1. Rather than finishing his homework on Saturday, Bob decided to _____ and do it on Sunday instead.

2. The slide machine used light to _____ an image onto a large screen.

3. Be careful so you don't hurt yourself on the table edges that _____ into the hallway.

4. The volcanoes _____ molten rock that will eventually cool and form a new mountain peak.

Using the Word List

dispersal   embankment   frantic   plodding

B. DIRECTIONS: *Underline the better definition for the italicized word in each sentence or phrase.*

1. The highway department built an *embankment* to hold the new interstate. (raised structure, tunnel)

2. *Plodding* through the mounds of snow, the backpackers decided to take a break. (running, trudging)

3. The *dispersal* of the seeds enabled the plants to spread over a wide area. (distribution, growth)

4. The turtle never seemed to make a *frantic* movement. (thoughtless, frenzied)

Name _____ Date _____

"The Turtle" *from* The Grapes of Wrath by John Steinbeck
Support for Writing

Prepare to write a research paper discussing the Dust Bowl and Great Depression and how *The Grapes of Wrath* reveals elements of these historic events. Use the chart below to record details of your research and your conclusions about how the Depression and "The Turtle" interconnect.

The Great Depression as Reflected in "The Turtle"

Basic Effects of Depression on American Farmers	Summary of Turtle Story	Conclusion About How the Depression and the Turtle Story Connect

On a separate page, introduce your research paper with a statement about how "The Turtle" helps to illuminate the plight of farmers during the Dust Bowl years. then support your ideas with your research and insights into the story. Be sure to include specific details from the story and from circumstances during the Great Depression. Provide citations for the sources of your information.

Name _____ Date _____

"Migrant Mother" by Dorothea Lange
"Dust Bowl Blues" by Woody Guthrie
Primary Sources: Photographs and Ballad

Primary sources, such as the photographs of Lange and the ballad of Guthrie, provide a glimpse of events specific to a particular time in history. By drawing inferences from these sources, you can better envision the time period when these pieces were created. To **draw inferences,** you make logical guesses about something that is not directly shown or stated. You look at details and then you consider what you already know about the time period and people and the world in general.

DIRECTIONS: *Read each question about the primary sources presented in this group and answer the questions.*

1. What feelings and concerns do you think lie behind the expression on the migrant mother's face in Lange's photographs? Explain.

   _____

   _____

   _____

2. Do you think that many of the recent experiences that are influencing the woman's thoughts in Lange's photographs are common to other people of the period? Explain your answer.

   _____

   _____

   _____

3. What can you infer about the family based on details you can observe about the tent, furniture, clothing, and other household implements in the pictures?

   _____

   _____

   _____

4. What can you infer about the circumstances of people of this era based on the tone and mood projected by Guthrie's ballad?

   _____

   _____

   _____

5. What can you infer about the experience of living through a dust storm from Guthrie's ballad?

   _____

   _____

   _____

"**Migrant Mother**" by Dorothea Lange
"**Dust Bowl Blues**" by Woody Guthrie
Vocabulary Builder

Using the Word List

agricultural   destitute   exposures   huddled   migrant   native

A. DIRECTIONS: *Rewrite each sentence, substituting a word from the Word List for each italicized word or phrase.*

1. When the cold winds blew, the farm workers *gathered closely* around the fire.

   _____

2. The workers *who moved from place to place* were looking for work and a home.

   _____

3. They were *living in complete poverty*.

   _____

4. *The sections of film where light fell* revealed a family struggling to survive.

   _____

5. The people *who considered farming as their main way of life* were forced from their land.

   _____

6. None of the people *belonged by birth* to this place.

   _____

B. DIRECTIONS: *For each item, choose the word pair that best expresses a relationship similar to that expressed in the numbered pair. Circle the letter of your choice.*

___ 1. NATIVE : FOREIGNER ::
    A. farmer : sailor
    B. consumer : producer
    C. traveler : explorer
    D. messenger : correspondent

___ 2. DESTITUTE :: IMPOVERISHED ::
    A. creative : imaginative
    B. sorrowful : reformed
    C. fundamental : resourceful
    D. strict : lenient

___ 3. AGRICULTURAL : FARM ::
    A. natural : factory
    B. medical : hospital
    C. urban : wasteland
    D. working : holiday

___ 4. HUDDLED : NESTLED ::
    A. rested : exhausted
    B. delivered : received
    C. thought : acted
    D. contributed : donated

"The Unknown Citizen" by W. H. Auden
Literary Analysis: Satire

Satire is writing that seeks to expose the faults of individuals, groups, or humanity at large in an effort to persuade readers to see the subject from the author's point of view. The tone of satiric writing will vary, depending upon the writer's approach to the subject. **Tone** is the writer's attitude toward the subject or the audience.

Public service announcements have used satire to promote particular points of view. For example, one anti-smoking campaign featured posters with the caption "Smoking Makes You Attractive," but with photographs of smokers who looked sick.

DIRECTIONS: *Think about how you might plan the following public service campaigns. Write a satirical slogan you would use and tell how you would use the slogan to satirize your subject.*

1. A campaign to educate drivers about the importance of obeying traffic signs.

_____

_____

_____

_____

2. A campaign to encourage everyone to have an annual physical checkup.

_____

_____

_____

_____

3. A campaign to get people to stop littering public beaches.

_____

_____

_____

_____

4. A campaign to warn teens about the dangers of drug abuse.

_____

_____

_____

_____

"The Unknown Citizen" by W. H. Auden
Reading Strategy: Relate Structure to Meaning

You can often relate a poem's **structure**—the way it is put together in words, lines, and stanzas—to its **meaning**—the central ideas the poet wants you to understand. For example, in "The Unknown Citizen," Auden uses uneven line lengths to evoke the rhythms and look of an official report. The rhythm it produces is matter-of-fact, almost institutional.

DIRECTIONS: *For each of the following passages from the poem, do the following: First, write the meaning of the passage. Second, write how one or more of the following structural elements reinforce that meaning:* **stanzas, rhymes, rhythm, syntax, capitalization, punctuation.**

1. Except for the War till the day he retired
   He worked in a factory and never got fired,
   But satisfied his employers, Fudge Motors Inc.
   Yet he wasn't a scab or odd in his views,
   For his Union reports that he paid his dues,
   (Our report on his Union shows it was sound)
   And our Social Psychology workers found
   That he was popular with his mates and liked a drink.

   Meaning: _____

   _____

   Structural Elements: _____

   _____

2. Both Producers Research and High-Grade Living declare
   He was fully sensible to the advantages of the Installment Plan
   And had everything necessary to the Modern Man.
   A phonograph, a radio, a car and a frigidaire.

   Meaning: _____

   _____

   Structural Elements: _____

   _____

Name _____ Date _____

"The Unknown Citizen" by W. H. Auden
Vocabulary Builder

Using the Greek Root *-psych-*

A. DIRECTIONS: *The following words contain the root -psych-, meaning "soul" or "mind." Determine the meaning of each of the following words. Then, write a sentence in which you use the word.*

1. psychobiography

_____

_____

2. psychological

_____

_____

3. psychologist

_____

_____

Using the Word List

conduct   psychology   sensible

B. DIRECTIONS: *Each sentence has a blank space indicating that a word has been omitted. Choose the lettered word that best completes the meaning of the sentence and write the word in the blank.*

1. A knowledge of _____ is important for people who work in teaching, marketing, and sports.

   A. psychosis   B. psychiatry   C. psychodrama   D. psychology

2. While talking, joking, and laughing are generally accepted as reasonable _____ in the workplace, any behavior that disrupts the workplace or interferes with getting the job done may be cause for dismissal.

   A. system   B. attitude   C. conduct   D. discussion

3. The citizen acted in a _____ manner, demonstrating that he was both emotionally and intellectually aware of the consequences of his actions.

   A. peculiar   B. sensible   C. ignorant   D. irresponsible

"**The Unknown Citizen**" by W. H. Auden
Support for Writing

Use the graphic organizer below to develop your ideas for your essay. Write a statement of Auden's view of society in the first box. Then add quotations from the poem that support that statement. Next, write another statement of Auden's views of society, and add examples to support that view.

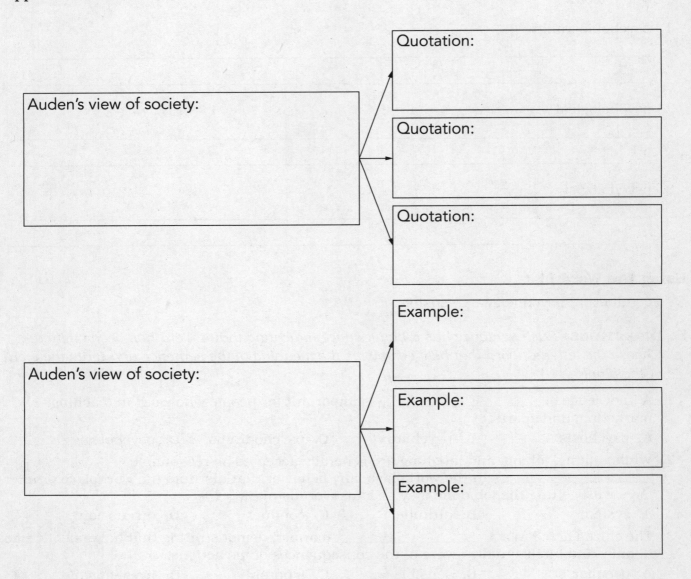

On a separate page, write your essay exploring Auden's view of modern society. Be sure to include details from Auden's poem to support general statements of Auden's views.

Name _____ Date _____

"old age sticks" and "anyone lived in a pretty how town" by E. E. Cummings
Literary Analysis: Author's Style

An **author's style** is the unique, individual way an author has of writing. Style is characterized by many different elements, such as word choice, imagery, speech, tone, rhyme, meter, and even by the arrangement of words on the page. E. E. Cummings has one of the most distinctive styles in American literature. It is readily identified by his unconventional syntax, unusual capitalization, minimal punctuation, elimination of spaces between some words and characters, and his use of typographical symbols within the text.

DIRECTIONS: *Read the following lines from "anyone lived in a pretty how town." Then answer the questions.*

anyone lived in a pretty how town
(with up so floating many bells down)
spring summer autumn winter
he sang his didn't he danced his did.

Women and men(both little and small)
cared for anyone not at all
they sowed their isn't they reaped their same
sun moon stars rain

1. How does Cummings's use of unconventional syntax influence the message conveyed by this poem?

   _____

   _____

2. How does Cummings's unusual use of upper and lowercase letters influence the message conveyed by this poem?

   _____

   _____

3. How does Cummings's minimal use of punctuation influence the message conveyed by this poem?

   _____

   _____

Name _____ Date _____

"old age sticks" and **"anyone lived in a pretty how town"** by E. E. Cummings
Reading Strategy: Paraphrase to Determine Meaning

Poetry condenses ideas, forcing readers to take lines apart and reconstruct them in ways they can understand. When poetry is experimental and the poet has an unusual style, as Cummings does, the meaning of a poem can become even more difficult. One effective way to get at the meaning of difficult lines or passages is to **paraphrase to determine meaning.** Record the difficult lines, and then read the lines to form a general impression of the meaning. Finally, put the passage in your own words as a way of extracting the meaning.

DIRECTIONS: *As you read the poems by Cummings, jot down difficult lines and passages. Then paraphrase them as a way of determining their meaning.*

Lines and Passages	Paraphrase

"old age sticks" and **"anyone lived in a pretty how town"** by E. E. Cummings
Vocabulary Builder

Using the Word List
reaped   sowed

A. DIRECTIONS: *Rewrite each sentence below, replacing the italicized word or phrase with an appropriate word from the Word List.*

1. The couple *gathered* in the rewards of all their hard work.

   _____

2. Over the years, they *scattered* much kindness throughout the community.

   _____

B. DIRECTIONS: *For each item, choose the word pair that best expresses a relationship similar to that expressed in the numbered pair. Circle the letter of your choice.*

___ 1. SOWED : HARVESTED ::
   A. hungered : consumed
   B. created : imagined
   C. begun : finished
   D. revived : suspended

___ 2. REAPED : CROPS ::
   A. prepared : prospered
   B. painted : picture
   C. planted : farmers
   D. analyzed : classified

"old age sticks" and **"anyone lived in a pretty how town"** by E. E. Cummings
Support for Writing

As you prepare for a poetry reading of works by Cummings, gather information for an **introduction** that provides background information on Cummings and briefly introduces the poems.

The Poetry of E. E. Cummings

What common themes are developed in Cummings's poems?

_____

_____

_____

What are the characteristics of Cummings's unique writing style?

_____

_____

_____

What is the significance of Cummings's unique writing style?

_____

_____

_____

Background of E. E. Cummings:

_____

_____

_____

On a separate page, write a draft of your introduction to the poetry reading. Give concrete examples from the poems to support the opinions you give. When you revise your work, be sure your details support your main points.

"Of Modern Poetry" by Wallace Stevens
"Ars Poetica" by Archibald MacLeish
"Poetry" by Marianne Moore
Literary Analysis: Theme

The **theme** of a poem is its central message or insight into life. Poets develop their theme in part with the use of imagery. **Imagery** is language that uses **images**, words that appeal to the senses: sight, sound, touch, taste, and smell. Poets may use **similes**, a comparison between two seemingly different things, to create images.

DIRECTIONS: *Read the following lines from the poems in this group. Then identify the theme it develops and explain how the imagery and similes contribute to it.*

1. "[The poem] has to be living, to learn the speech of the place./It has to face the men of the time and to meet/The women of the time. It has to think about war/And it has to find what will suffice. It has/To construct a new state. It has to be on that stage/And, like an insatiable actor, slowly and/With meditation, speak words. . . ."—"Of Modern Poetry"

_____

_____

_____

_____

_____

2. "A poem should be palpable and mute/As a globed fruit."—"Ars Poetica"

_____

_____

_____

_____

_____

_____

3. "I, too, dislike it [poetry]: there are things that are important beyond all this fiddle./Reading it, however, with a perfect contempt for it, one discovers in/it after all, a place for the genuine./Hands that can grasp, eyes/that can dilate, hair that can rise/if it must, these things are important. . . ."—"Poetry"

_____

_____

_____

_____

_____

_____

"Of Modern Poetry" by Wallace Stevens
"Ars Poetica" by Archibald MacLeish
"Poetry" by Marianne Moore

Reading Strategy: Analyze Philosophical Arguments

A poet has a philosophy or world view, a way of looking at things. In presenting a theme, the poet does not create something out of nothing, but rather builds upon his or her philosophy. Therefore, to understand the poem, readers must **analyze philosophical arguments** that the poet presents that support the theme.

DIRECTIONS: *As you read the poems in this group, identify an image or idea from each poem that reflects the poet's philosophy. Explain what the philosophy is and how it is represented in the image.*

Image or Idea	Poet's Philosophy

"Of Modern Poetry" by Wallace Stevens
"Ars Poetica" by Archibald MacLeish
"Poetry" by Marianne Moore

Vocabulary Builder

Using the Root -satis-

A. DIRECTIONS: *In "Of Modern Poetry," Wallace Stevens uses the word* insatiable *to describe an actor who must constantly perform. The root of* insatiable *is* -satis-, *which means "enough." The prefixes for the three words below are defined in parentheses. For each word, write a sentence in which the meaning of* satis *is demonstrated clearly.*

1. *dissatisfy* (*dis-* = "fail," "refuse to") _____

2. *insatiable* (*in-* = "no, not") _____

3. *unsatisfactorily* (*un-* = "the opposite") _____

Using the Word List

    derivative   insatiable   palpable   suffice

B. DIRECTIONS: *In the following excerpts from the poems, substitute the correct word from the Word List for the bracketed word or words and write it on the blank.*

1. "A poem should be [able to be handled] _____ and mute/As a globed fruit."

2. "It has to be on that stage/And, like an [unable to be satisfied] _____ actor, slowly and/Without meditation"

3. "When they become so [based on something else] _____ as to become/unintelligible"

4. "The poem of the mind in the act of finding/What will [be adequate]" _____.

"Of Modern Poetry" by Wallace Stevens
"Ars Poetica" by Archibald MacLeish
"Poetry" by Marianne Moore
Support for Writing

In order to **compare and contrast** the ideas in two of the poems in this selection, enter material into the chart below.

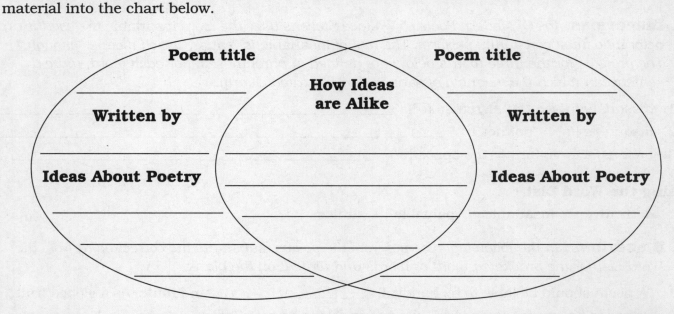

Below or on a separate page, write a draft of your comparison-and-contrast essay to show how the ideas of the two poets are either similar or different. When you revise, add more examples from the poems to support your opinions.

Contemporary Commentary
Tim O'Brien Introduces "Ambush"

DIRECTIONS: *Use the space provided to answer the questions.*

1. What does Tim O'Brien mean when he says that "Ambush" is a short story that can stand "entirely on its own"?

   _____

   _____

2. According to O'Brien, is the story fiction or nonfiction? Briefly explain O'Brien's comments on "an invented character who has my name."

   _____

   _____

   _____

   _____

3. Fill in the chart below to compare and contrast the factual and the fictional elements and details in "Ambush" as O'Brien describes them.

Factual Details	Fictional Details

4. Tim O'Brien says he will never know whether a bullet from his own weapon killed the young man, but that he is still responsible because he pulled the trigger. How do you evaluate O'Brien's statement? Do you agree or disagree? Briefly explain your answer.

   _____

   _____

   _____

   _____

   _____

5. According to O'Brien, what was his principal motivation, or purpose, in writing "Ambush"?

   _____

   _____

   _____

Tim O'Brien
Listening and Viewing

Segment 1: Meet Tim O'Brien
• What similarities can you find between writing fiction and performing magic?
• Why does Tim O'Brien care about truth in fiction writing?

_____

_____

_____

Segment 2: Tim O'Brien Introduces "Ambush"
• Why did Tim O'Brien write the story "Ambush" in the first person and name the narrator "Tim O'Brien"?
• How do you think this influences the reader's interpretation of the story?

_____

_____

_____

Segment 3: The Writing Process
• Do you agree with Tim O'Brien that revision is the most important step in the writing process?
• How does Tim O'Brien know when his story is finished?

_____

_____

_____

Segment 4: The Rewards of Writing
• Why does Tim O'Brien believe that stories can be powerful forces in our lives?
• How do you think writing can help you be your "ideal self"?

_____

_____

_____

Name _____ Date _____

"**In Another Country**" by Ernest Hemingway
Literary Analysis: Author's Style

An **author's style** is his or her use of language and includes diction, tone, and syntax. Diction is the author's word choices. Tone is the author's attitude toward his or her subject. Syntax is the complexity or simplicity of sentence and grammatical structures.

DIRECTIONS: *Complete the chart by identifying examples of Hemingway's style in "In Another Country." Briefly explain what each example displays.*

	Example	Explanation
Diction		
Tone		
Syntax		

"**In Another Country**" by Ernest Hemingway
Reading Strategy: Identifying With Characters

Ernest Hemingway included in his writing some characters that are outgoing and adventuresome, as well as some that are thoughtful and introspective. In each case, Hemingway presents the characters clearly and provides details to help readers connect with them and understand their motives and actions.

DIRECTIONS: *On the lines after each of the following passages, identify an emotion, a concept, or a goal that the passage suggests. Then write one or two sentences to explain how the character might act if he or she were more like the narrator in "In Another Country."*

1. The major, who had been the great fencer, did not believe in bravery, and spent much time while we sat in the machines correcting my grammar. He had complimented me on how I spoke Italian, and we talked together very easily. One day I had said that Italian seemed such an easy language to me that I could not take a great interest in it; everything was so easy to say. "Ah yes," the major said. "Why, then, do you not take up the use of grammar?" So we took up the use of grammar, and soon Italian was such a difficult language that I was afraid to talk to him until I had the grammar straight in my mind.

   _____

   _____

   _____

   _____

2. The boys at first were very polite about my medals and asked me what I had done to get them. I showed them the papers, which . . . really said, with the adjectives removed, that I had been given the medals because I was an American. After that their manner changed a little toward me, although I was their friend against outsiders. I was a friend, but I was never really one of them after they had read the citations, because it had been different with them and they had done very different things to get their medals. I had been wounded, it was true; but we all knew that being wounded, after all, was really an accident. . . . The three with the medals were like hunting-hawks; and I was not a hawk, although I might seem a hawk to those who had never hunted; they, the three, knew better and so we drifted apart.

   _____

   _____

   _____

   _____

Name _____ Date _____

"In Another Country" by Ernest Hemingway
Vocabulary Builder

Using the Word List

detached   disgrace   resign

A. DIRECTIONS: *Fill in each blank with the appropriate word from the Word List.*

1. The narrator did not feel any _____ regarding his medals even though they had been awarded because he was an American.

2. The doctor seemed _____ from the tragedy of the lives around him and went about his work in a brusque and matter-of-fact manner.

3. The major could not _____ himself to the fact that his wife had died while he, who had survived combat, would go on living.

B. DIRECTIONS: *Rewrite each sentence below, replacing the italicized word or phrase with an appropriate word from the Word List.*

1. The people at the café seemed to be *emotionally uninvolved* in the sufferings of the soldiers who were defending their country.

   _____

2. The soldier tried to *accept as unavoidable* the deaths of his comrades.

   _____

3. He forced himself to rush into combat knowing that failing to do so would be a *dishonor*.

   _____

Name _____ Date _____

"In Another Country" by Ernest Hemingway
Support for Writing

As you prepare for an essay on Hemingway's style, use the chart below to record evidence and examples from "In Another Country" to support your ideas.

Your opinion:	
Example	**What it demonstrates**

On a separate page, write a draft of your essay. When you revise your work, be sure your introduction clearly states your opinion, that the body gives evidence from the story, and that your conclusion summarizes your analysis.

Name _____ Date _____

"A Rose for Emily" and "Nobel Prize Acceptance Speech"
by William Faulkner
Literary Analysis: Conflict and Resolution

Conflict is the struggle between forces or characters that oppose each other. An **internal conflict** is a struggle between thoughts or emotions inside a character. You face an internal conflict, for example, when you know you have important work to complete, but you also want to talk to a friend on the phone. An **external conflict** is a struggle between a character and an outside force. For instance, society makes certain demands of us, as it does for Emily Grierson in "A Rose for Emily." The **resolution** to a conflict occurs when the struggle draws to a close.

A. DIRECTIONS: *On the lines provided, answer the following questions about conflict and resolution in "A Rose for Emily."*

1. What is the nature of the opening conflict between Emily Grierson and the Board of Aldermen in the town of Jefferson?

   _____

   _____

2. How does Miss Emily deal with the demand that is placed on her by the conflict?

   _____

   _____

3. Explain the nature of the conflict that is brought to the attention of Judge Stevens, the mayor of Jefferson.

   _____

   _____

4. Find at least one example that suggests that the narrator has an internal conflict about how he views Miss Emily.

   _____

   _____

5. How does finding the body of Homer Baron in the upstairs bedroom provide a resolution to the conflicting opinions about Miss Emily's unusual behavior?

   _____

   _____

B. DIRECTIONS: *In his "Nobel Prize Acceptance Speech," Faulkner describes the writer's responsibility to inspire others to face life with courage. Give an example of an internal or external conflict that people face that might lead them to seek courage through reading.*

   _____

   _____

   _____

   _____

"A Rose for Emily" and **"Nobel Prize Acceptance Speech"**
by William Faulkner

Reading Strategy: Clarify Ambiguities

Ambiguity occurs when some part of a story can be interpreted in at least two different ways. When Miss Emily buys arsenic in "A Rose for Emily" and won't tell the druggist its purpose, the reader wonders if she intends to kill rats or if she has something else in mind. **Clarifying ambiguity** in a literary work requires that you look for clues or details that can help you make a reasonable interpretation. Sometimes it's helpful to re-examine description, action, or characterization.

A. DIRECTIONS: *Examine the following ambiguous statements from "A Rose for Emily" and choose the best interpretation provided. Include details or clues from the story to support your choice.*

1. "So she vanquished them, horse and foot, just as she had vanquished their fathers thirty years before about the smell." Where does the smell come from?
   A. Miss Emily's unclean house
   B. the decaying body of Homer Baron
   C. a rat or snake that was killed in Miss Emily's yard

   Supporting details: _____

   _____

2. "She told them that her father was not dead." Why does Miss Emily tell the visiting ladies this information?
   A. She has a good imagination.
   B. Her father is not really dead.
   C. She is too proud to accept their pity.

   Supporting details: _____

   _____

3. "'Do you suppose it's really so?' they said to one another. 'Of course it is. What else could. . .'" What fact does this open-ended sentence refer to?
   A. Miss Emily's possible relationship with a laborer
   B. the fact that Miss Emily has no family in Jefferson
   C. her father's legal troubles over the estate of old lady Wyatt

   Supporting details: _____

   _____

B. DIRECTIONS: *In his "Nobel Prize Acceptance Speech," Faulkner insists that humans will never die because they have voices. What details might you add to this statement to clarify its ambiguity?*

_____

_____

"A Rose for Emily" and "Nobel Prize Acceptance Speech"
by William Faulkner
Vocabulary Builder

Using the Prefix *in-*

The prefix *in-* typically means "not," as in *indecisive, inedible,* and *injustice.* However, the same prefix may also suggest a "location or direction," as in *infield, ingrown,* and *insert.*

A. DIRECTIONS: *Examine the following words and their meanings. Decide if the prefix suggests negativity or direction. Write an "N" or a "D" next to each word along with a brief sentence.*

1. inhumane ("unkind") _____

2. ingrain ("to plant inside") _____

3. incoherent ("unable to be understood") _____

Using the Word List

    circumvent   encroached   inextricable   vanquished   vindicated   virulent

B. DIRECTIONS: *Briefly answer the following questions using words from the Word List.*

1. How might someone feel if his or her car slid into a snow bank and became *inextricable*?

   _____

2. What often happens to people who *circumvent* the rules of a game?

   _____

3. Why would it be surprising if a junior varsity team *vanquished* a varsity team?

   _____

4. If a defendant is *vindicated* during a trial, what does this suggest about his or her guilt?

   _____

5. If there were a *virulent* outbreak of chicken pox in town, what might doctors suggest?

   _____

6. If your little brother *encroached* on a personal phone call, what might you ask him to do next time?

   _____

   _____

"A Rose for Emily" and **"Nobel Prize Acceptance Speech"**
by William Faulkner
Support for Writing

To prepare to write a **critical review** of "A Rose for Emily" in terms of what Faulkner says is the duty of the writer, enter details into the graphic organizer below. Think about how the story helps people "endure [life] by lifting their hearts."

"A Rose for Emily"

Characters: _____ _____ _____ _____	How do the characters act with courage and honor? _____ _____ _____ _____
Summary of Plot: _____ _____ _____ _____	How does the plot help the reader feel pride or compassion? _____ _____ _____ _____
Theme: _____ _____ _____ _____	In what ways does the theme inspire a sense of glory? _____ _____ _____ _____

On a separate page, write the draft of your critical review of "A Rose for Emily." Make an introductory statement to tell whether or not the story fulfills Faulkner's guidelines. Then, give examples from the story to support your opinion. When you revise, be sure you have enough supporting material for your critical judgment.

Name _____ Date _____

"The Jilting of Granny Weatherall" by Katherine Anne Porter
Literary Analysis: Stream of Consciousness

The **stream-of-consciousness** technique in literature is based on real-life thinking processes. You probably realize that your thoughts often jump around. An ordinary sight, a certain sound, or a flash of memory can serve as a trigger, causing your thoughts to drift to the past or evoking a series of images that are yours alone.

Often, stream-of-consciousness narratives include the use of **flashback,** which is an interruption in the narrative to tell what happened earlier. Flashbacks give readers information so they can understand the background of events that are happening in the present.

A. DIRECTIONS: *In Porter's story, the following triggers cause Granny's thoughts to drift. For each one, write one or two sentences that discuss the thoughts, feelings, and images that come to Granny's mind. Indicate any that call up flashbacks.*

1. the sight of Doctor Harry

_____

_____

2. jobs to do tomorrow

_____

_____

3. the distance of her daughter Lydia

_____

_____

4. the feel of the pillow

_____

_____

5. the arrival of Father Connolly

_____

_____

B. DIRECTIONS: *From the list above, choose the trigger you find most interesting. Using the stream-of-consciousness technique, write a paragraph from the perspective of another character, either a character in the story or a character of your own choosing. Show how the trigger evokes thoughts, feelings, and images in the character's mind.*

_____

_____

_____

_____

_____

_____

_____

"The Jilting of Granny Weatherall" by Katherine Anne Porter

Reading Strategy: Clarify Sequence of Events

Events in Granny Weatherall's life are not told in the order they happened, which can cause confusion. To repair your comprehension, **clarify the sequence of events** by looking at breaks in the sequence of events and shifts from the present to the past.

DIRECTIONS: Granny Weatherall recalls that her father was interviewed by a reporter when he was 102 years old. Imagine that a reporter comes to interview Mrs. Weatherall just before her final illness. The reporter wants to tell about events of her life in sequence, and so poses the questions below. Reply to each question as if you were Granny Weatherall.

1. What did you look like when you were twenty years old?

   _____

   _____

   _____

2. What kind of relationship did you have with your husband?

   _____

   _____

   _____

3. As a young widow, what tasks did you take on alone?

   _____

   _____

   _____

4. How would you describe your relationship with your children when they were young? How has that relationship changed?

   _____

   _____

   _____

5. You seem to be very unconcerned about death. Could you please explain your reasons for this attitude?

   _____

   _____

   _____

6. During this interview, you've frequently muttered the name "George." Please explain who George is and tell us why he is so important.

   _____

   _____

   _____

"The Jilting of Granny Weatherall" by Katherine Anne Porter
Vocabulary Builder

Using the Prefix dys-

A. DIRECTIONS: *The word* dyspepsia *combines the prefix* dys-, *meaning "difficult" or "bad," and the word root* pepsis, *meaning "digestion". The word* dyspepsia, *therefore, means "indigestion." The prefix* dys- *is often used in medical terminology. Using the information following each word and what you know about the prefix* dys-, *write the letter of the definition on the line next to the word it defines.*

___ 1. *dyscrasia* (*krasis* = a mixing)
___ 2. *dysgraphia* (*graphia* = writing)
___ 3. *dyskinesia* (*kin[e]sis* = motion)
___ 4. *dyslexia* (*lexis* = word)
___ 5. *dysphagia* (*phag[ein]* = to eat)
___ 6. *dysphonia* (*ph[o]n[e]* = voice)
___ 7. *dyspnea* (*pnein* = breathing)

A. impairment of the ability to read
B. difficulty in swallowing
C. impairment of the ability to write
D. an abnormal imbalance in some part of the body, especially in the blood
E. shortness of breath
F. impairment of the ability to produce speech sounds
G. impairment of body movement

Using the Word List

dyspepsia   piety   tactful

B. DIRECTIONS: *Choose the word that best completes the meaning of each sentence and write it in the blank.*

1. Granny thought she was being tactful, but she ended up _____ them.
   A. insulting
   B. humoring
   C. ignoring
   D. consulting

2. His piety was demonstrated by his desire to _____
   A. spend
   B. sleep
   C. pray
   D. play

3. When her dyspepsia would act up, her _____ would hurt badly.
   A. back
   B. elbow
   C. head
   D. stomach

"The Jilting of Granny Weatherall" by Katherine Anne Porter
Support for Writing

To prepare to write your **monologue,** enter stream-of-consciousness writing in the chart below. You may write a monologue as yourself or as a character you create.

Words and Phrases That Relate to _____

Actions _____	Feelings _____
_____	_____
_____	_____
_____	_____
Comments _____	Attitudes _____
_____	_____
_____	_____
_____	_____

Below or on a separate page, write your monologue to focus on one or two major memories of your character. When you revise, be sure to show how the memories blend into one another without transitions.

Name _____ Date _____

"A Worn Path" by Eudora Welty
Literary Analysis: Archetype of the Hero's Quest

An **archetype** is a symbol, character, idea, or event that reappears in different forms in literature and mythology of many different cultures. The **hero's quest,** which is typified by "A Worn Path," is one archetypal image.

DIRECTIONS: Complete the following chart to track elements of the hero's quest through "A Worn Path."

Object or purpose of journey:	
Obstacles faced:	**How obstacles are overcome:**
What journey symbolizes:	

Name _____ Date _____

Reading Strategy: Generate Questions to Make and Confirm Predictions

To better understand and enjoy literature, **generate questions** as you read. Then **make predictions** based on events and details in the story. As you read further, **confirm** your predictions.

DIRECTIONS: *As you read "A Worn Path," consider information the narrator gives you about Phoenix, her journey, and the events that befall her. Then make a prediction based on that information. As you read further, confirm your predictions.*

Detail or Event from Story	Prediction

"A Worn Path" by Eudora Welty
Vocabulary Builder

Using the Word List

grave   limber   obstinate   persistent

A. DIRECTIONS: *Fill in each blank with the appropriate word from the Word List.*

1. The child's illness was a matter of _____ concern.

2. Phoenix was _____ and would not be quiet regardless of how long or difficult the walk.

3. The cane was so _____ that it was a wonder that it did not bend under her weight and allow her to fall.

4. The child's cough was _____; it would not go away.

B. DIRECTIONS: *For each item, choose the word pair that best expresses a relationship similar to that expressed in the numbered pair. Circle the letter of your choice.*

___ 1. LIMBER : BRANCH ::
   A. helpful : illness
   B. reflective : mirror
   C. joke : laughter
   D. praise : pride

___ 2. PERSISTENT : CONTINUAL ::
   A. relentless : successful
   B. realistic : impractical
   C. strenuous : exhausting
   D. relieved : anxious

___ 3. OBSTINATE : RESIGNED ::
   A. violent : peaceful
   B. obscure : vague
   C. adventurous : eventful
   D. excellent : wonderful

___ 4. GRAVE : INJURY ::
   A. profitable : purchase
   B. hesitant : determination
   C. relaxing : mystery
   D. exciting : competition

Name _____ Date _____

"A Worn Path" by Eudora Welty
Support for Writing

To prepare for writing your sequel to Welty's "A Worn Path," use the following story map to plan and organize your characters and plot.

Characters:

Setting:

Problem:

Events:

Resolution:

On a separate page, write a draft of your story. When you revise your work, be sure you clearly introduce the problem and that the sequence of your events is clear and that they are related by cause and effect.

Name _____ Date _____

"The Night the Ghost Got In" by James Thurber
Literary Analysis: Humorous Essay

A **humorous essay** is nonfiction writing that is intended to entertain and be funny. In "The Night the Ghost Got In," Thurber takes an everyday event and expands on events with the use of **hyperbole**, **understatement**, and **idioms**.

DIRECTIONS: *Read the following passages from "The Night the Ghost Got In" and identify any examples of hyperbole, understatement, and idioms that it contains. Tell how these elements contribute to the humor of the passage.*

1. "After the walking had gone on for perhaps three minutes, I tiptoed to Herman's room. 'Psst!' I hissed, in the dark, shaking him. 'Awp,' he said in the low, hopeless tone of a despondent beagle. . . ."

_____

_____

_____

2. "Downstairs, we could hear the tromping of the other police. Police were all over the place; doors were yanked open, drawers were yanked open, windows were shot up and pulled down, furniture fell with dull thumps. A half-dozen policemen emerged out of the darkness of the front hallway upstairs. They began to ransack the floor: pulled beds away from walls, tore clothes off hooks in the closets, pulled suitcases and boxes off shelves."

_____

_____

_____

3. "'No sign o'nuthin',' said the cop who had first spoken to mother. 'This guy,' he explained to the others, jerking a thumb at me, 'was nekked. The lady seems historical.' They all nodded, but said nothing; just looked at me. . . ."

_____

_____

_____

4. "The cops were reluctant to leave without getting their hands on somebody besides grandfather; the night had been distinctly a defeat for them. Furthermore, they obviously didn't like the 'layout'; something looked—and I can see their viewpoint—phony."

_____

_____

_____

"The Night the Ghost Got In" by James Thurber
Reading Strategy: Analyzing Cause and Effect

The humor of "The Night the Ghost Got In" rests firmly on the cause-and-effect relationship between events as one event leads to another and each one becomes more and more humorous.

DIRECTIONS: *On the lines following each passage from "The Night the Ghost Got In," tell what happens next.*

1. "After the walking had gone on for perhaps three minutes, I tiptoed to Herman's room. 'Psst!' I hissed. . . ."

_____

_____

2. "'Don't either of you go a step,' said mother. 'We'll call the police.' Since the phone was downstairs, I didn't see how we were going to call the police. . . ."

_____

_____

3. "The police were on hand in a commendably short time. . . . 'Open Up!' cried a hoarse voice. "We're men from Headquarters!"

_____

_____

4. "Their lights played all over the living-room and crisscrossed nervously in the dining-room, stabbed into hallways, shot up the front stairs and finally up the back. They caught me standing in my towel at the top."

_____

_____

5. "One of them found an old zither. . . . 'What is it?' he asked me."

_____

_____

6. "In the small silence we all heard a creaking in the attic. Grandfather was turning over in bed. 'What's 'at?' snapped Joe."

_____

_____

7. "The reporter looked at me with mingled suspicion and interest. 'Just what the heck is the real lowdown here, bud?' he asked."

_____

_____

"The Night the Ghost Got In" by James Thurber
Vocabulary Builder

Using the Word List

despondent   reluctant   intervene   blaspheming

A. DIRECTIONS: *Rewrite each sentence, substituting a word from the Word List for each italicized word or phrase.*

1. The narrator wanted to *take action in order* to prevent his grandfather from being descended upon by the police.

    _____

2. The man next door was sick and was *without courage or hope.*

    _____

3. The neighbor was *disinclined* to lend out his lawn mower.

    _____

4. The movie has an R rating because of the *strong language.*

    _____

B. DIRECTIONS: *Select the word from the Word List that is best related to each situation or thing and write it in the blank.*

1. the wounded officer started shouting angrily _____

2. the narrator did not act to stop his mother from throwing her shoe _____

3. Grandfather was discouraged because the soldiers were leaving _____

4. the police were unwilling to leave without the suspect _____

Name _____ Date _____

"The Night the Ghost Got In" by James Thurber
Support for Writing

Consider Thurber's comment that "the humorist makes fun of himself, but in so doing, he identifies himself with people—that is, people everywhere, not for the purpose of taking them apart, but simply revealing their true nature." To prepare to write your **essay** applying his comment to "The Night the Ghost Got In," enter information from the selection in the graphic organizer.

Thurber pokes fun at himself	Connection to others
Example:	
Example:	
Example:	
Conclusion about human nature	

Below or on a separate page, write your draft. Begin with an introduction stating how well you think the quotation applies to "The Night the Ghost Got In." In the body of the essay, cite your examples and give reasons and details to support your ideas. Finally, present your conclusion about human nature.

Name _____ Date _____

"Chicago" and **"Grass"** by Carl Sandburg
Literary Analysis: Personification

Personification is a figure of speech in which a nonhuman subject, such as a city, is given human characteristics. **Apostrophe** takes this literary device one step further; it is a literary technique that directly addresses a person or thing as if it were present. This technique is frequently used in romantic poetry or funeral songs in which the speaker of the poem directly addresses the loved one, or death. For example, the clown in Shakespeare's play *Twelfth Night* addresses his love, "O mistress mine! where are you roaming?" *In Much Ado About Nothing*, a group of singers open a funeral song with, "Pardon, Goddess of the night,/Those that slew thy virgin knight;"/In a more modern example, the poet Sandburg is using apostrophe on lines such as this one from "Chicago":

Hog Butcher for the world, . . . They tell me you are wicked. . .

DIRECTIONS: *Read "Chicago." Then answer the questions below.*

1. List three clues that show that Sandburg is using apostrophe in this poem.

   _____

   _____

   _____

   _____

   _____

   _____

2. Who is being addressed in "Chicago"?

   _____

   _____

3. Suppose that the speaker of "Chicago" is responding to a previous conversation. What would that conversation have been like? Who would have participated in it?

   _____

   _____

   _____

   _____

   _____

   _____

4. How might the structure of this poem have been different if Sandburg had *not* used the technique of apostrophe?

   _____

   _____

   _____

   _____

   _____

Name _____ Date _____

Reading Strategy: Effects of Repetition on Clarity

Sandburg, like many other poets, uses repetition to emphasize ideas and clarify meaning. As you read the poems, think about how the recurrence of an idea or phrase helps clarify Sandburg's ideas.

DIRECTIONS: *On the lines following each passage from "Chicago" and "Grass" tell what the effect of the repetition is.*

1.
They tell me you are wicked and I believe them, for I have seen your painted women
    under the gas lamps luring the farm boys.
And they tell me you are crooked and I answer: Yes, it is true I have seen the gunman kill and
    go free to kill again.
And they tell me you are brutal and my reply is: On the faces of women and children I
    have seen the marks of wanton hunger.

_____

_____

2.
Under the smoke, dust all over his mouth, laughing with white teeth,
Under the terrible burden of destiny laughing as a young man laughs,

_____

_____

3.
  And pile them high at Gettysburg
  And pile them high at Ypres and Verdun.

_____

_____

4.
  I am the grass; I cover all.
  . . . .
  I am grass.
  Let me work.

_____

_____

"Chicago" and "Grass" by Carl Sandburg
Vocabulary Builder

Related Words: *brutal*

A. DIRECTIONS: *Knowing that the word* brutal *means "cruel," "crude," or "harsh," write the letter of the best description of the italicized word in each sentence.*

____ 1. An editor who criticizes a writer's work *brutally* is most likely to
   A. give the writer a physical beating.
   B. physically tear up the paper the work is written on.
   C. write unnecessarily severe comments about the work.
   D. suggest helpful changes in the writer's work.

____ 2. "The *brutalization* of prisoners of war" probably refers to
   A. beatings and torture.   C. censorship of letters.
   B. lack of clean water.   D. unfair imprisonment.

____ 3. Because her bus was a half hour late, Sarah growled her anger *brutishly*.
   A. charmingly   C. quietly
   B. harshly   D. whiningly

Using the Word List

   brutal   cunning   wanton

B. DIRECTIONS: *Fill in each blank with a word from the Word List. Two words are used more than once.*

1. Stealthy and _____, the tiger crept through the grass.
2. Unable to find what she was looking for, Marisa began smashing the store's crystal with _____ abandon.
3. The temperature was bitterly cold and the wind was _____.
4. The _____ reality was that Harold had no job, no money, and no place to live.
5. With a _____ disregard for Joseph's feelings, Darnell painted over the portrait that his friend had painstakingly rendered through months of effort.

Name _____ Date _____

"Chicago" and "Grass" by Carl Sandburg
Support for Writing

To prepare to write your **essay** on Sandburg's use of repetition, enter material from the poems into the chart below.

Repetition in Sandburg's Poems

"Chicago": Examples of repetition	Effect of repetition on listener
"Grass": Examples of repetition	Effect of repetition on listener

Below or on a separate page, write a draft of your essay. Summarize each poem briefly. Then, give examples of the repetitions used by the poet and the effects these have on the listener. When you revise, be sure your ideas are clear. Add more examples from the poems if you need to.

Robert Frost's Poetry
Literary Analysis: Blank Verse and Pastorals

Robert Frost was a versatile poet equally skilled at writing in rhymed and unrhymed formats. In his poem "Stopping by Woods on a Snowy Evening," for example, he uses the technique of rhyming first, second, and fourth lines until the final stanza, which has end rhymes on all four lines:

> The woods are lovely, dark and deep,
> But I have promises to keep,
> And miles to go before I sleep,
> And miles to go before I sleep.

Despite this formal rhyme scheme, the poem has an unforced musical quality that reveals both the speaker's joy at the beauty of nature and his wistfulness at the many obligations he must fulfill before his day is done.

However, in "The Gift Outright," "Birches," and " 'Out, Out—'," Frost writes in quite a different style. These poems are written in **blank verse**, which is composed of unrhymed lines of **iambic pentameter**. The basic unit of this type of meter is the iamb, which is made up of one unstressed syllable immediately followed by a stressed syllable. In iambic pentameter, there are five iambs per poetic line. This meter re-creates the flow of human speech patterns. Poems written in iambic pentameter, therefore, lend themselves to being read aloud.

While Frost uses both rhymed and blank verse for the poems in this group, all the poems are pastorals. **Pastorals** are poems that deal with rural settings. Traditionally, pastorals idealize rural life, evoking the beauty and gentleness found in natural settings. Frost incorporates this tradition in poems like "Birches" and "Stopping by Woods on a Snowy Evening." However, he does not hesitate to introduce a realistic element into his pastorals. In poems such as "Out, Out" and even in "Birches," Frost acknowledges that rural life can also be violent and unpleasant.

A. DIRECTIONS: *Read the following excerpt from Robert Frost's poem "Birches." Underline each stressed syllable. Then, read the excerpt aloud to observe the poem's rhythm.*

> And so I dream of going back to be.
> It's when I'm weary of considerations,
> And life is too much like a pathless wood
> Where your face burns and tickles with the cobwebs
> Broken across it, and one eye is weeping
> From a twig's having lashed across it open.

B. DIRECTIONS: *Identify elements of the pastoral in the excerpt above. Which elements are not traditional?*

Robert Frost's Poetry
Reading Strategy: Read Poetry in Sentences

While the rhythm of poetry is part of the appeal of poems, the rhythm can distract readers and interfere with comprehension. When you begin losing understanding of meaning, repair your comprehension by **reading poetry in sentences** rather than in poetic lines.

A. DIRECTIONS: *Rewrite the following lines from "Birches" as complete sentences.*

> When I see birches bend to left and right
> Across the lines of straighter darker trees,
> I like to think some boy's been swinging them.
> But swinging doesn't bend them down to stay
> As ice storms do. Often you must have seen them
> Loaded with ice a sunny winter morning
> After a rain. They click upon themselves
> As the breeze rises, and turn many colored
> As the stir cracks and crazes their enamel.

_____

_____

_____

_____

_____

_____

_____

_____

_____

B. DIRECTIONS: *As you read the six Frost poems, use this chart to note first the number of sentences in each. Then remember how to fix any difficulties in comprehension by reading the poems in sentences.*

Poem	Number of Sentences
"Birches"	
"Stopping By Woods on a Snowy Evening"	
"Mending Wall"	
"Out, Out—"	
"The Gift Outright"	
"Acquainted With the Night"	

Robert Frost's Poetry
Vocabulary Builder

Using the Root *-lum-*

A. DIRECTIONS: *The following words contain the root* -lum-, *meaning "light." Look carefully at each word and its definition; then write a sentence in which you use the word. Pay close attention to the part of speech of each word.*

1. *luminary, n,* a person of prominence or brilliant achievement

   _____

   _____

2. *luminary, adj,* giving off light

   _____

   _____

3. *luminous, adj,* emitting or reflecting steady, suffused, or glowing light

   _____

   _____

4. *luminosity, n,* the quality or state of being luminous

   _____

   _____

5. *illuminate, vt,* 1: to enlighten spiritually or intellectually 2: to supply or brighten with light

   _____

   _____

Using the Word List

   luminary   poise   rueful

B. DIRECTIONS: *Fill in each blank with the vocabulary word that best completes the sentence.*

1. The moon cast its _____ glow against the night sky.
2. In the poem "'Out, Out—,'" the young boy's first expression of shock about his accident is a _____ laugh.
3. The neighbor in the poem "Mending Wall" shows his _____ with the repeated comment "Good fences make good neighbors."

Robert Frost's Poetry
Support for Writing

Prepare your **critical essay** on the 20th- and 21st-century pastoral by completing the chart that follows.

Frost's Depiction of Nature	Your Experiences with Nature
How your experiences are similar to Frost's:	
How your experiences are different from Frost's:	

On a separate page, write your draft of your essay. In your introduction, state your opinion of the question: Does the pastoral have usefulness, relevance, or importance in today's world? Develop your ideas in the body of the essay, being sure to support your ideas with specific details from your experiences and Frost's poems.

"The Negro Speaks of Rivers," "Dream Variations," "I, Too," and "Refugee in America"
by Langston Hughes
Langston Hughes: Biography

Langston Hughes's early life was one of trials and difficulties, which prepared him for a life of risk-taking and for undertaking the hard work needed to succeed. His effort paid off as he became one of the great American writers of the twentieth century. His importance stems not only from his greatness as a poet, but from his role in defining the movement that became known as the Harlem Renaissance. That movement in turn inspired and brought to public awareness the skills and accomplishments of many other African American artists of the early twentieth century.

A. DIRECTIONS: *What are the two most important or interesting pieces of information you found in each section of Hughes's biography?*

Humble Beginning: _____

_____

_____

Writing and Wandering: _____

_____

_____

Renaissance Man: _____

_____

_____

B. DIRECTIONS: *What three questions would you like to ask Hughes about any of the topics introduced in his biography? Why do the answers interest you?*

1. _____

_____

_____

2. _____

_____

_____

3. _____

_____

_____

Name _____ Date _____

"The Negro Speaks of Rivers," "Dream Variations," "I, Too,"
and "Refugee in America"
by Langston Hughes
Literary Analysis: Speaker and Multiple Themes

The **speaker** is the voice of a poem. There are several possibilities as to who the speaker may be: the author, another person, an imaginary person, a group of people, an animal, or an object. This grouping of poems also contains **multiple themes** relating to racial identity, perseverance, and pride. Clues from the poem can help the reader figure out who the speaker is and what the themes are.

DIRECTIONS: Reread each poem in the group and decide who the speaker is and what racial theme is developed for each. Then tell what clues helped you figure out who the speaker is and what the theme is.

"The Negro Speaks of Rivers" Speaker: _____

Clues: _____

Themes: _____

Clues: _____

"Dream Variations" Speaker: _____

Clues: _____

Themes: _____

Clues: _____

"I, Too" Speaker _____

Clues: _____

Themes: _____

Clues: _____

"Refugee in America" Speaker: _____

Clues: _____

Themes: _____

Clues: _____

Name _____ Date _____

Reading Strategy: Apply Critical Perspectives

To **apply critical perspective** to a piece of literature, consider the point of view of the writer and the **social** or **historical perspective** of the time and situation in which the work was written. You may also look at the **archetypal perspective**—considering the author, speaker, or work as an archetype, or general example of something.

DIRECTIONS: *Review the poems from a critical perspective, and then answer the questions that follow.*

1. How does knowledge of historical perspective help you understand the poem "Refugee in America"?

   _____

   _____

   _____

2. What archetypal perspective is the speaker using in "The Negro Speaks of Rivers"?

   _____

   _____

   _____

3. What insights does a social and historical perspective give you into the meaning of "I, Too"?

   _____

   _____

   _____

4. How does a social perspective give you insight into "Dream Variations"?

   _____

   _____

   _____

"The Negro Speaks of Rivers," "Dream Variations," "I, Too,"
and "Refugee in America"
by Langston Hughes
Vocabulary Builder

Using the Root -liber-

A. DIRECTIONS: *The latin root word* -liber- *means "free."*

Complete each of the sentences below with one of the words or phrases in the box. To help figure out which word or phrase to use, determine which part of speech—noun, verb, adverb—is missing in the sentence.

> liberal arts   liberalize   liberally   libertarian

1. Since basketball games often did not end until about 11:00 P.M., Anthony began a campaign to _____ the curfew laws.

2. Literature, philosophy, and history are considered to be part of the _____ because studying them helps students to develop their general ability to think and reason.

3. Scowling at the steamed broccoli, Maura poured cheese sauce over it _____.

4. A person who believes that liberty should be absolute and unrestricted is a _____.

Using the Word List

> dusky   liberty   lulled

B. DIRECTIONS: *In each blank, write the letter of the one best answer.*

____ 1. A baby would most likely be lulled to sleep by
   A. a deep bellow.   C. a loud yell.
   B. a sharp screech.   D. a soft song.

____ 2. It is *dusky* outside when
   A. it is completely dark.   C. the sun is high in the sky.
   B. it is almost dark.   D. the sun is behind clouds.

____ 3. A prisoner who is told that he is at *liberty* to go may safely assume that
   A. he may leave and go wherever he wants to.
   B. he may leave if he keeps in touch with authorities.
   C. he is only free to go home and go to work.
   D. he must stay in prison.

Name _____ Date _____

Grammar and Style: Pronoun-Antecedent Agreement

Pronouns are words that take the place of nouns. An antecedent is the noun or pronoun that a pronoun refers back to. A pronoun must agree in number, gender, and person with its antecedent.

Agrees in number: **Erica** decided **she** needed to spend time in the library.

Agrees in gender: Each **student** chose the topic **he or she** wanted to research.

Agrees in person: **Hughes** wrote about **his** life in Harlem.

A. DIRECTIONS: *Circle the correct pronoun in each sentence to agree with the antecedent.*

1. Every student took (their; his or her) time completing the assignment.
2. Marcia could not find (her; its) place in the book.
3. Each of the poems has (his or her; its) distinct theme and perspective.
4. One of the poets wrote (their; his) poem in the 1920s.
5. All of the poems present (their; its) own interesting ideas.

B. DIRECTIONS: *Read each sentence. If the sentence has correct pronoun-antecedent agreement, write Correct. If the sentence has incorrect pronoun-antecedent agreement, rewrite the sentence correctly.*

1. Most readers have his or her favorite poems by Langston Hughes.

_____

2. The theme of that poem is its most interesting element.

_____

3. Each of the poets in this anthology have their own perspectives on life and society.

_____

4. Adam and Greta have decided to work together on their research project.

_____

5. The poem about rivers was interesting because they create images of many times and places.

_____

"The Negro Speaks of Rivers," "Dream Variations," "I, Too,"
and **"Refugee in America"**
by Langston Hughes

Support for Writing

Prepare your **multi-genre response to literature**, by completing the chart below as you do your research. Jot down the time period Hughes refers to as he evokes each river, what the river might symbolize, and why it is significant to African American readers.

River	Time	What it symbolizes	Significance to African American
Euphrates			
Congo			
Nile			
Mississippi			

On a separate page, write your draft of your essay. In your introduction briefly state the theme of "The Negro Speaks of Rivers." In the body of your essay, discuss each of the stanzas and rivers and tell how they relate to the theme. Summarize your ideas in your conclusion.

Name _____ Date _____

"Study the Masters" by Lucille Clifton
"For My Children" by Colleen McElroy
Literary Analysis: Poetry of Cultural Identity

Culture is the way of life of a group of people and is recognizable by their manner of dressing and talking, the rituals they keep, their beliefs, their art forms, and other details of their daily lives. The **poetry of cultural identity** is poetry that targets the culture of a particular group. The poetry of Lucille Clifton and Colleen McElroy expresses a cultural identity very similar to that of Langston Hughes, such as a common African American heritage, pride in their heritage, patterns of speech, and art forms.

DIRECTIONS: *Complete the following chart as you read "study the masters" and "For My Children" to identify examples of cultural identity displayed in these two poems.*

Aspects of cultural identity	"Study the Masters" by Lucille Clifton	"For My Children" by Colleen McElroy
African roots and history		
Cultural knowledge and values		
Language and patterns of speech		
Art forms		

Name _____ Date _____

Vocabulary Builder

Using the Word List

effigies   handiwork   rituals

A. DIRECTIONS: *Rewrite each sentence, substituting a word from the Word List for each italicized word or phrase.*

1. The *figures* of a Bantu chief and a Watusi warrior stood upon the shelf, two reminders of her African heritage.

_____

2. She sat quietly, waiting for the *ceremonial* acts to begin.

_____

3. The blanket represented beautiful *work done by hand* that had been passed down for generations.

_____

B. DIRECTIONS: *Write an original sentence using each of the words from the Word List.*

1. _____

_____

2. _____

_____

3. _____

_____

Name _____ Date _____

"Study the Masters" by Lucille Clifton
"For My Children" by Colleen McElroy
Support for Writing

Prepare for writing your **essay** by completing the chart below. Jot down details from each poem that identify the elements in the column heads. Include words, quotations, or other details to use in your essay.

	Speaker	Details that suggest gender	Elements of cultural identity	Message of each speaker
"The Negro Speaks of Rivers"				
"Dream Variations"				
"I, Too"				
"Refugee in America"				
"study the masters"				
"For My Children"				

On a separate page, write a draft of your essay. When you revise your essay, be sure you have included details from each poem to support your ideas.

Name _____ Date _____

"The Tropics in New York" by Claude McKay
"From the Dark Tower" by Countee Cullen
"A Black Man Talks of Reaping" by Arna Bontemps

Literary Analysis: Stanza Structure

All the poems in this group have a **stanza structure,** which refers to the manner in which the poet divides up the lines. Each stanza contains a distinct main idea, like a paragraph in prose. Certain kinds of poetic structures, such as the sonnet, require a fixed number of lines in each stanza. A sonnet has 14 lines.

DIRECTIONS: *Answer these questions about the poems in this group.*

1. What stanza structure does McKay use in "The Tropics in New York"?

   _____

2. What is the main idea of each stanza in "The Tropics in New York"?

   _____

   _____

   _____

3. What poetic form does Cullen use in "From the Dark Tower"?

   _____

4. What is the main idea of each stanza of "From the Dark Tower"?

   _____

   _____

   _____

5. What stanza structure does Bontemps use in "A Black Man Talks of Reaping"?

   _____

6. What is the main idea of each stanza in "A Black Man Talks of Reaping"?

   _____

   _____

   _____

"The Tropics in New York" by Claude McKay
"From the Dark Tower" by Countee Cullen
"A Black Man Talks of Reaping" by Arna Bontemps

Reading Strategy: Apply a Political Approach to Literary Criticism

When you **apply a political approach to literary criticism,** you use what you know about the political events of a time to help you understand the literary work. Details in the works often refer to specific events or situations.

DIRECTIONS: *Review the poems from a critical perspective. Look for details that refer to political and social situations of the period in which they were written. Then answer the questions that follow.*

1. Does your knowledge of the political situation in the first half of the twentieth century in America contribute to your understanding of "The Tropics in New York"? Explain.

   _____

   _____

   _____

   _____

2. What insights into "From the Dark Tower" do you get by applying a political approach to criticism?

   _____

   _____

   _____

   _____

3. How does a political approach to literary criticism help you understand "A Black Man Talks of Reaping"?

   _____

   _____

   _____

   _____

Name _____ Date _____

"The Tropics in New York" by Claude McKay
"From the Dark Tower" by Countee Coullen
"A Black Man Talks of Reaping" by Arna Bontemps
Vocabulary Builder

Using the Word List

beguile   benediction   countenance   increment

A. DIRECTIONS: *Choose the word that best completes the meaning of each sentence and write it in the blank.*

1. He did not countenance their behavior; that is to say, he would not _____ their talking and laughing in class.
   A. like   B. acknowledge   C. understand   D. tolerate

2. His paycheck increment reflected his _____ responsibilities.
   A. increased   B. lavish   C. marginal   D. commited

3. The dance beguiled, or _____, the audience.
   A. bored   B. angered   C. delighted   D. puzzled

4. In the benediction, he _____ the people who were still struggling to find work and to survive in the city.
   A. cursed   B. pitied   C. blessed   D. chastised

B. DIRECTIONS: *For each item, choose the word pair that best expresses a relationship similar to that expressed in the numbered pair. Circle the letter of your choice.*

___ 1. BENEDICTION : BLESSING ::
   A. poet : teacher
   B. avenue : city
   C. livelihood : job
   D. praise : demand

___ 2. COUNTENANCE :: DISAPPROVE ::
   A. pardon : forgive
   B. despise : respect
   C. relax : enjoy
   D. inspect : discover

___ 3. BEGUILE : CHARM ::
   A. revive : deplete
   B. measure : mileage
   C. restrict : expand
   D. puzzle : confuse

___ 4. INCREMENT : LOSS ::
   A. profit : debt
   B. cease : discontinue
   C. fraction : quantity
   D. equality : rights

"The Tropics in New York" by Claude McKay
"From the Dark Tower" by Countee Cullen
"A Black Man Talks of Reaping" by Arna Bontemps
Support for Writing

Prepare for writing your **essay** by completing the comparison-and-contrast chart below. Write details from each poem that demonstrate how the imagery is used differently in the three poems and how the imagery is used in the same way.

	"From the Dark Tower"	**"A Black Man Talks of Reaping"**
Imagery & Figurative Language		
Diction		
Sound		
Message		
Other Features		

On a separate page, write your draft of your essay. Give examples from the poetry to support your comparison-and-contrast development. When you revise, add descriptive language that supports your opinions.

from **Dust Tracks on a Road** by Zora Neale Hurston

Literary Analysis: Social Context in Autobiography

Zora Neale Hurston's autobiography, *Dust Tracks on a Road,* is clearly written from the point of view of an adult reflecting on her childhood in the segregated South. Although she remembers these early events in great detail, she makes it clear that her interpretation happened long after the incidents occurred. She is able to fit her own story into the social context of the time period in which she grew up. For example, in the second paragraph Hurston comments on the white travelers' allowing her to accompany them a short way: "I know now that I must have caused a great deal of amusement among them, but my self-assurance must have carried the point, for I was always invited to come along." As a child she was not aware of why asking to walk along with white people was frowned upon by her family, but as an adult, she places her behavior in a social context and sees how her actions were very unusual among African Americans at that time.

By combining narration and reflection on the social situation, autobiographers not only reveal something about themselves and their social context, they also lead us to contemplate our own social context and its influence upon us.

DIRECTIONS: *For each of the following quotations, discuss what Zora Neale Hurston reveals about the social context of her writing. Then briefly explain how each quotation might relate to something in your current social context.*

1. "Git down offa dat gate-post! You li'l sow, you! Git down! Setting up dere looking dem white folks right in de face! They's gowine to lynch you, yet. And don't stand in dat doorway gazing out at 'em neither. Youse too brazen to live long."

   _____

   _____

   _____

2. The village seemed dull to me most of the time. If the village was singing a chorus, I must have missed the tune.

   _____

   _____

   _____

3. The whites that came down from the North were often brought by their friends to visit the village school. A Negro school was something strange to them, and while they were always sympathetic and kind, curiosity must have been present.

   _____

   _____

   _____

from **Dust Tracks on a Road** by Zora Neale Hurston
Reading Strategy: Analyzing Author's Purpose and Its Impact on Meaning

Writers usually have one or more **purposes** in mind when they write. The words, characters, events, and details of their works are chosen to achieve their purposes or goals. In her autobiography, Zora Neale Hurston wrote to describe her own personal experiences, her own character, and the vital African American community in which she grew up. By identifying her purpose, readers gain insight into her character and meaning.

DIRECTIONS: *The first column of the chart below lists summaries of scenes, events, and comments from Zora Neale Hurston's autobiography. Read the summaries and, in the second column, record your analysis of the author's purpose in choosing each scene. Then choose one more scene, event, or comment, summarize it in the first column, and analyze its purpose in the second. If necessary, use extra paper. Finally, summarize how identifying Hurston's purpose added to your understanding of the selection.*

Scene, Event, or Comment of Writer	Analysis of Writer's Purpose
1. Zora marvels at the fingers of the white women with their pink tips.	
2. The white ladies ask Zora to read from a magazine when she visits them in their hotel.	
3. Zora finds Hercules a moving hero because he chooses duty over pleasure. She likes David because he is a strong, active character.	
4.	
5. How purpose contributes to meaning	

Name _____ Date _____

from **Dust Tracks on a Road** by Zora Neale Hurston
Vocabulary Builder

Using the Word List

brazenness   caper   duration   exalted

A. DIRECTIONS: *Match each word in the left column with its definition in the right column.*

___ 1. duration   A. filled with joy or pride; elated
___ 2. brazenness   B. the time something lasts
___ 3. caper   C. prank
___ 4. exalted   D. shamelessness; boldness

B. DIRECTIONS: *Decide whether each statement below is true or false. Circle* **T** *or* **F.** *Then use the space provided to explain each of your answers.*

1. People who act with *brazenness* lack confidence in themselves.
   T / F _____

2. During the *duration* of an hour, you have enough time to eat lunch and visit with friends.
   T / F _____

3. Students almost always feel *exalted* when they do really poorly on an examination.
   T / F _____

4. When they planned the *caper*, they probably thought it would be great fun.
   T / F _____

Name _____ Date _____

from **Dust Tracks on a Road** by Zora Neale Hurston
Support for Writing

Prepare to write a **personal narrative** about an event in your life that changed you in some important way by inspiring you. Think about some of your hobbies or interests and how you first gained an interest in them. Enter information in the graphic organizer below.

How This Event Changed My Life

How old I was and what the event was:
What I thought and felt while the event was happening:
What I did that was new after the event happened:
How the event has changed the way I think or feel today:

On a separate page, begin your essay by stating how the event changed your life. Then, analyze how the cause created certain effects in your life. When you revise, be sure the connection between the event and your life today is clear.

Name _____ Date _____

Essential Questions Workshop—Unit 4

In their stories, poems, and nonfiction, the writers in Unit Four express ideas that relate to the three Essential Questions framing this book. Review the literature in the unit. Then, for each Essential Question, choose an author and at least one passage from his or her writing that expresses a related idea. Use this chart to complete your work.

Essential Question	Author/Selection	Literary Passage
How does literature shape or reflect society?		
What is the relationship between place and literature?		
What makes American literature American?		

Unit 5 Introduction
Names and Terms to Know

A. DIRECTIONS: *Write a brief sentence explaining each of the following names and terms. You will find all of the information you need in the Unit Introduction in your textbook.*

1. The Cold War: _____

2. The Silent Generation: _____
   _____

3. Sputnik: _____
   _____

4. *The Crucible:* _____

5. John Hersey: _____

6. Martin Luther King, Jr. _____
   _____

B. DIRECTIONS: *Use the hints below to help you answer each question.*

1. Contrast the 1950s and the 1960s. *[Hints: What was the Age of Anxiety, and what caused it? What was the Age of Aquarius, and what caused it?]*
   _____
   _____
   _____
   _____

2. What was the effect of suburbia on American life? *[Hints: What brought "suburbia" into existence? What did it replace?]*
   _____
   _____
   _____

3. How did the Civil Rights movement affect American life? *[Hints: What did the Civil Rights movement accomplish? How did these accomplishments affect the lives of African Americans?]*
   _____
   _____
   _____

Unit 5 Introduction

Essential Question 1: How does literature shape or reflect society?

A. DIRECTIONS: *Answer the questions about the first Essential Question in the Introduction, about the relationship between the writer and society. All the information you need is in the Unit 5 Introduction in your textbook.*

1. *Political and Social Events*

   a. What international conflicts affected life in the 1950s and 1960s? _____
   _____

   b. Two important movements pressing for change in American society were _____
   _____

2. *American Values and Attitudes*

   a. What was the Age of Anxiety, and what did it value? _____
   _____

   b. What was the Age of Aquarius, and what did it value? _____
   _____

3. *These Values and Attitudes in American Literature*

   a. Which writers treated postwar life with irony? _____
   _____

   b. What purposes did writers pursue during this period? _____
   _____

   c. List examples of pop culture favorites in the 1950s and 1960s. _____
   _____

B. DIRECTIONS: *Complete the sentence stems that include the Essential Question Vocabulary words.*

1. Adele's *conformity* to her friends' choices kept her from _____

2. D.B.'s *anxiety* about college acceptance led him to _____

3. Her friends value Jeanie's *idealism* because _____

Name _____ Date _____

Unit 5 Introduction

Essential Question 2: What makes American literature American?

A. DIRECTIONS: *On the lines provided, answer the questions about the second Essential Question in the Introduction, about what makes American literature American. All the information you need is in the Unit 5 Introduction in your textbook.*

1. *Themes Expressed by American Writers*

   a. What questions did writers in the prosperous 1950s raise about the American Dream?
   _____

   b. How was the rebellion in the 1960s different from that of the American Revolution?
   _____

   c. How did the issue of race affect the writing of the period? _____
   _____

2. *Roles Played by American Writers*

   a. How did writers assume the role of "Witness" during this period? _____
   _____

   b. How did writers assume the role of "Nonconformist" during this period? _____
   _____

   c. How did writers assume the role of "Standard-Bearer" during this period? _____
   _____

3. *Building on the Past*

   a. Give examples of writers who used events from American history to illuminate the present. _____

   b. Which writers kept earlier forms and styles alive, and how? _____
   _____

   c. Which writers further developed the style of Modernism? _____
   _____

B. DIRECTIONS: *Complete the following sentence stems that include the Essential Question Vocabulary word.*

1. The Bronsons' new *prosperity* allowed them to _____

2. One way to create a new *identity* for yourself is to _____

3. Drew's *alienation* from his friends was caused by _____

All-in-One Workbook
© Pearson Education, Inc. All rights reserved.
275

Unit 5 Introduction

Essential Question 3: What is the relationship between place and literature?

A. DIRECTIONS: *On the lines provided, answer the questions about the third Essential Question in the Introduction, about the relationship between place and literature. All the information you need is in the Unit 5 Introduction in your textbook.*

1. *Wartime Settings*

   a. Which writers wrote about their World War II experiences? _____
   _____

   b. How did post–World War II writing differ from the writing that arose after World War I?
   _____

2. *Urban Life*

   a. Novels and plays that took place in cities included works by _____
   _____

   b. How did the image of the city influence American poetry? _____
   _____

3. *Growth of Suburbia and American Literature*

   a. The suburbs offered the middle class _____
   _____

   b. What less than rosy view of the American Dream emerged at this time, and which writers expressed this view? _____
   _____

B. DIRECTIONS: *Complete the sentence stems based on the Essential Question Vocabulary words.*

1. In our family, *discord* always arises when _____

2. The *destruction* of our old town library led to _____

3. Life in *suburbia* is different from life "out in the country" because _____
   _____

Unit 5 Introduction

Following-Through Activities

A. CHECK YOUR COMPREHENSION: *Use this chart to complete the Check Your Comprehension activity in the Unit 5 Introduction. In the middle boxes, fill in two key concepts for each Essential Question. Then in the right box, fill in a key author for each key concept. One key concept for Literature and Society is completed for you.*

Place and Imagination	Key Concept	Key Author
Place and Imagination	1. 2.	1. 2.
American Literature	1. 2.	1. 2.
Literature and Society	1. Individuality and nonconformity 2.	1. Lawrence Ferlinghetti 2.

B. EXTEND YOUR LEARNING: *Use this graphic organizer to plan and conduct your interview for the Extend Your Learning activity. (Q = Question; A = Answer).*

INTERVIEW SUBJECT: _____

Q: What were your reactions to the assassinations of President John F. Kennedy and Martin Luther King, Jr.?

A: _____
_____

Q: What social issues captured your imagination in those years?

A: _____
_____

Q: What was school like in the 1960s?

A: _____
_____

Q: What songs, movies, and TV shows did you enjoy? What books meant the most to you?

A: _____
_____
_____

Q: What public figures did you admire?

A: _____
_____

Q: How do you think America has changed since that time?

A: _____
_____
_____

from **Hiroshima** by John Hersey
"The Death of the Ball Turret Gunner" by Randall Jarrell
Literary Analysis: Implied Theme

The **theme** is the central idea or message about life that a writer conveys in a literary work. A writer will rarely state a theme outright. Often theme is stated indirectly, or **implied,** through the writer's portrayal of characters and events, use of literary devices, and choice of details.

To understand theme, notice whether or not the narrator presents personal feelings. Your analysis can help you identify the **author's perspective,** the point of view from which a work is written. Works can be objective, subjective, or a mixture of both.

DIRECTIONS: *For each of the following excerpts from* Hiroshima *and "The Death of the Ball Turret Gunner," (a) identify whether the author's perspective is objective or subjective and explain why, and (b) briefly explain what theme is implied in the excerpt.*

from **Hiroshima**

1. The Reverend Mr. Tanimoto got up at five o'clock that morning. He was alone in the parsonage, because for some time his wife had been commuting with their year-old baby to spend nights with a friend in Ushida, a-suburb to the north. Of all the important cities of Japan, only two, Kyoto and Hiroshima, had not been visited in strength by *B-san,* or Mr. B, as the Japanese, with a mixture of respect and unhappy familiarity, called the B-29; and Mr. Tanimoto, like all his neighbors and friends, was almost sick with anxiety.

   a. Perspective—subjective or objective? Why? _____

   _____

   b. Implied theme: _____

   _____

2. The ceiling dropped suddenly and the wooden floor above collapsed in splinters and the people up there came down and the roof above them gave way; but principally and first of all, the bookcases right behind her swooped forward and the contents threw her down. . . . There, in the tin factory, in the first moment of the atomic age, a human being was crushed by books.

   a. Perspective—subjective or objective? Why? _____

   _____

   b. Implied theme: _____

   _____

"The Death of the Ball Turret Gunner"

3. Six miles from earth, loosed from its dream of life,/I woke to black flak and the nightmare fighters./When I died they washed me out of the turret with a hose.

   a. Perspective—subjective or objective? Why? _____

   _____

   b. Implied theme: _____

   _____

Name _____ Date _____

from **Hiroshima** by John Hersey
"The Death of the Ball Turret Gunner" by Randall Jarrell
Reading Strategy: Analyze Political Assumptions

When a writer addresses a historical topic, he or she often brings a clearly stated or implied political viewpoint to the events being recounted. It is therefore useful to **analyze the political assumptions** that each writer makes—in this case, about the nature of war in general and World War II in particular.

DIRECTIONS: *In the following chart, record details, descriptions of characters, and literary devices that strike you as significant and that help to reveal the political ideas of the writer of each selection. Then, summarize the author's political assumptions about war in general and World War II in particular that those details reveal.*

Selection	Details/Events and Characters/Literary Devices	Author's Political Assumptions
from Hiroshima		
"The Death of the Ball Turret Gunner"		

from **Hiroshima** by John Hersey
"The Death of the Ball Turret Gunner" by Randall Jarrell
Vocabulary Builder

Words from Other Languages

A rendezvous was originally a place for assembling of military troops. The word comes from the French words *rendez vous*, meaning "present yourself." Many other words related to the military and warfare have their origins in other languages.

A. DIRECTIONS: *Fill in the blanks with the most appropriate word from the following list of military words that are derived from other languages.*

barricade   blitz   coup   khaki   reconnaissance

1. As our unit approached our objective, we found that we had to climb over an elaborate steel and wooden _____ that had been built by the enemy to thwart our advance.

2. Once our unit was ready to advance again, we sent two soldiers ahead to conduct _____ on the enemy's positions and manpower.

3. To conceal the movements of our troops in the lush vegetation, we wore green camouflage uniforms instead of the usual _____ ones.

4. At all times we surveyed the skies to keep on the lookout for an unexpected _____ by enemy bombers.

5. In an unexpected _____ of good fortune, we found that the enemy troops had abandoned their positions and fled before we reached our objective.

Using the Word List

convivial   evacuated   incessant   rendezvous   volition

B. DIRECTIONS: *For each Word List word, choose the word or phrase that is most similar in meaning. Circle the letter of your choice.*

1. evacuated:
   A. departed   B. replenished   C. canceled   D. ended

2. volition:
   A. unwillingness   B. resolution   C. will   D. speed

3. rendezvous:
   A. meeting   B. dance   C. song   D. tradition

4. incessant:
   A. hopeless   B. constant   C. violent   D. clear

5. convivial:
   A. reluctant   B. angry   C. sociable   D. conflicting

Name _____ Date _____

from **Hiroshima** by John Hersey
"The Death of the Ball Turret Gunner" by Randall Jarrell
Support for Writing

Both John Hersey and Randall Jarrell present powerful messages about war, but in different ways. Each author has a unique perspective and method for conveying his views and feelings about the experience and consequences of warfare. Write an essay in which you **compare and contrast** each author's views of war and the ways in which they communicate those views. Cite examples from *Hiroshima* and Jarrell's poem to support your analysis.

Before you begin to compare and contrast, review each author's work separately. Try to summarize the basic message about war that each author presents. Then begin your comparison by looking for key similarities and differences. Arrive at a solid overall evaluation before you begin to draft. As an aid in preparing your draft, answer the following questions about the selections.

1. Are the authors' messages about war similar or different? Explain your answer. (This thesis will be the guiding focus for your paper. As you write, refer back to your thesis to be sure you are staying on topic.)

   _____

   _____

   _____

   _____

2. How do the authors' methods of presenting their messages differ? Are the methods the same in any respects?

   _____

   _____

   _____

   _____

3. What are some key quotations from each work that illustrate the author's message about war?
   from *Hiroshima*:

   _____

   _____

   _____

   _____

   "The Death of the Ball Turret Gunner":

   _____

   _____

   _____

   _____

Once you have gathered these details, use them to begin writing a first draft of your comparison-and-contrast essay.

Name _____ Date _____

Editorial: "Backing the Attack"
Editorial Cartoon: "The Battle of the Easy Chair"
Advertisement Poster: "Junk Rally"
Primary Sources Worksheet

The three selections in this grouping are all concerned with the same topic: winning World War II. Each uses methods unique to its form in order to persuade the reader or viewer to think or act a certain way. These methods include visual elements, verbal elements, and persuasive techniques (logical and emotional appeals).

DIRECTIONS: *Use the table below to identify and compare the methods used in the primary source selections. Some boxes may be blank.*

	Editorial	**Editorial Cartoon**	**Poster**
Thesis (stated or implied main idea)			
Facts and figures			
Visual elements			
Humor			
Quotations			
Catchy phrases			
Appeal to emotion			
Appeal to logic			

Editorial: "Backing the Attack"
Editorial Cartoon: "The Battle of the Easy Chair"
Advertisement Poster: "Junk Rally"
Vocabulary Builder

Using the Word List

canvass	civilian	collective	estimates
expenditures	license	receipts	undertaking

A. DIRECTIONS: *Answer each questions with an explanation that clarifies the meaning of the word in italics.*

1. If you behaved with *license* at a party, is it likely that you offended someone?

   _____

2. Is a serious *undertaking* something a lazy person would welcome?

   _____

3. To *canvass* a neighborhood, would one person or a team of five be better?

   _____

4. If a hundred people let out a *collective* sigh, would it take longer than one person sighing?

   _____

5. What are some *expenditures* you have over the course of a week?

   _____

6. Are *estimates* of a home's value usually the precise price it would sell for?

   _____

7. Do a company's *receipts* represent its income or its costs?

   _____

8. Would a *civilian* be likely to wear a military uniform?

   _____

B. DIRECTIONS: *Circle the letter of the word that best completes each analogy.*

1. expenditures : costs : : undertaking :
   A. difficulty   B. endeavor   C. overtaking   D. winning
2. estimates : precise : : license :
   A. wild   B. strict   C. loose   D. expensive
3. civilian : military : : collective :
   A. grouped   B. rich   C. lengthy   D. single
4. receipts : income : : canvass :
   A. solicit   B. run   C. travel   D. oilcloth

Name _____ Date _____

"The Life You Save May Be Your Own" by Flannery O'Connor
Literary Analysis: Grotesque Characters

Flannery O'Connor included in her writing some characters that are **grotesques.** Such characters have a one-track mind; they are controlled by a single emotion, concept, or goal.

On the lines after each of the following passages, identify an emotion, a concept, or a goal that the passage suggests. Then write one or two sentences to explain how the character might act if he or she were a grotesque, controlled by the way of thinking that you have identified.

1. "Is she your baby girl?" he asked.
   "My only," the old woman said, "and she's the sweetest girl in the world. I would give her up for nothing on earth. She's smart too. She can sweep the floor, cook, wash, feed the chickens, and hoe. I wouldn't give her up for a casket of jewels."
   "No," he said kindly, "don't ever let any man take her away from you."
   "Any man come after her," the old woman said, "'ll have to stay around the place."

   _____

   _____

   _____

2. He had raised the hood and studied the mechanism and he said he could tell that the car had been built in the days when cars were really built. You take now, he said, one man puts in one bolt and another man puts in another bolt and another man puts in another bolt so that it's a man for a bolt. That's why you have to pay so much for a car: you're paying all those men. Now if you didn't have to pay but one man, you could get you a cheaper car and one that had had a personal interest taken in it, and it would be a better car.

   _____

   _____

   _____

3. Mr. Shiftlet felt that the rottenness of the world was about to engulf him. He raised his arm and let it fall again to his breast. "Oh Lord!" he prayed. "Break forth and wash the slime from this earth!"

   _____

   _____

   _____

   _____

"The Life You Save May Be Your Own" by Flannery O'Connor
Reading Strategy: Draw Conclusions from Details

"The Life You Save May Be Your Own" contains a wealth of revealing details about characters and their motivations, setting, and plot. It can enrich your appreciation of a story if, as you read, you **draw conclusions from details** to evaluate the significance of specific story elements, such as a character's name or a suggestive gesture or action or remark. Attention to such details can often help you to draw conclusions about what characters are likely to do or how the story is likely to turn out.

DIRECTIONS: *On the lines following each excerpt, explain how the details in the excerpt allow you to draw conclusions about what is likely to happen next in the story.*

1. "Although the old woman lived in this desolate spot with only her daughter and she had never seen Mr. Shiftlet before, she could tell, even from a distance, that he was a tramp and no one to be afraid of."

   _____

   _____

2. "The old woman watched from a distance, secretly pleased. She was ravenous for a son-in-law."

   _____

   _____

3. "'Saturday,' the old woman said, 'you and her and me can drive into town and get married.'"

   _____

   _____

4. "'I'm only saying a man's spirit means more to him than anything else. I would have to take my wife off for the weekend without no regards at all for cost. I got to follow where my spirit says to go.'"

   _____

   _____

5. "As they came out of the courthouse, Mr. Shiftlet began twisting his neck in his collar. He looked morose and bitter as if he had been insulted while someone held him."

   _____

   _____

6. "'Give it to her when she wakes up,' Mr. Shiftlet said. 'I'll pay for it now.'"

   _____

   _____

"The Life You Save May Be Your Own" by Flannery O'Connor
Vocabulary Builder

Using the Root -sol-

A. DIRECTIONS: *The root -sol- comes to English from the Latin adjective* solus, *meaning "alone." Use each of the following words in a sentence to demonstrate your understanding of its meaning.*

1. solitary _____

2. sole _____

3. solely _____

4. solitude _____

Using the Word List

> desolate   listed   morose   ominous   ravenous

B. DIRECTIONS: *Use one of the Word List words as you write each sentence according to the instructions given. Use the context of the sentence instructions to determine which word to use.*

1. Write a sentence about something that tilts.

   _____

   _____

2. Write a sentence about the isolated setting of a story.

   _____

   _____

3. Write a sentence about someone who is gloomy or sullen.

   _____

   _____

4. Write a sentence about someone who is extremely eager about something.

   _____

   _____

5. Write a sentence about a situation that is threatening or sinister.

   _____

   _____

Name _____ Date _____

"The Life You Save May Be Your Own" by Flannery O'Connor
Support for Writing

The title and ending of a story contain essential information that helps you interpret the story's meaning. Write an essay in which you explain the fate of each character in Flannery O'Connor's "The Life You Save May Be Your Own" and interpret the title. Be sure to answer these questions in your essay: What happens to each character at the end of the story? Whose life, if anyone's, is saved?

Use the chart below as in aid in organizing your ideas by reviewing each character's final moments in the story. Try to connect each character's fate with the idea that "the life you save may be your own."

Character	What happens to the character in the end?	How does the character's fate connect to the title?
Mrs. Crater		
Lucynell		
Mr. Shiftlet		

On a separate page, use the ideas and details you have gathered in your chart to begin to draft an introduction in which you present your interpretation of the title. You might begin by writing a one-paragraph sketch about each of the three main characters. Then explain how the final image of each character relates to the key idea of the title. Summarize and extend your analysis in your conclusion. When you are satisfied that your rough draft contains all the ideas and details that are essential to your essay, begin to write your final draft.

Name _____ Date _____

"The First Seven Years" by Bernard Malamud

Literary Analysis: Plot and Epiphany

A story follows a sequence of events called a **plot.** The plot reaches a high point of interest or suspense at the **climax.** In this story, Malamud builds toward an **epiphany,** a climax in which a character has a flash of insight that affects the conflict or causes a character to re-examine long-held assumptions.

DIRECTIONS: *On the lines below each of the following quotations, explain why that moment of the plot does or does not represent a true epiphany for Feld, the shoemaker.*

1. Neither the shifting white blur outside, nor the sudden deep remembrance of the snowy Polish village where he had wasted his youth could turn his thoughts from Max the college boy. . . .

   _____

   _____

   _____

   _____

2. An old wish returned to haunt the shoemaker: that he had had a son instead of a daughter. . . .

   _____

   _____

   _____

   _____

3. Maybe he could awaken in her a desire to go to college; if not—the shoemaker's mind at last came to grips with the truth—let her marry an educated man and live a better life.

   _____

   _____

   _____

   _____

4. That night the shoemaker discovered that his new assistant had been all the while stealing from him, and he suffered a heart attack.

   _____

   _____

   _____

   _____

5. Feld had a sudden insight. In some devious way, with his books and commentary, Sobel had given Miriam to understand that he loved her.

   _____

   _____

   _____

   _____

Name _____ Date _____

Reading Strategy: Summarizing

One useful strategy for monitoring your comprehension is **summarizing.** Pause after a significant scene or at a section break and review the events and the developing relationships between the characters. Your summary should state the main points of the scene.

DIRECTIONS: *Use the chart below to summarize Feld's relationship with the three other main characters in "The First Seven Years." In the middle column, write a phrase or short summary of how Feld relates to that character. In the right-hand column, summarize what Feld learns about each of these characters.*

Character	Summary of Relationship with Feld	Summary of What Feld Learns about This Character
Miriam		
Sobel		
Max		

"The First Seven Years" by Bernard Malamud
Vocabulary Builder

Using the Root -litera-

A. DIRECTIONS: *Explain how the meaning of each of the following words is related to the root word -litera- meaning "letter."*

1. literate (*adj.*) _____

_____

_____

2. literature _____

_____

_____

Using the Word List

diligence   discern   illiterate   repugnant   unscrupulous

B. DIRECTIONS: *Answer the following questions to demonstrate your understanding of the Word List words.*

1. Why does Feld think Max has *diligence* and Miriam does not?

_____

_____

2. Why are Sobel and Miriam *not* described as *illiterate*?

_____

_____

3. What might an *unscrupulous* employee have done to Feld?

_____

_____

4. What did Feld think he could *discern* that Miriam could not?

_____

_____

5. Why was the idea of sending Miriam to Sobel's boarding house *repugnant*?

_____

_____

Name _____ Date _____

"The First Seven Years" by Bernard Malamud
Support for Writing

Prepare a personality profile for one of the characters in "The First Seven Years" to help persuade a television producer that a show starring this character would be a big hit. Enter information about that character from the story in the graphic organizer below.

Profile of Mr. Feld

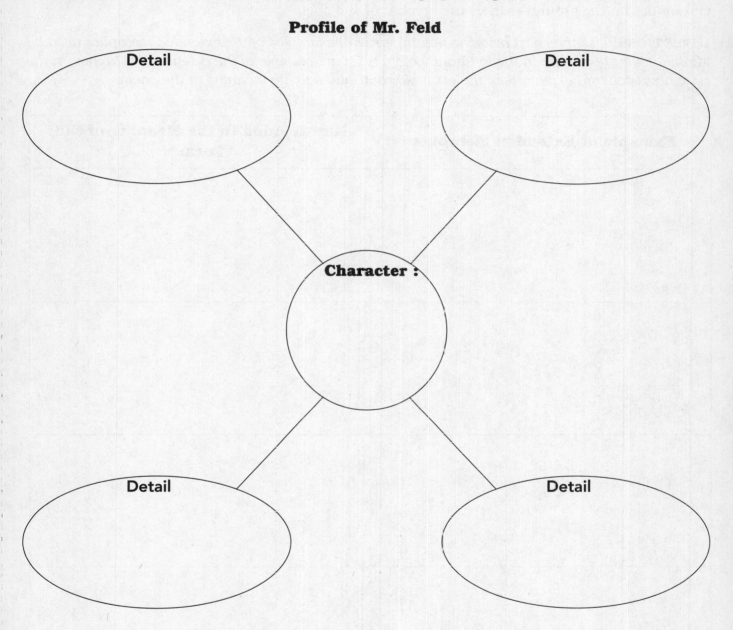

On a separate page, draft your personality profile by introducing the character you have chosen using each detail from your graphic organizer. Expand your profile until you have used all the details. When you revise, compare your cluster diagram with that of one of your classmates who has chosen the same character to see if you (or your classmate) have missed any important details. Then, add those details to your profile.

Name _____ Date _____

"Constantly Risking Absurdity" by Lawrence Ferlinghetti
Literary Analysis: Extended Metaphor

In "Constantly Risking Absurdity," Lawrence Ferlinghetti builds the entire poem on a single **extended metaphor**—in this case, a long, sustained comparison between the craft of poetry and the physical skills required of the acrobat. One false step, he implies, and someone could end up flat on the ground—either the acrobat or the poet.

DIRECTIONS: *Use the chart below to identify several examples of the extended metaphor used by Ferlingheti in this poem. In the left-hand column, list an example of the extended metaphor; in the right-hand column, explain how the example contributes to the meaning of the poem.*

Example of Extended Metaphor	How It Adds to the Meaning of the Poem

Name _____ Date _____

"**Constantly Risking Absurdity**" by Lawrence Ferlinghetti
Reading Strategy: Visualize or Picture the Action

In "Constantly Risking Absurdity," Ferlinghetti uses phrases and line breaks rather than punctuation to signal units of meaning. As you read each line, **visualize or picture the action** being described. If you lose track of the meaning, return to the last line you could clearly picture, and then read from that point forward. Sometimes you will find that an image extends beyond one line—in that case, keep reading until you feel that you have a complete mental picture of the poet's image.

DIRECTIONS: *Use the chart below as in aid in visualizing or picturing the action of various lines from the poem. The left-hand column gives several examples of lines from the poem. In the right-hand column, briefly explain how you picture or visualize the passage from the poem.*

Passage from the Poem	How I Visualize or Picture the Action
1. the poet like an acrobat climbs on rime to a high wire of his own making	
2. performing entrechats and sleight-of-foot tricks	
3. above a sea of faces	
4. little charleychaplin man	

"Constantly Risking Absurdity" by Lawrence Ferlinghetti
Vocabulary Builder

Word List

absurdity   taut   realist

A. DIRECTIONS: *Think about the meaning of the underlined Word List word in each sentence. Then, answer the question.*

1. During their animated discussion about politics, Juana declared that she thought that Gerald's desire to have a national voter ID card was an <u>absurdity.</u> Was she agreeing with Gerald's position? How do you know?

   _____

   _____

2. The movie critic described the movie's plot as "<u>taut.</u>" Was the critic paying a compliment to the movie? How do you know?

   _____

   _____

3. Tariq said that his proposals for this year's student council would reflect the fact that he considers himself a <u>realist.</u> Do you think that Tariq's program would include any unreasonable demands? How do you know?

   _____

   _____

B. DIRECTIONS: *On each line, write the letter of the word or phrase that is most nearly* opposite *in meaning to the Word List word.*

____ 1. absurdity
   A. caution
   B. seriousness
   C. fragility
   D. sincerity

____ 2. taut
   A. authentic
   B. understood
   C. slack
   D. unsightly

____ 3. realist
   A. idealist
   B. artist
   C. creator
   D. director

Name _____ Date _____

Support for Writing

Using "Constantly Risking Absurdity" as a model, write a poem using an extended metaphor. In the poem, compare something abstract to a concrete object or a physical activity.

Before you begin, make a list of ways the two things are alike. Use the graphic organizer below as an aid in identifying the abstract idea, the concrete object or physical activity, and the ways in which they are alike.

Metaphor or Image	**Summary of What It Means**

"Mirror" by Sylvia Plath

"Courage" by Anne Sexton

Literary Analysis: Figurative Language

To communicate emotions in a vivid, concrete way to the reader, both Sylvia Plath and Anne Sexton use **figurative language,** or language used imaginatively rather than literally. In particular, they use two figures of speech that compare seemingly dissimilar things.

- A **simile** is a comparison that uses a connecting word such as *like* or *as:* "The child's first step,/as awesome as an earthquake."

- A **metaphor** is a comparison that does not use a connecting word. Instead, the comparison is either implied or directly stated: "Now I am a lake."

DIRECTIONS: *Use the chart below to identify four examples of figurative language—metaphors or similes—from either poem. In the middle column, identify which kind of figure of speech it is—metaphor or simile. Then, in the right-hand column, briefly explain the meaning of the figure of speech.*

Example of Figure of Speech	Metaphor or Simile	Meaning of Figure of Speech

"Mirror" by Sylvia Plath

"Courage" by Anne Sexton

Reading Strategy: Interpreting the Connotations of Words

In most poems, the central message is not directly stated. Instead, it is up to you to look for the poem's underlying meaning. Because poets choose every word with great care, you can often gain clues to a poem's meaning by **interpreting the connotations** of individual words. To do this, consider the associations and feelings a word calls to mind, and then try to determine what common thread ties the words together.

For example, in line 14 of "Mirror" the woman in the poem is said to "reward" the mirror "with tears and an agitation of hands." How would the unhappiness shown by tears and agitation be considered a reward? The unusual use of *reward* in this line encourages you to think about the specific connotation of this word in this context and how it adds to the overall impact of the poem.

DIRECTIONS: *Answer the following questions about the connotations of key words in "Mirror" and "Courage."*

1. In line 2 of "Mirror," the mirror states, "Whatever I see I swallow immediately." What is the connotation of *swallow* in this line? How does that connotation contribute to the poem's overall message?

_____

_____

_____

2. In line 12 of "Mirror," the mirror says that the woman "turns to those liars, the candles or the moon." In what sense would candles and the moon be considered liars in the view of the mirror? What does the connotation of *liars* in this line explain about the mirror's view of the world around it?

_____

_____

_____

3. In the third stanza of "Courage," the poet writes, "Later, if you have endured a great despair,/then you did it alone,/getting a transfusion from the fire. . . ." In what sense would one get a "transfusion" from the fire of a "great despair"? How does the unusual connotation of this word in this context contribute to the poet's meaning?

_____

_____

_____

4. In the second stanza of "Courage," the poet writes, "Later, if you faced the death of bombs and bullets/you did not do it with a banner,/you did it with only a hat to/cover your heart." What is the connotation of the word *banner* in this passage? What does it say about what motivates the courage of the person she writes about?

_____

_____

_____

"Mirror" by Sylvia Plath
"Courage" by Anne Sexton
Vocabulary Builder

Word List

    endured   preconceptions   transformed   transfusion

A. DIRECTIONS: *Think about the meaning of the underlined Word List word in each sentence. Then, answer the question.*

1. If your teacher wrote that your essay was filled with <u>preconceptions,</u> does that mean that she thought that you approached your topic with an open mind? How do you know?

    _____

    _____

2. If a book critic wrote that he had "<u>endured</u>" a new science fiction novel, is it likely that he gave it an unfavorable review? How do you know?

    _____

    _____

3. If you were going to the hospital for a <u>transfusion</u> of blood, would you be donating the blood? How do you know?

    _____

    _____

4. If your friend said that the movie she saw last night had left her <u>transformed</u>, does that mean that the movie had a powerful effect on her? How do you know?

    _____

    _____

B. DIRECTIONS: *On each line, write the letter of the word or phrase that is closest in meaning to the Word List word.*

____ 1. preconceptions
    A. prejudices   C. predicaments
    B. predictions   D. preferences

____ 2. endured
    A. withstood   C. investigated
    B. persisted   D. stretched

____ 3. transfusion
    A. judgment   C. transfer
    B. travel   D. creation

____ 4. transformed
    A. understood   C. pretended
    B. altered   D. propelled

"Mirror" by Sylvia Plath
"Courage" by Anne Sexton
Support for Writing

Both "Mirror" and "Courage" address the full sweep of a human life, from youth to adulthood to old age. However, the poets' portrayals of these stages of life are extremely different. Write an **analytical essay** comparing and contrasting how each speaker sees the process or progress of life.

To help you define and organize your thoughts before you begin writing, answer the following questions about the poems:

1. Do the poets have similar or different attitudes toward aging? What words would you use to describe the speaker's attitude toward aging in each poem?

   _____

   _____

   _____

   _____

2. How does each poet use language—metaphors, similes, and striking connotations for familiar words—to convey her attitudes and ideas about aging? What are the key images that convey these attitudes and ideas?

   _____

   _____

   _____

   _____

   _____

3. Which poem's portrayal of old age strikes you as more truthful and more powerful? Or is each equally powerful and truthful in its way? Why?

   _____

   _____

   _____

   _____

After you have answered these questions, use the thoughts and ideas you have gathered to begin writing a rough draft of your essay.

Name _____ Date _____

"**Cuttings**" and "**Cuttings (*later*)**" by Theodore Roethke
Literary Analysis: Sound Devices

Roethke's poems often rely on **sound devices** to achieve their impact. Among the sound devices he uses in "Cuttings" and "Cuttings (*later*)" are the following:

- **Alliteration** is the repetition of a consonant sound at the beginnings of words: "What <u>s</u>aint <u>s</u>trained <u>s</u>o much,/Rose on <u>s</u>uch <u>l</u>opped <u>l</u>imbs to a new <u>l</u>ife?"

- **Assonance** is the repetition of a vowel sound in stressed syllables with dissimilar consonant sounds: "I qu<u>ai</u>l, l<u>ea</u>n to beginnings, sh<u>ea</u>th-wet."

- **Consonance** is the repetition of consonant sounds in stressed syllables in the middle or at the end of words: "The sma<u>ll</u> ce<u>ll</u>s bu<u>lg</u>e."

DIRECTIONS: *Use the chart below to identify the device used in each of the four examples given (there could be more than one device used in a given example), and underline the letters, words, or syllables involved in the device. Then, in the far-right column, explain how the example highlights or extends the poem's meaning.*

Example	Device	Effect on Meaning
1. This urge, wrestle, resurrection of dry sticks, . . .		
2. What saint strained so much, . . .		
3. I can hear, underground, that sucking and sobbing. . . .		
4. When sprouts break out, . . .		

"Cuttings" and "Cuttings (later)" by Theodore Roethke

Reading Strategy: Using Background Knowledge

When you read a piece of literature, **using background knowledge** can often help you to gain better understanding of important details and central ideas in the piece. You can gather background information from a variety of sources, including an introduction, footnotes, an author biography, or even from your own experiences.

"Cuttings" and "Cuttings (later)" both use processes of plant growth to explore and evoke basic truths of life. Background knowledge for these poems is provided by the author biography and the background section of your textbook. Think about how this background information helped your understanding as your read these two poems.

DIRECTIONS: *Answer the following questions, based on background information provided in your textbook about this selection.*

1. Where did Theodore Roethke's grandparents immigrate from? Where did they settle? What business did they go into after they settled in the United States?

   _____

   _____

2. What business did Roethke's father and uncle go into? How did they end up in that business? How did they do in their business?

   _____

   _____

3. Where did Roethke spend countless hours of his childhood, and what did he learn there?

   _____

   _____

4. What is a cutting?

   _____

   _____

5. What role does diffusion play in the creation of new plants from a cutting?

   _____

   _____

6. What role does water pressure play in the growth of new cells, stems, and leaves?

   _____

   _____

Name _____ Date _____

"Cuttings" and "Cuttings (later)" by Theodore Roethke
Vocabulary Builder

Word List

intricate   seeping   quail

A. DIRECTIONS: *Think about the meaning of the underlined Word List word in each sentence. Then, answer the question.*

1. The professor proposed an <u>intricate</u> method of solving the equation. Was his solution a simple one? How do you know?

   _____

   _____

2. I noticed that water was <u>seeping</u> from the bottom of the pitcher. Was the water leaking quickly? How do you know?

   _____

   _____

3. I started to <u>quail</u> during the climactic scene of the movie. Was the movie scary? How do you know?

   _____

   _____

B. DIRECTIONS: *On each line, write the letter of the word or phrase that is most nearly* opposite *in meaning to the Word List word.*

____ 1. seeping
    A. plodding   C. gushing
    B. glaring   D. laughing

____ 2. intricate
    A. delicate   C. safe
    B. unsightly   D. simple

____ 3. quail
    A. pretend   C. deny
    B. confront   D. limit

"Cuttings" and "Cuttings (*later*)" by Theodore Roethke
Support for Writing

Your assignment is to write an essay in which you compare and contrast the information in a science text with the depiction of plant growth in Roethke's poems, evaluating the merits of each type of writing. Use the chart below to help you to organize your basic information and ideas for the essay.

Source	Type of Language Used	Author's Purposes	Author's Perspectives
Roethke's poems			
Science text			

Then, answer this question: In your view, which presentation of plant growth is more engaging and effective? Why?

_____

_____

_____

On a separate piece of paper, write a rough draft of your essay based on the information and ideas you have gathered on this page.

Name _____ Date _____

"The Explorer" by Gwendolyn Brooks
"Frederick Douglass" by Robert Hayden

Literary Analysis: Repetition and Parallelism

Two common rhetorical devices that are prominent in these two poems are **repetition** and **parallelism**.

- Repetition is the repeating of key words or concepts: "<u>this man,</u> this Douglass . . . <u>this man,</u> superb in love and logic, <u>this man</u> / shall be remembered. . . ."

- Parallelism is the repetition of a grammatical structure: "<u>There were</u> no bourns. / <u>There were</u> no quiet rooms."

Rhetorical devices emphasize a message or excite an emotion.

Directions: *For each poem in this grouping, provide one example of repetition and parallelism. In each case, state whether the basic purpose of the device is to emphasize a message, excite an emotion, or both.*

"The Explorer"

1. **Example of repetition:** _____

_____

_____

Purpose: _____

2. **Example of parallelism:** _____

_____

_____

Purpose: _____

"Frederick Douglass"

1. **Example of repetition:** _____

_____

_____

Purpose: _____

2. **Example of parallelism:** _____

_____

_____

Purpose: _____

"The Explorer" by Gwendolyn Brooks
"Frederick Douglass" by Robert Hayden

Reading Strategy: Read the Poems Aloud

When poets use repeated or parallel words or phrases, they are often trying to emphasize a point or give added intensity to an emotion. When we read a text silently, though, we sometimes fail to grasp the full impact of these repetitions or parallel phrasings—they often convey their full impact only if read aloud. To enhance your appreciation of the author's message, **read the poems aloud.** When you encounter a repetition or parallel structure, slow down and emphasize it. What message becomes clear? What emotions do you feel?

DIRECTIONS: *Use the chart below to write a passage that you read aloud in each of the poems in this grouping. For each passage, identify the main technique used—parallelism or repetition—and then, in the final column briefly state how reading the passage aloud enhanced your understanding of the meaning of the poem.*

"The Explorer"

Passage I Read Aloud	Technique Used in Passage	How Reading Aloud Enhanced Meaning

"Frederick Douglass"

Passage I Read Aloud	Technique Used in Passage	How Reading Aloud Enhanced Meaning

Name _____ Date _____

"The Explorer" by Gwendolyn Brooks
"Frederick Douglass" by Robert Hayden

Vocabulary Builder

Word/Phrase Relationships

The meaning of a descriptive word can change when it is connected to other words in a phrase. For example, the adjective *smooth* means "having a continuous surface" if applied to an object you are touching, but it means "serene" or "suave" if you are talking about someone's manner or disposition.

A. DIRECTIONS: *Read each pair of sentences below. Then, explain how the meaning of the word differs in the context of each underlined phrase.*

1. a. My blanket was so <u>frayed</u> that it had begun to fall into pieces.
   b. My patience was <u>frayed</u> by my inability to solve the math problem after countless attempts.

Difference in meaning between *a and b*: _____

_____

_____

2. a. The hotel was comfortable, but we were put off by the <u>gaudy</u> decor of the lobby.
   b. The speaker made a <u>gaudy</u> recitation of his credentials in the area of political science.

Difference in meaning between *a and b*: _____

_____

_____

Using the Word List

    frayed   wily   gaudy

B. DIRECTIONS: *For each Word List word, chose the word or phrase that is most clearly opposite in meaning. Circle the letter of your choice.*

1. frayed
A. cooked   B. typical   C. intact   D. peaceful

2. wily
A. stupid   B. large   C. sad   D. respectful

3. gaudy
A. dark   B. patient   C. tasteful   D. unique

"The Explorer" by Gwendolyn Brooks
"Frederick Douglass" by Robert Hayden
Support for Writing

"The Explorer" and "Frederick Douglass" can be read in two different ways: (a) from a **social perspective,** as a reflection of the struggles of African Americans during the mid-twentieth century and (b) from an **archetypal perspective,** as an expression of universal human longings. Prepare to write an essay in which you examine both poems from each of these perspectives. Use the questions below to help you begin to gather information and organize your thoughts in preparation for your first draft.

"The Explorer"

1. **Connections between details in the poem and events or issues in mid-1900s America:**

   _____

   _____

   _____

   _____

   _____

2. **How the poem expresses universal human problems and longings:**

   _____

   _____

   _____

   _____

   _____

   _____

"Frederick Douglass"

1. **Connections between details in the poem and events or issues in mid-1900s America:**

   _____

   _____

   _____

   _____

   _____

2. **How the poem expresses universal human problems and longings:**

   _____

   _____

   _____

   _____

   _____

On a separate page, gather your information and thoughts together in a first draft of your essay. Identify points in your draft at which you make important general statements about the poem. Strengthen your analysis by adding accurate quotations from the poem to support your interpretation.

Name _____ Date _____

"One Art" and **"Filling Station"** by Elizabeth Bishop

Literary Analysis: Diction

Elizabeth Bishop carefully crafts her poems to create a sense of intimacy with and connection to the reader. A major formal element that she uses to connect with the reader is **diction,** or word choice. Consider the rhyming words in the following lines from "One Art":

> *The art of losing isn't hard to <u>master</u>;*
> *so many things seem filled with the intent*
> *to be lost that their loss is not <u>disaster</u>.*

The words *master* and *disaster* are common, everyday words, yet the way in which she places and repeats them throughout the poem gives them fresh meaning. In "Filling Station," Bishop creates a strong sense of place through the skillful diction with which she describes key details of the filling station and the people who work and live there.

DIRECTIONS: *Use the graphic organizer below to list four examples of vivid words or phrases in "Filling Station" that vividly evoke the reality of this place for the reader.*

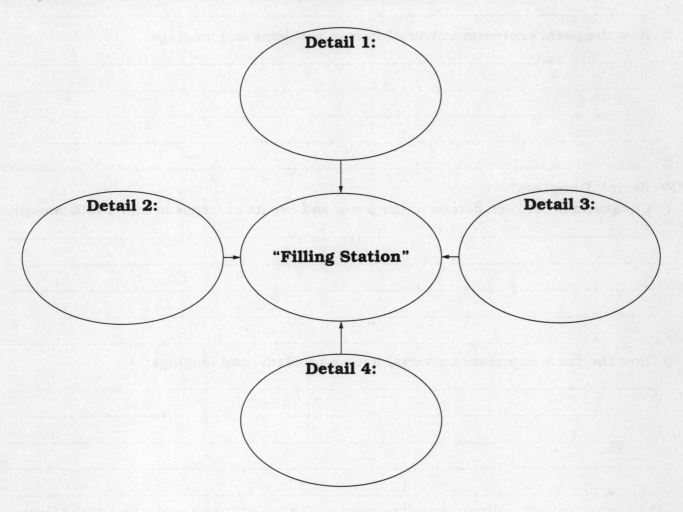

"One Art" and **"Filling Station"** by Elizabeth Bishop

Reading Strategy: Read According to Punctuation

Many poems—including "One Art" and "Filling Station"—are written in sentences and use the same punctuation marks that you find in prose. To better understand the meaning of a poem, **read according to punctuation.** Instead of pausing at line breaks, pause only when you encounter a comma, a colon, a semicolon, a dash, or an end mark.

DIRECTIONS: *Write your answer to the following questions on the lines provided.*

1. The first line of "Filling Station" ends with an exclamation point ("Oh, but it is dirty!"). How does this punctuation affect the impact and meaning of that line?

   _____

   _____

2. How many sentences or complete thoughts are expressed in the following lines from "Filling Station"?

   > Some comic books provide
   > the only note of color—
   > of certain color. They lie
   > upon a big dim doily
   > draping a taboret
   > (part of the set), beside
   > a big hirsute begonia.

   _____

3. Each line of the fifth stanza of "One Art" ends with a stop—a period or comma. Is it reasonable to conclude that each line expresses a single thought? Why or why not?

   _____

   _____

   _____

4. Which stanza of "One Art" expresses the most complete thoughts? Explain your answer.

   _____

   _____

"One Art" and **"Filling Station"** by Elizabeth Bishop
Vocabulary Builder

Using the Root -extra-

A. DIRECTIONS: *The root -extra- means "additional," "outside," or "beyond." Tell what the meaning of each of these words has to do with these meanings.*

1. extraterrestrial _____

2. extrapolate _____

3. extralegal _____

4. extramarital _____

Using the Word List

extraneous   intent   master   permeated

B. DIRECTIONS: *Circle the letter of the answer that is closest in meaning to the Word List word.*

1. MASTER
   A. learn   B. judge   C. rule   D. define

2. INTENT
   A. goal   B. concentration   C. analysis   D. force

3. PERMEATED
   A. diluted   B. requested   C. spread   D. founded

4. EXTRANEOUS
   A. diverting   B. inessential   C. complicated   D. courteous

Name _____ Date _____

Support for Writing

Use the following chart to help get started in creating a multigenre response to either "One Art" or "Filling Station." First, illustrate the poem with drawings, paintings, or photographs of your own, or with a collage of images you find in other sources. Next, write an explanation of your choices. Finally, combine the images with the written text to create a poetry display. Post your display in the classroom, if possible.

Use the chart below as an aid in generating ideas for your project.

Type of Drawing, Painting, or Photograph	Is Image Realistic or Symbolic?	Why I Chose This Image

"The Rockpile" by James Baldwin
Literary Analysis: Setting

Every story has a **setting,** a particular time and place in which it occurs. The setting of a story affects how the characters feel and how they behave. Setting encompasses details that fall into several categories, such as location, weather, geography, time of day, season, and atmosphere. The social and economic conditions that prevail in a story are also an important aspect of its setting.

A specific story setting might also be a **symbol,** which is a person, place, or object that has a meaning in itself but also suggests a larger meaning. For example, in this story, the rockpile represents both failure in the community and conflict in the family.

A. DIRECTIONS: *Each of the following passages from the selection reflects or symbolizes a particular category of setting. Review the categories listed below. On the line before each passage, write the letter of the category (or the letters of the categories) that best applies to the passage. You will not use every category.*

A. location	B. geography	C. weather	D. time of day
E. social and economic conditions		F. season	G. atmosphere

_____ 1. "At the end of the street nearest their house was the bridge which spanned the Harlem River . . ."

_____ 2. ". . . John and Roy sat on the fire escape and watched the forbidden street below."

_____ 3. "Dozens of boys fought each other in the harsh sun . . ."

_____ 4. "One Saturday, an hour before his father would be coming home, Roy was wounded on the rockpile and brought screaming upstairs."

_____ 5. "They filled the air, too, with flying weapons: stones, sticks, tin cans, garbage, whatever could be picked up and thrown."

B. DIRECTIONS: *In each of the sentences in Part A, at least one word is related to a particular category (or categories) of setting. Change the setting of each sentence by replacing the word or words with your own. On the lines below, rewrite each sentence with your new words. Your new sentences can make the setting imaginative and fun.*

_____

_____

_____

_____

_____

_____

_____

_____

_____

Name _____ Date _____

When you **identify cause and effect** relationships in fiction, you can take several approaches. You might figure out what causes characters to behave as they do. You might note the effects that one character's words or actions have on other characters. Identifying cause and effect in fiction can help you understand a story's action and meaning.

DIRECTIONS: *Complete the following flow charts to identify cause and effect in "The Rockpile."*

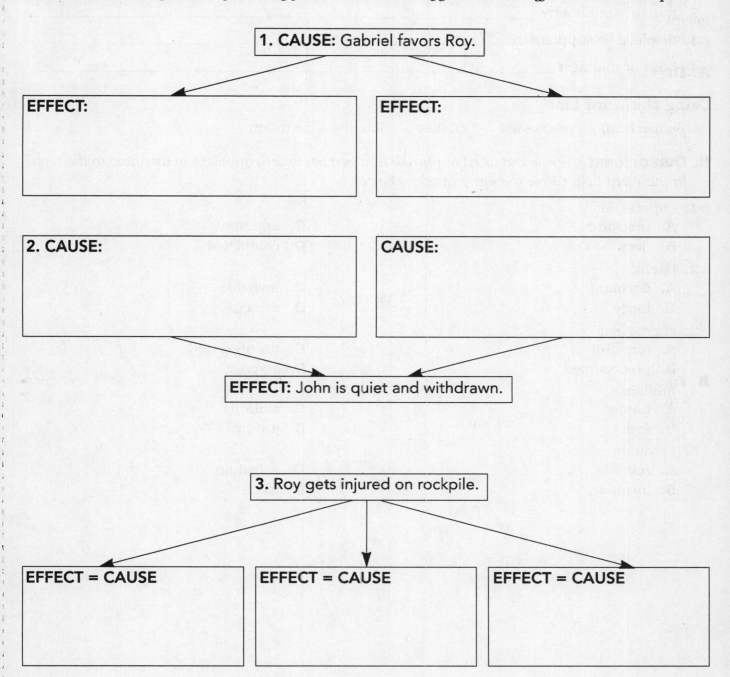

1. CAUSE: Gabriel favors Roy.

EFFECT:

EFFECT:

2. CAUSE:

CAUSE:

EFFECT: John is quiet and withdrawn.

3. Roy gets injured on rockpile.

EFFECT = CAUSE

EFFECT = CAUSE

EFFECT = CAUSE

"The Rockpile" by James Baldwin
Vocabulary Builder

Using the Latin Prefix *super-*

A. DIRECTIONS: *The prefix* super- *means "over, above, beyond." For each word or phrase that follows, write a synonym that contains the prefix* super-.

1. of higher rank or quality _____

2. naughty or snobby _____

3. displace or supplant _____

4. boss or manager _____

Using the Word List

superficial   engrossed   jubilant   latent   perdition

B. DIRECTIONS: *Choose the word or phrase that is most nearly* opposite *in meaning to the word in the Word List. Circle the letter of your choice.*

1. superficial:
   A. unaware
   B. deep
   C. apparent
   D. completed

2. latent:
   A. dormant
   B. tardy
   C. invisible
   D. evident

3. engrossed:
   A. forgetful
   B. preoccupied
   C. uninterested
   D. serene

4. jubilant:
   A. happy
   B. sad
   C. skillful
   D. jumpy

5. perdition:
   A. relief
   B. intuition
   C. salvation
   D. focus

"The Rockpile" by James Baldwin
Grammar and Style: Avoiding Shifts in Verb Tense

A **verb** has different forms, called **tenses,** to show the time of the action. Generally, use the same tense. When your verbs **shift** unnecessarily from one tense to another, it's difficult to follow your meaning. Here's an example of consistent use of verb tenses:

When I *finished* this story, I *knew* more about life in Harlem in the 1930s

However, you can shift tenses if you want to show a change in time:

"The Rockpile" *was* so interesting that I *am* now eager to read more of Baldwin's work.

Here is an example of an inconsistent shift in verb tense of the kind you should avoid:

I *sit* on the couch while I *did* my homework.

The present-tense action of *sit* conflicts with the past-tense shift to *did*. The unnecessary shift in verb tense is corrected in the examples below:

I *sit* on the couch while I *do* my homework.

I *sat* on the couch while I *did* my homework.

DIRECTIONS: *Rewrite each sentence below to correct any unnecessary shift in verb tense. If the sentence is correct, write correct on the line.*

1. I will write a thank-you note to all the guests when I got home.

   _____

2. There are lots of exciting music acts at the concert I attended.

   _____

3. It is the duty of all citizens to help all those who were in need.

   _____

4. Last year's basketball team had a losing record despite the high hopes we have for it.

   _____

5. The movie we are watching now is not as interesting as the one we saw last week.

   _____

"The Rockpile" by James Baldwin
Support for Writing

A radio drama can capture the sounds and emotions of a story, while allowing the listeners to imagine for themselves what the characters and settings look like. Work with a group of classmates to prepare an adaptation of "The Rockpile" as a **radio play.** Answer the questions below as an aid in organizing the details and tasks you will have to consider in putting on your radio play. Sketch your answers on the lines below or on a separate sheet of paper.

1. Who should draft the script for the play? Should it be one person or a group? Which would work better? If it's one person, who should that be; if it's a group, who should be in the group?

   _____

   _____

   _____

2. How many scenes will there be in the play, and where in the plot will each scene begin and end?

   _____

   _____

   _____

   _____

3. Make a list of characters, and think about what the characters are thinking and feeling in each scene.

   _____

   _____

   _____

   _____

4. Make a list of appropriate sound effects and music to give the audience a feeling for the time and place of the story.

   _____

   _____

   _____

   _____

Once you have prepared a draft of the script of the play and have gathered your sound effects and music, rehearse the play until you are satisfied with the results. Then present the play to the rest of your classmates. If other groups in the class have prepared different versions of a radio play of "The Rockpile," compare your adaptation with those of other groups.

"Life in His Language" by Toni Morrison

Literary Analysis: Eulogy and Mood

A **eulogy** is a speech or essay written to pay tribute to someone who has died, to honor his or her life and accomplishments. An effective eulogy can help an audience understand the subject's personality and unique contributions.

Because most eulogies are written shortly after the subject's death, they focus on that person's strengths and positive features and are thus usually written in a respectful tone. **Mood** is the feeling created in the reader by a literary work. Elements that can influence the mood of a work include word choice, tone, and rhythm. Even though all eulogies are respectful, they do not all have the same mood: some might be somber, while others are celebratory or angry.

DIRECTIONS: *Use the graphic organizer below to help you identify the basic overall mood of Morrison's eulogy "Life in His Language." Once you have identified the basic mood, provide four examples of language from the eulogy that expresses that mood.*

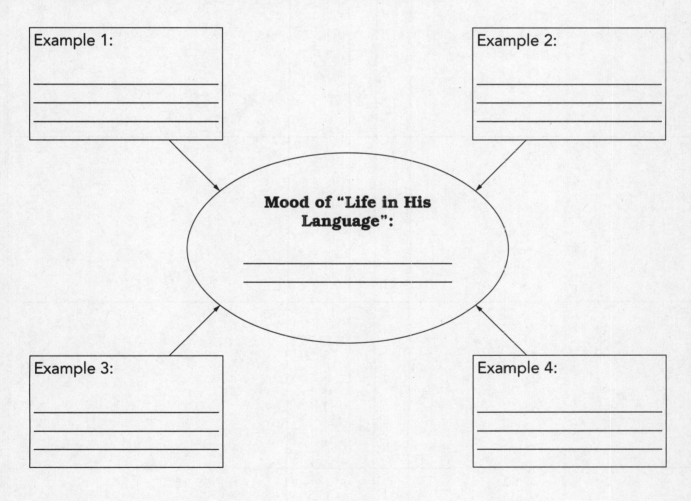

Name _____ Date _____

Reading Strategy: Analyze Syntax and Patterns of Organization

Syntax is the order of words and their relationships. **Analyzing syntax and patterns of organization**—looking at grammar and placement of words and phrases—can be a useful tool in understanding an essay.

Patterns of organization reveal the structure of ideas in an essay. In this essay, Morrison's discussion of the "three gifts" that Baldwin shared with others is a key example of such a pattern.

DIRECTIONS: *Use the chart below to analyze each of Baldwin's "three gifts." In the first column, identify each gift. In the second column, briefly explain the significance and meaning of the gift.*

GIFT	Significance and Meaning of Gift
1.	
2.	
3.	

Name _____   Date _____

"Life in His Language" by Toni Morrison
Vocabulary Builder

Word List

appropriate   platitudes   scenario   summation

A. DIRECTIONS: *Write whether each statement is true or false. Then, explain your answer using the meaning of the word in italics.*

1. Jury members can expect to hear the *summation* of a lawyer's argument at the beginning of his remarks.

   _____

2. A chief executive who wants to make the right decision will ask his assistants to present him with the consequences of every conceivable *scenario*.

   _____

3. An essay that is notable for its originality will not rely on *platitudes*.

   _____

4. A writer who tends to *appropriate* the ideas of other authors is usually very careful about citing and acknowledging his sources.

   _____

B. DIRECTIONS: *Circle the letter of the word that is closest in meaning to the word in CAPITAL LETTERS.*

1. SUMMATION
   A. peak
   B. interval
   C. trial
   D. conclusion

2. SCENARIO
   A. sensation
   B. pace
   C. situation
   D. enclosure

3. PLATITUDES
   A. investigations
   B. feelings
   C. crowds
   D. cliches

4. APPROPRIATE
   A. receive
   B. prepare
   C. accuse
   D. steal

Name _____ Date _____

"Life in His Language" by Toni Morrison
Support for Writing

"Life in His Language" is Toni Morrison's moving account of the ways in which James Baldwin influenced and inspired her work and those of other African American writers and activists. Write an **essay of tribute** to honor someone who has inspired you. Your subject might be someone you know or someone whose work affected you. Organize your essay using a clear pattern of three—start out by sketching three key ways in which your subject's life and/or work has inspired and influenced you, using Morrison's description of Baldwin's "three gifts" as your model.

Answer the questions below as an aid in organizing your thoughts for this essay:

1. Who is the person who has had the greatest impact on me?

_____

2. Briefly summarize the life and key accomplishments, personal or professional, of the person you have chosen.

_____
_____
_____
_____

3. What are three major ways in which that person has influenced and/or inspired me?

A. _____
_____
_____

B. _____
_____
_____

C. _____
_____
_____

Using the material you have gathered in your answers to these questions, write a first draft of your essay. Include the following:

- an introduction that identifies your subject and focus

- one paragraph for each of the three features or elements you will discuss

- a conclusion that summarizes and extends your view of this person

Name _____   Date _____

"Inaugural Address" by John F. Kennedy;
from "Letter from Birmingham City Jail" by Martin Luther King, Jr.
Literary Analysis: Persuasion

Persuasion is writing or speech meant to get a reader or listener to think or act in a particular way. To make their words persuasive, both Kennedy and King use a variety of **rhetorical devices.** Some of the rhetorical devices that are prominent in Kennedy's speech and King's letter are as follows:

- **Parallellism** is the repetition of grammatical structures to express similar ideas: "born in this century, tempered by war, disciplined by a hard and bitter peace . . ."

- **Antithesis** is a form of parallelism in which strongly contrasting words, phrases, clauses, or sentences are repeated: "not as a call to battle, . . but as a call to bear the burden of a long twilight struggle. . . ."

Use the chart below to give another example of each of these rhetorical devices from either selection. Then, in the right-hand column, explain briefly how the use of the device helps to make the work more persuasive.

Example of Rhetorical Device	**How It Makes the Work More Persuasive**
Parallellism:	
Antithesis:	

"Inaugural Address" by John F. Kennedy;
from **"Letter from Birmingham City Jail"** by Martin Luther King, Jr.

Reading Strategy: Identify Main Ideas and Supporting Details

The **main ideas** in a selection are the key points that the writer or speaker wants to express. The **supporting details** are the facts, examples, or reasons that explain or justify those main ideas. For example, when Martin Luther King, Jr., writes of African Americans, "Our destiny is tied up with the destiny of America," he supports this main idea with the following historical facts:

- Before the Pilgrims landed at Plymouth, we were here.

- Before the pen of Jefferson etched across the pages of history the majestic words of the Declaration of Independence, we were here.

- For more than two centuries our foreparents labored in this country without wages; they made cotton king; and they built the homes of their masters in the midst of brutal injustice and shameful humilation.

On the graphic organizer below, identify a main idea from each of the two selections and the details that support the main idea.

Selection:		
Main Idea:		
Supporting Detail	**Supporting Detail**	**Supporting Detail**

Selection:		
Main Idea:		
Supporting Detail	**Supporting Detail**	**Supporting Detail**

"Inaugural Address" by John F. Kennedy;
from **"Letter from Birmingham City Jail"** by Martin Luther King, Jr.
Vocabulary Builder

Using the Latin Root -*vert*- or -*vers*-

The Latin root -*vert*- or -*vers*- means "to turn." For example, the word *reverse* means "to turn completely around in direction."

A. DIRECTIONS: *Complete the following sentences by circling the word containing the root -vert- or -vers- that best fits the meaning of the sentence. Use a dictionary if necessary.*

1. When Stephanie lost control of her motorcycle, I quickly (averted/converted) my eyes for fear of what I might see.

2. The police immediately began (conversing/diverting) traffic away from the accident.

3. The medical helicopter that took Stephanie to the hospital flew (vertically/inversely) before heading to the northeast.

4. While Stephanie had suffered a few scrapes and bruises, she mostly complained about (vertigo/conversion).

5. She said that while she loved the thrill of riding on two wheels, she might (reverse/convert) to four-wheel transportation in the near future.

Word List

    adversary   alliance   eradicate   flagrant   invective   profundity

B. DIRECTIONS: *Show that you understand the meaning of the italicized words from the Word List by briefly answering the following questions.*

1. Why might countries form an *alliance*?

   _____

2. Why might one country be the *adversary* of another?

   _____

3. What kind of substance might I wish to *eradicate* from my carpet?

   _____

4. Why might a philosopher spoke with *profundity* about life?

   _____

5. Why might a politician appear shocked if another politician shouted an *invective* at her or him?

   _____

6. How was segregation *flagrant* in its lack of obedience to the nation's law?

   _____

"Inaugural Address" by John F. Kennedy;
from **"Letter from Birmingham City Jail"** by Martin Luther King, Jr.
Grammar and Style: Use Active, Not Passive, Voice

A verb is in the **active voice** when the subject of the sentence performs the action. A verb is in the **passive voice** when the subject of the sentence receives the action. The passive voice uses a form of *to be* together with a past participle.

Active Voice: King emphasized the importance of using moral means to achieve moral ends.

Passive Voice: The importance of using moral means to achieve moral ends was emphasized by King.

Use the active voice whenever possible. It is livelier and more direct than the passive voice. Use the passive voice only if the person or thing performing the action is unknown or unimportant.

A. PRACTICE: *Read each sentence and write* A *above any verbs or verb phrases in the active voice and* P *above any in the passive voice.*

1. When the influence of Gandhi's philosophy on King was posed by the questioner, the lecturer affirmed that King considered himself a disciple of Gandhi's philosophy of nonviolence.

2. Many presidents have delivered forgettable or undistinguished inaugural addresses; Kennedy's address, by contrast, is considered among the finest and most memorable by many historians.

3. Ask not what your country can do for you.

4. . . . we were carrying our whole nation back to those great wells of democracy which were dug deep by the Founding Fathers. . . .

B. Writing Application: *Rewrite the following sentences, changing all verbs in the passive to the active voice.*

1. All this will not be finished by us in the first 100 days.

_____

2. Only a few generations have been granted the role of defending freedom in its hour of maximum danger.

_____

_____

3. Let us hope that the deep fog of misunderstanding will be lifted from our fear-drenched communities.

_____

_____

4. Dr. Martin Luther King, Jr., has been honored throughout the country in the many communities that have named schools and streets after him.

_____

_____

Name _____ Date _____

"Inaugural Address" by John F. Kennedy;
from "Letter from Birmingham City Jail" by Martin Luther King, Jr.
Support for Writing

To prepare to write a letter to the editor on an issue about which you feel strongly, first enter information into the chart below.

Letter from [_____: your name] about [_____: issue]

Issue:
_____
_____
Opinion Statement:
_____
_____

Persuasive Support		
Logical:	**Emotional:**	**Ethical:**
_____	_____	_____
_____	_____	_____
_____	_____	_____

On a separate page, draft your letter. Begin by presenting your main idea about the issue in the form of an opinion statement. In your draft, support your main idea with details, using logical, emotional, and ethical appeals. Use parallel structure as a device. As you revise, be sure you have supported your opinion statement with enough persuasive evidence.

All-in-One Workbook
325

Contemporary Commentary
The Words of Arthur Miller on *The Crucible*

DIRECTIONS: *Use the space provided to answer the questions.*

1. Briefly identify the "correspondence" Arthur Miller says he perceived in two widely separated periods of American history as he started to write *The Crucible*.

   _____

   _____

   _____

2. How does Miller connect the Salem witch hunt with poetry?

   _____

   _____

3. What specific similarities does Miller identify between the prosecutions and the confessions of the accused?

   _____

   _____

   _____

   _____

4. According to Miller, why has *The Crucible* become his most-produced play?

   _____

   _____

5. What questions for further research or investigation does this commentary leave you with? Identify at least two issues you would like to pursue as you read the play.

   _____

   _____

   _____

   _____

   _____

   _____

Arthur Miller
Listening and Viewing

Segment 1: Meet Arthur Miller
- What are the titles of Arthur Miller's most famous plays?
- How do you think growing up during the Depression influenced Arthur Miller's writing?

_____

_____

_____

_____

Segment 2: *The Crucible*
- How is Senator Joseph McCarthy historically significant?
- How does *The Crucible* reflect what was going on in America in the 1950s?

_____

_____

_____

_____

Segment 3: The Writing Process
- According to Arthur Miller, why is theater a "changeable art"?
- Why do you think dramas written long ago are still relevant today?

_____

_____

_____

_____

Segment 4: The Rewards of Writing
- How does Arthur Miller's writing reflect his political concerns?
- What do you think is Arthur Miller's greatest contribution to American society and literature?

_____

_____

_____

_____

Name _____ Date _____

Biography: Arthur Miller

DIRECTIONS: *Fill in the time line with important events from playwright Arthur Miller's life.*

1932:

1947:

1949:

1953:

1956:

1956:

Name _____ Date _____

The Crucible, *Act I,* by Arthur Miller
Literary Analysis: Plot and Dramatic Exposition

Arthur Miller's *The Crucible* is a **political drama** because it is both a historical narrative about the Salem witch hunts of the 1600s and a commentary on American politics during the "Red Scare" of the 1950s, when Senator Joseph McCarthy ran "witch hunts" to expose communists and communist sympathizers in the United States. The **plot,** or series of events, of *The Crucible* can be interpreted as a metaphor for the events of the Red Scare and the political climate it created. In Act I, Miller uses **dramatic exposition,** or the revealing of background information through stage directions and dialogue, to set up this extended metaphor.

DIRECTIONS: *Refer to Act I of* The Crucible *as you answer the following questions.*

1. Miller uses lengthy prose commentaries for much of his dramatic exposition in Act I. What kind of information does he reveal in these commentaries?

   _____

   _____

2. Why do you think Miller uses this unusual expository strategy for his drama?

   _____

   _____

3. How would the experience of reading the play be different without this type of dramatic exposition?

   _____

   _____

4. At what point does the rising action begin?

   _____

   _____

5. What conflict prompts the beginning of the rising action?

   _____

   _____

6. What do you feel is the most important piece of information revealed in Act I? Why?

   _____

   _____

The Crucible, *Act I*, by Arthur Miller
Reading Strategy: Dialogue and Stage Directions

Arthur Miller's **stage directions** in *The Crucible* are extensive, detailed, and full of historical information. They provide the setting, background on the situation, and information about characters' backgrounds, motives, and personalities. A reader of the play benefits from Miller's background information by gaining an understanding of the characters as people and why they act the way they do.

Still, *The Crucible* is a play. As in all plays, the **dialogue** carries the burden of communicating to the audience. From the dialogue a reader or an audience member learns how the characters think, how they express themselves, and how they feel about one another and about the situation at hand. It is only through the dialogue that the plot develops.

DIRECTIONS: *Refer to dialogue, stage directions, and background information in Act I as you fill in the chart.*

Question	Answer	Where You Found the Information
1. What do you learn about Reverend Parris's relationship with the community in Act I?		
2. What are Abigail's circumstances? What led her to reside with her uncle?		
3. What relationship exists between Abigail and Proctor?		
4. What kind of person is Goody Putnam? What makes her this way?		
5. Why is Mary Warren embarrassed and fearful when John Proctor enters the room?		

Name _____ Date _____

The Crucible, *Act I,* by Arthur Miller
Vocabulary Builder

Using the Root *-grat-*

A. DIRECTIONS: *The root -grat- means "pleasing" or "grateful." Explain how the meaning of the word root -grat- contributes to the meaning of each of the following words.*

1. gratitude _____

   _____

   _____

2. gratuitous _____

   _____

   _____

Using the Word List

> calumny   evade   dissembling   inculcation
> ingratiating   predilection   propitiation

B. DIRECTIONS: *Match each word in the left column with its definition in the right column. Write the letter of the definition on the line next to the word it defines.*

___ 1. predilection   A. charming
___ 2. calumny   B. slander
___ 3. propitiation   C. escape
___ 4. evade   D. instilling
___ 5. ingratiating (adj.) E. appeasement
___ 6. inculcation   F. lying
___ 7. dissembling   G. preference

The Crucible, *Act I*, by Arthur Miller
Support for Writing: Newspaper Article

DIRECTIONS: *Fill in the chart below to help you write your newspaper article reporting Betty's sudden illness and the accusations of witchcraft in Salem that followed. Collect your information from Act I of The Crucible. You may use your imagination to fill in more details, but remember that your article should be made up of objective facts rather than your personal opinions.*

Who (is involved)?	
What (happened)?	
When (did it happen)?	
Where (did it happen)?	
Why (did it happen)?	
How (did it happen)?	

The Crucible, *Act II*, by Arthur Miller
Literary Analysis: Allusion

An **allusion** is a reference to some well-known thing or idea. In our society, for example, people often allude to sports phenomena: "This project is the Super Bowl for us." Common allusions often take their reference from the surrounding society, so it's little wonder that the Salem Puritans in *The Crucible* make **Biblical allusions** as knowledgeably and as frequently as we allude to sports

DIRECTIONS: *Use a dictionary or other reference work to explain the italicized allusion in each of the following items.*

1. At the beginning of Act II, a kind of *cold war* exists between John and Elizabeth because of past events.

   _____

   _____

2. Although an honest and strong man, John Proctor has an *Achilles heel*—his relationship to Abigail.

   _____

   _____

3. Something between a *siren* and a *harpy*, Abigail proves to be Proctor's undoing.

   _____

   _____

4. Reverend Hale brings an *ivory-tower* approach to his examination that ill fits the world he finds.

   _____

   _____

5. With the sword of Damocles above his head, Proctor flusters and cannot remember the Ten Commandments.

   _____

   _____

6. When Abigail walks through the courtroom, the crowd *parts like the Red Sea.*

   _____

   _____

Name _____ Date _____

The Crucible, *Act II,* by Arthur Miller
Reading Strategy: Make and Confirm Predictions

As you read a complicated drama such as *The Crucible,* you can use your **background knowledge** to help you **make predictions** about what will happen next in the story. Your background knowledge about life in seventeenth-century New England, along with what you have already observed in the first act of the play, plus your understanding of human nature in general, can help you form predictions about future events in the story. Pay attention to the author's hints about what might be coming up. You can **confirm your predictions** as you read and at the end of the play.

DIRECTIONS: *Before and during your reading of Act II, make predictions about future events in The Crucible in the chart below. Then explain what background knowledge made you think each event might happen. If you can confirm or disprove a prediction by the end of Act II, do so in the third column. You may come back when you have finished reading the entire play to confirm or disprove your other predictions.*

Prediction	Background Knowledge	Confirm or Disprove
1.		
2.		
3.		
4.		
5.		

The Crucible, *Act II,* by Arthur Miller
Vocabulary Builder

Using the Suffix *-ology*

The most common meaning of the suffix *-ology* is "the science or study of." The suffix derives from a Greek word meaning "reason" or "word."

A. DIRECTIONS: *Use a dictionary to discover and define the root of each of the following words. Then write the meaning of the root of each, and explain how the suffix -ology combines with the meaning of the root to make the word.*

1. sociology _____

2. ontology _____

3. entomology _____

4. zoology _____

Using the Word List

    ameliorate   avidly   base   deference   pallor   theology

B. DIRECTIONS: *Choose the word or phrase most nearly similar in meaning to the Word List word. Circle the letter of your choice.*

1. pallor:
   A. ease
   B. majesty
   C. paleness
   D. sitting room

2. ameliorate:
   A. nourish
   B. improve
   C. criticize
   D. plot

3. avidly:
   A. rapidly
   B. loftily
   C. eagerly
   D. coolly

4. base:
   A. degraded
   B. faded
   C. safe
   D. planned

5. deference:
   A. distinction
   B. citation
   C. delay
   D. respect

6. theology:
   A. study of legal issues
   B. study of religious philosophy
   C. study of life forms
   D. study of ancient books

The Crucible, *Act II,* by Arthur Miller
Support for Writing: Persuasive Letter

DIRECTIONS: *You will be writing a persuasive letter in which one character from the play tries to persuade another character to take a different course of action. To help you with your prewriting, review the first two acts of* The Crucible *and choose the character and position you will represent in your persuasive letter. In the chart below, record facts, examples, and personal experiences that can be used to support the course of action you want the reader of your letter to take. Remember that you are writing from the point of view of a character in the play.*

Character and position you will represent:

Evidence to Support Your Position

Facts	Examples	Personal Experience
1.		
2.		
3.		

Name _____ Date _____

The Crucible, *Act III,* by Arthur Miller
Literary Analysis: Dramatic and Verbal Irony

In real life, things are often different from what they seem. When this occurs—both in life and in literature—it is called **irony.** Writers and playwrights make use of two forms of irony to surprise and entertain their readers and viewers.

In **dramatic irony,** the characters think one thing to be true, but the audience knows something else to be true. This creates interest and tension in a story or play. In **verbal irony,** words seem to say one thing but mean something quite different.

DIRECTIONS: *Explain the verbal or dramatic irony that exists in the following passages.*

1. Upon hearing Proctor's and Mary's statements, Danforth is shaken by the idea that Abigail and the girls could be frauds. Danforth challenges Proctor with this: "Now, Mr. Proctor, before I decide whether I shall hear you or not, it is my duty to tell you this. We burn a hot fire here; it melts down all concealment."

   _____

   _____

   _____

2. Parris, to save his own reputation, is eager to support Abigail's claims and the court's decisions. He accuses several people of making attacks upon the court. Hale's response is this: "Is every defense an attack upon the court? Can no one—?"

   _____

   _____

   _____

3. Proctor reminds Mary of a biblical story about the angel Raphael and a boy named Tobias. In the story, the boy frees a woman from the devil and cures his father of blindness.

   _____

   _____

   _____

4. Proctor is informed that Elizabeth has said she is pregnant. Proctor says he knows nothing of it but states that his wife does not lie. Later, when questioned about her husband's fidelity, Elizabeth lies, thinking she is protecting her husband and his reputation.

   _____

   _____

   _____

Name _____ Date _____

Reading Strategy: Evaluate Arguments

Evaluate arguments in the court scene in Act III by determining if the evidence used to support the accusation is believable and logical. Watch for **logical fallacies,** which are ideas or arguments that appear logical even though they are based on completely incorrect assumptions. For example, Judge Danforth explains his reasoning for believing the accusations of witchcraft. Though his thoughts seem logical, all of them are based on a mistaken premise.

DIRECTIONS: *Fill in the chart to help you evaluate the arguments of each character in the trial scene.*

Character	Argument	Logical?	Believable Evidence?
1. Judge Danforth			
2. John Proctor			
3. Reverend Parris			
4. Reverend Hale			
5. Giles Corey			

The Crucible, *Act III,* by Arthur Miller
Vocabulary Builder

Using Legal Terms

Scenes that take place in courtrooms are usually full of special words and phrases that have particular meaning for the judges, lawyers, and others present. This is true of Act III of *The Crucible.*

A. DIRECTIONS: *Find out what the following words mean. Then use each in a sentence about the action in Act III.*

1. affidavit _____

2. deposition _____

3. prosecutor _____

4. warrant _____

Using the Word List

anonymity   contentious   deposition   effrontery   imperceptible   incredulously

B. DIRECTIONS: *Choose the word or phrase that is most nearly* opposite *in meaning to the Word List word. Circle the letter of your choice.*

1. anonymity:
   A. obscurity
   B. fame
   C. solitude
   D. recklessness

2. contentious:
   A. competitive
   B. agreeable
   C. inclusive
   D. smoldering

3. deposition:
   A. shifting
   B. trial
   C. putting in place
   D. informal chat

4. effrontery:
   A. decoration
   B. rearward
   C. politeness
   D. lying

5. imperceptible:
   A. obvious
   B. untouchable
   C. understandable
   D. off track

6. incredulously:
   A. contemptuously
   B. dismissively
   C. skeptically
   D. trustfully

Name _____ Date _____

The Crucible, *Act III,* by Arthur Miller
Support for Writing: "Friend of the Court" Brief

DIRECTIONS: *You will be writing an Amicus Curiae—or "Friend of the Court"—brief, as if you are a respected member of a neighboring community who is advising the Salem court. To help you with your prewriting, fill in the chart below by stating your position and recording detailed supporting evidence and counterarguments.*

My position regarding the Salem witch trials is:

Evidence that supports my position:	1. 2. 3.
Arguments that might be made against my position:	1. 2. 3.
How I will defend my position:	1. 2. 3.

The Crucible, *Act IV,* by Arthur Miller

Literary Analysis: Tragedy and Allegory

Tragedy is a dramatic form in which the main character—the **tragic hero**—is involved in a struggle that ends in disaster. The hero is usually a well-respected person whose downfall comes as a result of fate or a **tragic flaw.** The audience or readers feel sorry for the main character, who usually learns something profound and displays honor or nobility at the end.

An **allegory** is a story with more than one layer of meaning: a literal meaning and one or more symbolic meanings. The characters, setting, and themes in an allegory are symbols of ideas and qualities that exist outside the story.

A. DIRECTIONS: *Refer to Act IV of* The Crucible *as you answer the following questions.*

1. Who is the tragic hero of *The Crucible?* How do you know?

_____

_____

2. What is this character's tragic flaw? How does it lead to his or her downfall?

_____

_____

3. What does the hero learn at the end of the play? How does this affect his or her actions?

_____

_____

B. DIRECTIONS: *On the lines below, write a paragraph explaining how* The Crucible *is an allegory. Identify both its literal meaning and its symbolic meaning. Then evaluate the effectiveness of the play as an allegory and explain your assessment.*

_____

_____

_____

_____

_____

_____

_____

_____

_____

_____

_____

Name _____ Date _____

Reading Strategy: Evaluate the Influences of the Historical Period

The philosophical, political, religious, ethical, and social influences of the historical period portrayed in *The Crucible* shape the characters, setting, actions, and message of the play. Though some elements of the story could take place any time and in any place, many aspects of the play are completely dependent on the time period for their meaning.

DIRECTIONS: *Refer to Act IV to fill in the graphic organizer. In each circle, identify and briefly evaluate the influences of the historical period in the categories specified.*

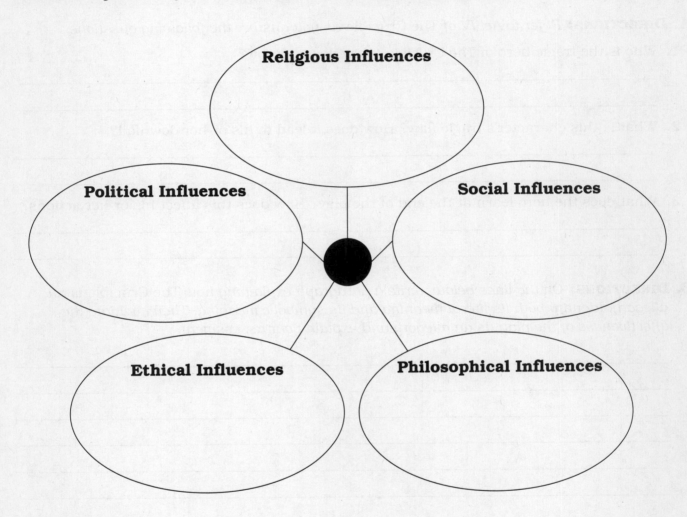

The Crucible, *Act IV,* by Arthur Miller
Vocabulary Builder

Using Words From Myths

Myths are fictional stories that account for natural phenomena or explain actions of gods. As English was developing, many writers and speakers were familiar with classical learning, including mythology. Thus, English includes names and stories from the myths of various cultures, and many words originate in these ancient tales.

A. DIRECTIONS: *Use a dictionary or other resource to explain the mythological origins of the following words.*

1. echo _____

   _____

2. volcano _____

   _____

3. Wednesday _____

   _____

4. museum _____

   _____

Using the Word List

| adamant | beguile | cleave | conciliatory | mercy |
| penitence | principle | retaliation | salvation | tantalized |

B. DIRECTIONS: *Match each word in the left column with its definition in the right column. Write the letter of the definition on the line next to the word it defines.*

___ 1. conciliatory   A. tempted

___ 2. beguile   B. belief

___ 3. cleave   C. resolute

___ 4. tantalized   D. deliverence

___ 5. retaliation   E. charm

___ 6. adamant   F. reprisal

___ 7. principle   G. compassion

___ 8. penitence   H. appeasing

___ 9. salvation   I. regret

___10. mercy   J. cling

Name _____ Date _____

The Crucible, *Act IV*, by Arthur Miller
Grammar and Style: Sentence Fragments and Run-Ons

Sentence fragments are incomplete sentences that may lack either a subject or a verb. Fragments are therefore parts of sentences incorrectly punctuated as though they were complete. A **run-on** is two or more complete sentences that are not properly joined or separated. To correct fragments and run-ons, follow these steps:

1. Decide if a problematic sentence is a fragment or a run-on.
2. If it is a fragment, add information to make a complete thought or combine the fragment with another sentence.
3. If it is a run-on, split it into two sentences. You might also add a comma or a conjunction to make it a correct single sentence.

A. PRACTICE: *On the space before each number, identify each of the following problematic sentences as a fragment or a run-on.*

_____ 1. Tried to get the prisoners to confess.

_____ 2. Proctor was not guilty he was willing to confess to save his life he wanted to be with his wife and children.

_____ 3. Although he spoke his confession willingly.

_____ 4. Rebecca Nurse bravely willing to die rather than confess to being a witch.

_____ 5. Proctor changed his mind he could not write his confession down and lose his honesty.

B. Writing Application: *On the lines below, revise each sentence in Practice A so that it is no longer a fragment or a run-on.*

1. _____
   _____

2. _____
   _____

3. _____
   _____

4. _____
   _____

5. _____
   _____

The Crucible, *Act IV*, by Arthur Miller
Support for Writing: Literary Criticism

DIRECTIONS: *You will write an essay in which you interpret* The Crucible's *main themes by exploring how the events, characters, and messages presented in the play both reflect the play's historical context then transcend that context to become universal. For your prewriting, review the play and generate a list of themes you think are important. Fill in the diagram below to record the themes and your interpretation of them.*

Theme

1.

2.

3.

↓

Historical Meaning

1.

2.

3.

↓

Universal Meaning

1.

2.

3.

The Crucible by Arthur Miller
from **Good Night and Good Luck** by George Clooney and Grant Heslov
Comparing Political Drama Past and Present

The two selections in this pairing are examples of political drama, or drama that has an openly political topic and purpose. Whereas Arthur Miller's play focuses on the Salem witch trials of the seventeenth century, its underlying message concerns the McCarthy era of the twentieth century, which is also the focus of *Good Night and Good Luck*.

Directions: *Complete the following chart by explaining how each selection reflects the features of political drama.*

Features of political drama	The Crucible	Good Night and Good Luck
Reflects the author's political opinion		
Characterizes a politician or describes a series of political events		
Questions inequities and injustices of contemporary society		
Examines a political issue from the past or present or uses past events to comment on current problems		

The Crucible by Arthur Miller
from **Good Night and Good Luck** by George Clooney and Grant Heslov
Vocabulary Builder

A. DIRECTIONS: *Revise each sentence so that the underlined vocabulary word is used logically. Be sure not to change the vocabulary word.*

Example: We greeted the insurmountable task with joy.
We greeted the insurmountable task with dread.

1. Sylvia's vulnerability to accusations of incompetence made her an excellent candidate for president. _____

_____

2. Because Justin decided to disregard the ringing of his cell phone, he was on the phone all day. _____

_____

3. Maureen acknowledges the applause of the audience by leaving the stage immediately.

_____

4. The statute explained the punishment that the criminal would suffer. _____

_____

Using the Word List

    acknowledges   disregard   statute   vulnerability

B. DIRECTIONS: *Write a complete sentence to answer each question. For each item, use a word from the Word List to replace each underlined word without changing its meaning.*

1. How might you help a friend whose exposure to food temptations has caused health problems? _____

_____

2. What might happen to someone who tended to ignore symptoms of illness? _____

_____

3. If a judge recognizes the validity of certain pieces of evidence, how should the jury respond?

_____

4. What is the law regarding dogs and leashes in your neighborhood? _____

_____

Name _____ Date _____

The Crucible by Arthur Miller
from **Good Night and Good Luck** by George Clooney and Grant Heslov
Support for Writing

Directions: *Use these charts to organize your thoughts for your compare-and-contrast essay.*

Characters from *The Crucible*	Actions That Represent Author's Political Opinion	Language That Represents Author's Political Opinion

Characters from *Good Night . . .*	Actions That Represent Authors' Political Opinion	Language That Represents Author's Political Opinion

Essential Questions Workshop—Unit 5

In their stories, poems, and nonfiction, the writers in Unit Five express ideas that relate to the three Essential Questions framing this book. Review the literature in the unit. Then, for each Essential Question, choose an author and at least one passage from his or her writing that expresses a related idea. Use this chart to complete your work.

Essential Question	Author/Selection	Literary Passage
How does literature shape or reflect society?		
What is the relationship between place and literature?		
What makes American literature American?		

Unit 6 Introduction
Names and Terms to Know

A. DIRECTIONS: *Write a brief sentence explaining each of the following names and terms. You will find all of the information you need in the Unit 6 Introduction in your textbook.*

1. Ronald Reagan: _____
   _____

2. 9/11: _____
   _____

3. Watergate: _____
   _____

4. Sally Ride: _____

5. Al Gore: _____

6. Bicentennial: _____
   _____

B. DIRECTIONS: *Use the hints below to help you answer each question.*

1. How has the Internet changed the way people communicate? [*Hints: What is the Internet? What are the various ways people communicate on the Internet? How are these different from communication by letter, telephone, or mass media?*]

   _____

   _____

   _____

2. What challenges did the new millennium present to Americans? [*Hints: What new dangers did Americans face after 2000? What new problems did the U.S. face overseas?*]

   _____

   _____

   _____

3. What problems or controversies marked American politics during this time? [*Hints: What was Watergate? What happened to President Nixon? What happened during the 2000 election?*]

   _____

   _____

   _____

Unit 6 Introduction

Essential Question 1: How does literature shape or reflect society?

A. DIRECTIONS: *Answer the questions about the first Essential Question in the Introduction, about whether literature shapes or reflects society. All the information you need is in the Unit 6 Introduction in your textbook.*

1. *Political and Social Events with the Greatest Impact*

    a. Give examples of the ways in which computers became part of daily life. _____
    _____

    b. How have historians changed their views about the cultural contributions of minority populations?_____
    _____

    c. How did the terrorist attacks on September 11, 2001, affect Americans in general?
    _____

2. *American Values and Attitudes*

    a. How do computers enhance both self-expression and anonymity? _____
    _____

    b. What has become the American toward maintaining individual cultural identities? ___
    _____

3. *Expression of Values and Attitudes in American Literature*

    a. List the various types of diversity reflected in American literature of this period.
    _____

    b. How does the new technology affect the way literature now reaches Americans?
    _____

    c. List some of the themes explored by American writers during this time.
    _____

B. DIRECTIONS: *Answer the questions that include the Essential Question Vocabulary words.*

1. Would *diversity* on a menu suggest many or few choices? Explain. _____
2. What would a *commercial* view of a product be likely to involve? _____
3. From which of the mass *media* do you get most of your news? _____

Name _____ Date _____

Unit 6 Introduction

Essential Question 2: What is the relationship between place and literature?

A. DIRECTIONS: *On the lines provided, answer the questions about the second Essential Question in the Introduction, about the relationship between place and literature. All the information you need is in the Unit 6 Introduction in your textbook.*

1. *Places Americans Write About*

   a. What are "ordinary places," and what contemporary American writers write about these ordinary places? _____

   _____

   b. Give examples of ways in which Americans are writing about "ordinary places transformed." _____

   _____

2. *Global Awareness*

   a. What environmental problems are explored in contemporary American writings?

   _____

   b. Give examples of contemporary writers whose nonfiction, fiction, and poetry develops environmental themes. _____

   _____

3. *Impact of Electronic Technology*

   a. How has electronic technology changed the way characters, authors, and readers communicate with one another? _____

   _____

   b. Contemporary literature includes many references to such areas of popular culture as

   _____

   c. What is cyberliterature? _____

   _____

B. DIRECTIONS: *Answer the following questions based on Essential Question Vocabulary words.*

1. Would a story set in *cyberspace* be old-fashioned or futuristic? Explain. _____

   _____

2. Would local property taxes be a *global concern?* _____

   _____

3. If you were to *transform* your house, what would be the first thing you'd do? _____

   _____

Unit 6 Introduction

Essential Question 3: What makes American literature American?

A. DIRECTIONS: *On the lines provided, answer the questions about the third Essential Question in the Introduction, about what makes American literature American. All the information you need is in the Unit 6 Introduction in your textbook.*

1. *Qualities in Contemporary American Literature*

   a. Why would you expect American literature to display cultural diversity? _____
   _____

   b. How has the definition of "literature" expanded in recent decades?
   _____

2. *Postmodern American Literature*

   a. What does it mean to say a literary work is "self-conscious"?
   _____

   b. Why is contemporary literature "released" from the need to mean something?
   _____

   c. What attitude toward the past does much contemporary literature display?
   _____

3. *Growth of Suburbia and American Literature*

   a. Give examples of American prose writers whose works look toward the future.
   _____

   b. List some twenty-first century American poets.
   _____

B. DIRECTIONS: *Answer the questions based on the Essential Question Vocabulary words.*

1. What might a poet who wants to experiment with a different *genre* write? _____
2. Name one *innovation* in contemporary automobiles. _____
3. Is someone who is *self-conscious* likely to be relaxed or nervous? Explain. _____
   _____

Name _____ Date _____

Following-Through Activities

A. CHECK YOUR COMPREHENSION: *Use this chart to complete the Check Your Comprehension activity in the Unit 6 Introduction. In the middle box, fill in a key concept in contemporary American literature. In the right box, fill in a key author. The concept-author pairing for American Literature has been done for you.*

Common Theme	New / Changed Form	Element of Style
Place and Imagination		
American Literature	Cultural Identity	Amy Tan
Literature and Society		

B. EXTEND YOUR LEARNING: *Use this graphic organizer to help you compare directions to a real-world location and a location on the Internet.*

Real-World Location:
_____
_____
_____
_____
_____
_____
_____
_____

Internet Location
_____
_____
_____
_____
_____
_____
_____
_____

Travel Directions:
_____
_____
_____
_____
_____
_____

Travel Directions:
_____
_____
_____
_____
_____
_____

Name _____ Date _____

Julia Alvarez Introduces "Antojos"

DIRECTIONS: *Use the lines provided to answer these questions based on Alvarez's introduction to the story "Antojos."*

1. According to Alvarez's first paragraph, what did "Antojos" eventually become?

    _____

    _____

2. What explanation does Alvarez give for writing a short story first, not a novel?

    _____

    _____

3. How did studying Emily Dickinson apparently affect Alvarez's writing?

    _____

    _____

4. How did reading about Thomas Wolfe help inspire Alvarez to write "Antojos"?

    _____

    _____

5. On what real-life person is the main character of "Antojos" based, and on what experience of that person?

    _____

    _____

6. What main point about going home does Alvarez suggest "Antojos" expresses?

    _____

    _____

7. According to Alvarez, how does "Antojos" differ from an essay?

    _____

    _____

8. Why did Alvarez include the Palmolive poster in "Antojos"? As what does the poster come to be seen?

    _____

    _____

Julia Alvarez
Listening and Viewing

Segment 1: Meet Julia Alvarez

- Where did Alvarez spend her childhood, and what was her family there like?

- After coming to America, what good and bad treatment did she encounter in school?

_____

_____

_____

_____

Segment 2: Julia Alvarez on the Short Story

- According to Alvarez, where should the action in a short story start?

- Citing Chekhov, where does Alvarez think a short story should end?

_____

_____

_____

_____

Segment 3: Julia Alvarez on the Writing Process

- What does Alvarez mean by "the habit of writing"?

- What does she say about trying to write a story or novel from beginning to end?

_____

_____

_____

_____

Segment 4: Julia Alvarez on the Rewards of Writing

- For Alvarez, what role do rewards from the larger world play in writing?

- According to Alvarez, how does writing help her in life?

_____

_____

_____

_____

"Antojos" by Julia Alvarez
Literary Analysis: Plot Structure

Plot structure is the sequence of events in a literary work. A plot usually begins by introducing the setting, the characters, and the basic situation. However, authors sometimes begin *in medias res*, in the middle of an action. For example:

For the first time since Yolanda had reached the hills, there was a shoulder on the left side of the narrow road.

Writers use *in medias res* to grab readers' attention by cutting to the climax or to an interesting part of the story. They then go back to the beginning to fill in the details. To accomplish this, writers make use of flashbacks, which highlight a scene or event from an earlier time, thus providing valuable information about the characters' backgrounds, personalities, and motives. Writers also add interest through foreshadowing, the use of clues to suggest events that have yet to occur.

Use the chart below to provide examples from "Antojos" of each of these techniques: *in medias res*, flashback, and foreshadowing. In each case, explain the use of the technique and what it adds to the development of the plot.

Example of Technique	Explanation of Technique	What It Adds to the Story
In medias res:		
Flashback:		
Foreshadowing:		

"**Antojos**" by Julia Alvarez
Reading Strategy: Make Predictions

As you read a selection, you often wonder how a story will end. One strategy for understanding the way a story unfolds is to pause and make predictions about what will happen. Often a story contains hints that foreshadow things to come.

DIRECTIONS: *On the lines following each excerpt from "Antojos," record what predictions you might make about the rest of the story.*

1. She [Yolanda] would have to wait until she got to the coast to hear news of the hunger march in the capital.

   _____

   _____

2. It crossed her mind that her family had finally agreed to loan her a car because they knew she'd be far safer on the north coast than in the capital city where revolutions always broke out.

   _____

   _____

3. She hadn't seen her favorite *antojo*, guavas, since her last trip seven years ago.

   _____

   _____

4. —She was going up north? By herself? A woman alone on the road! "This is not the States." Her old aunts had tried to dissuade her. "Anything can happen."

   _____

   _____

5. "You must excuse him, Doña," she apologized. "He's not used to being among people." But Yolanda knew the old woman meant, not the people in the village, but the people with money who drove through Altamira to the beaches on the coast.

   _____

   _____

6. Branches scraped the sides and pebbles pelted the underside of the car. Yolanda wanted to turn back, but there was no room to maneuver the car around.

   _____

   _____

"Antojos" by Julia Alvarez
Vocabulary Builder

Word Orgins: Borrowed Words

A *machete* is a large, heavy knife used to cut down vegetation. The word is taken directly from Spanish, in which it has the same meaning. Many other words in English come from Spanish.

A. DIRECTIONS: *The following words are derived from Spanish. Consult a dictionary, and then write down their different meanings. Tell which words are taken directly from Spanish, like machete, and which have been changed slightly.*

1. hammock _____

2. plaza _____

3. patio _____

4. cocoa _____

Using the Word List

appease   collusion   dissuade   docile   maneuver   machetes

B. DIRECTIONS: *For each Word List word, choose the word or phrase that is most similar in meaning. Circle the letter of your choice.*

1. dissuade
   A. persuade   B. destroy   C. discourage   D. encourage

2. appease
   A. apply   B. control   C. provoke   D. satisfy

3. machetes
   A. artillery   B. shovels   C. knives   D. machines

4. collusion
   A. argument   B. conspiracy   C. disruption   D. interpretation

5. docile
   A. harmful   B. angry   C. obedient   D. foolish

6. maneuver
   A. move   B. neglect   C. reflect   D. take

"Antojos" by Julia Alvarez
Support for Writing

As you work on a new version of the story "Antojos," choose one of the men who help Yolanda when her tire goes flat. Tell the story through his eyes from a first-person point of view. Reread the story and enter information into the chart below.

"A Flat Tire," by _____

What we were doing that day	
What we thought when we first saw Yolanda	
Yolanda's behavior toward us/how we felt	
How we felt when Yolanda offered to pay us	

On a separate page, draft your new version of the event. Use your new information from the chart, along with information from the story. Provide dialogue and background for your character and other characters who may be in your new version. When you revise, check to be sure you have kept the viewpoint of the new character.

"**Everyday Use**" by Alice Walker
Literary Analysis: Characterization

Characterization is the revelation of characters' personalities. In "Everyday Use," the author uses language to show different sides of characters' personalities. For example, the story's narrator uses Standard English to reveal her internal thoughts:

Maggie attempts to make a dash for the house, in her shuffling way, but I stay her with my hand.

The narrator uses dialect, however, in her outward expressions:

"I reckon she would," I said. "I promised to give them quilts to Maggie, for when she marries John Thomas."

This duality of language causes readers and Dee to have very different perceptions of the narrator. Use the chart below to provide two examples of each kind of expression used by the narrator—Standard English and dialect. For each example, explain what the use of language reveals about the narrator's character.

Standard English, Example 1:	What it reveals about narrator's character:
Standard English, Example 2:	What it reveals about narrator's character:
Dialect, Example 1:	What it reveals about narrator's character:
Dialect, Example 2:	What it reveals about narrator's character:

"Everyday Use" by Alice Walker
Reading Strategy: Contrast Characters

Good writers use specific details to depict characters. In depicting characters who are very different, writers use contrasting details. For example, recall the ways in which the three female characters in "Everyday Use" are dressed:

The narrator: I wear flannel nightgowns to bed and overalls during the day.

Maggie: her thin body enveloped in pink skirt and red blouse

Dee: A dress down to the ground, in this hot weather. A dress so loud it hurt my eyes. There are yellows and oranges enough to throw back the light of the sun. . . . Earrings gold, too, and hanging down to her shoulders.

Nowhere does Alice Walker come out and write, "The narrator was practical; Maggie was plain, simple, and solid; Dee, on the other hand, was flashy and bold." Instead of making such "telling" remarks, Walker shows us how the characters are different by using specific and concrete details and letting us draw our own conclusions.

Below are several specific details, some drawn from "Everyday Use." After each, describe a contrasting detail. (It, too, may be from "Everyday Use.") An example is given.

Example: The mother opened her arms and ran across the room to embrace her daughter.

Answer: Her arms folded across her chest, the mother stared at her daughter from across the room.

1. He smiles broadly; his teeth shiny white as pearls.

   _____

   _____

2. She cooked the freshly killed pork over an open fire.

   _____

   _____

3. She hung back in the kitchen, her scarred hands hidden in the folds of her tattered skirt.

   _____

   _____

4. She rifled through the trunk to find the precious quilts.

   _____

   _____

5. She talked a blue streak over the sweet potatoes and the rest of the meal.

   _____

   _____

"Everyday Use" by Alice Walker
Vocabulary Builder

Using the Roots -doc-/-doct-

The roots -doc- and -doct- mean "teach." The Word List word *doctrines*, which means "ideas, beliefs, or rules that are taught," is formed from the root -doct-.

A. DIRECTIONS: *Complete each of the following sentences by choosing the best word for each sentence. Use context clues and what you know about the meaning of -doc-/-doct- to make your selection.*

docent   doctorate   doctrinaire   documented

1. She received her _____ in veterinary science from the state university.
2. Wanting a record of their family reunion, the Hernandez family _____ the event on videotape.
3. The _____ who teaches our honors class is not a regular faculty member.
4. The tutor's inflexible and _____ methods did not inspire his students.

Using the Word List

furtive   cowering   homely   doctrines

B. DIRECTIONS: *Choose the word or phrase that is most nearly* opposite *in meaning to each numbered Word List word. Circle the letter of your choice.*

1. furtive
   A. shifty
   B. hidden
   C. honest
   D. annoying
2. cowering
   A. retreating
   B. swaggering
   C. thriving
   D. despising
3. homely
   A. ordinary
   B. unusual
   C. attractive
   D. free
4. doctrines
   A. beliefs
   B. doubts
   C. creeds
   D. theories

"Everyday Use" by Alice Walker

Grammar and Style: Transitional Expressions

Writers often use **transitional expressions**—transitions and transitional phrases—to show the relationships between ideas. A transition is a single word, and a transitional phrase is a group of words. Transitions and transitional phrases show time relationships, comparisons, degrees of importance, and spatial relationships. Read the following examples from "Everyday Use":

Maggie will be nervous *until after* her sister goes. . . . (shows a time relationship)

This house is in pasture, too, *like* the other one. (shows a comparison)

A. PRACTICE: For each sentence, underline the transition or transitional phrase. Then tell whether it shows a time relationship, a comparison, or a spatial relationship.

1. One winter I knocked a bull calf straight in the brain between the eyes with a sledge hammer. . . .

   _____

2. But that was before we raised the money, the church and me, to send her to Augusta to school.

   _____

3. The dress is loose and flows, and as she walks closer, I like it.

   _____

4. "You must belong to those beef-cattle people down the road," I said.

   _____

5. You didn't even have to look close to see where hands pushing the dasher up and down to make butter had left a kind of sink in the wood.

   _____

6. "Some of the pieces, like those lavender ones, come from old clothes her mother handed down to her," I said. . . .

   _____

B. WRITING APPLICATION: *Write a paragraph based on the characters and/or situations portrayed in "Everyday Use." Use transitions and transitional phrases to show the relationships between ideas.*

   _____

   _____

   _____

   _____

   _____

   _____

   _____

   _____

Name _____ Date _____

Support For Writing

To write a critical review of "Everyday Use," begin by rereading the story and noting your reactions. Enter your responses in the chart below.

Review of "Everyday Use"

Story Plot	My Opinion	Examples from Story
_____	_____	_____
_____	_____	_____
Story Characters	**My Opinion**	**Examples from Story**
_____	_____	_____
_____	_____	_____
Story Message	**My Opinion**	**Examples from Story**
_____	_____	_____
_____	_____	_____

Summary of My Opinion:

_____

_____

_____

_____

On a separate page, begin your draft by making a general statement about your opinion of the story. Then, write individual paragraphs to address each of the items in your chart. When you revise your work, replace weak modifiers with strong and precise adjectives.

Name _____ Date _____

"Everything Stuck to Him" by Raymond Carver
Literary Analysis: Author's Style

Every work of fiction reflects its **author's style**—the author's choice and arrangement of words and details and how these elements work together to establish mood and meaning. Some authors use detailed descriptions in their narratives, whereas others avoid elaborate descriptions in favor of simple dialogue or a spare recounting of events. Raymond Carver usually favors an economical, pared-down approach that features an economy of words and a minimum of description. Critics have often labeled Carver's style as minimalist, a term used to describe work that has been reduced to its bare essentials.

DIRECTIONS: *The left column of the chart below lists several notable features of Carver's minimalist approach in "Everything Stuck to Him." In the right column, briefly explain how that feature adds to the overall impact of the story*

Minimalist Feature	How It Adds to Impact of the Story
No quotation marks in dialogue	
No names given to the father and daughter	
The husband and wife are called "boy and girl"	
No descriptions of physical features of characters	
Simple, direct language	

"Everything Stuck to Him" by Raymond Carver
Reading Strategy: Ask Questions

When you read news articles, poems, or short stories, you may sometimes need to **ask questions** about what is happening, why things happen, or why the writer expresses something in a particular way. Do you pay attention, or do you just read on? If you do pay attention to the questions in your mind, you may gain fuller understanding of what you are reading. For example, readers may find themselves asking questions about the time shifts in "Everything Stuck to Him."

DIRECTIONS: *As you read "Everything Stuck to Him," ask yourself these questions. It is possible that you might not be able to answer the questions right way. You might have to piece together information or clues to come up with the answers after you finish the story.*

1. What is the relationship of the two characters who are speaking to each other as the story opens? How can you tell?

_____

_____

_____

2. Who narrates the "outer" story that opens and closes "Everything Stuck to Him"? Who narrates the "inner story" that comes in between?

_____

_____

3. At one point "boy" expresses some romantic interest in "girl's" two sisters. What does this admission say about the possible future of the marriage between "boy" and "girl"?

_____

_____

4. What has happened to the marriage of "boy" and "girl" by the time the scene shifts back to the "outer" story toward the end of "Everything Stuck to Him"? How can you tell?

_____

_____

5. What do you think is the meaning of the title "Everything Stuck to Him"?

_____

_____

"Everything Stuck to Him" by Raymond Carver
Vocabulary Builder

Word List

ambitions   coincide   fitfully   striking

A. DIRECTIONS: *Think about the meaning of the underlined Word List word in each sentence. Then, answer the question.*

1. His birthday often seemed to <u>coincide</u> with one of his final exams. Was the boy often free of exam pressures on his birthday? How do you know?

_____

_____

2. Juanita is known for her <u>ambitions</u>. Does Juanita lack goals that she wants to achieve? How do you know?

_____

_____

3. The hotel was known for the <u>striking</u> decor of its lobby? Would people be likely to notice the decor of the hotel lobby? How do you know?

_____

_____

4. If someone said that he had slept <u>fitfully</u>, would he have slept soundly through the night? How do you know?

_____

_____

B. DIRECTIONS: *On each line, write the letter of the word or phrase that is closest in meaning to the Word List word.*

___ 1. coincide
   A. delight
   B. predict
   C. declare
   D. overlap

___ 2. ambitions
   A. encounters
   B. aspirations
   C. triumphs
   D. schemes

___ 3. striking
   A. tiring
   B. pressuring
   C. noticeable
   D. fulfilling

___ 4. fitfully
   A. faithfully
   B. sporadically
   C. diligently
   D. carelessly

Name _____ Date _____

"Everything Stuck to Him" by Raymond Carver
Support for Writing

When you finished reading "Everything Stuck to Him," did you find the ending happy or unhappy or somewhere in between? Try to sketch arguments for all sides of this issue before settling on the viewpoint you will take in your essay on this subject. Answer the questions below to help you organize your thoughts before you write your essay. Think about plot elements, key bits of dialogue, and the main characters' reactions to events, memories, and each other.

1. What arguments can be made for viewing the ending as happy?

   _____

   _____

   _____

   _____

2. What arguments can be made for viewing the ending as unhappy?

   _____

   _____

   _____

   _____

3. What arguments can be made for viewing the ending as neither happy nor unhappy, but somewhere in between?

   _____

   _____

   _____

   _____

After you decide which of these three views of the ending is the most convincing to you, write a rough draft of an essay in which you defend your opinion. Support your opinion with clear logic and details from the story.

Name _____ Date _____

Literary Analysis: Epiphany

Characters in literature or speakers in poems sometimes have a sudden flash of insight, which is called an **epiphany**. At the moment of the epiphany, the character may realize something significant about himself or herself, about another character, or about life in general.

DIRECTIONS: *On the lines below each of the following quotations, explain why that moment in the specified poem does or does not represent a true epiphany for the speaker.*

"Traveling Through the Dark"

1. Traveling through the dark I found a deer / dead on the edge of the Wilson River road.

   _____

   _____

   _____

2. I thought hard for us all—my only swerving— / then pushed her over the edge into the river.

   _____

   _____

   _____

"The Secret"

3. Two girls discover / the secret of life / in a sudden line of / poetry.

   _____

   _____

   _____

4. "I love them . . . / for wanting to know it, / for / assuming there is / such a secret, yes, / for that / most of all.

   _____

   _____

   _____

"The Gift"

5. To pull the metal splinter from my palm / my father recited a story in a low voice.

   _____

   _____

   _____

6. And I did not lift up my wound and cry, / Death visited here! / I did what a child does / when he's given something to keep. / I kissed my father.

   _____

   _____

   _____

"Traveling Through the Dark" by William Stafford
"The Secret" by Denise Levertov **"The Gift"** by Li-Young Lee
Reading Strategy: Interpret Poetry

To deepen your understanding of a poem, you must *interpret*, or search to find meaning in its words, images and other elements, You can interpret by looking closely at a particular element, such as the poem's title, the identity of its speaker, or a particular image and then deciding how the element relates to the poem's central message. You can also use your understanding of a poet's overall meaning or social context to interpret its individual elements.

DIRECTIONS: *Practice your interpretation skills by answering the following questions, which are based on the poems you have read.*

1. Who is the speaker in Denise Levertov's poem "The Secret"? Use your knowledge of the speaker to interpret the following lines from the poem:

   I love them / for finding what / I can't find, and for loving me / for the line I wrote, / and for forgetting it / so that / a thousand times, till death / finds them, they may / discover it again, in other / lines / in other / happenings.

   _____

   _____

   _____

   _____

2. How does the title of the poem "Traveling Through the Dark" relate to its central message? How does the title help you understand the poem as you begin reading?

   _____

   _____

   _____

   _____

3. In the poem "The Gift," significant images are presented in the following lines:

   Had you entered that afternoon / you would have thought you saw a man / planting something in a boy's palm, / a silver tear, a tiny flame.

   How do you interpret the images "silver tear" and "tiny flame," and how do they relate to the overall meaning of the poem?

   _____

   _____

   _____

   _____

"Traveling Through the Dark" by William Stafford
"The Secret" by Denise Levertov **"The Gift"** by Li-Young Lee
Building Vocabulary

Using Related Words: *exhaust*

A. DIRECTIONS: *Complete each sentence with one of the following words related to the word* exhaust: exhausted, exhaustively, exhaustible.

1. Our current use of fossil fuels is depleting _____ energy sources.

2. At the end of their twelve-hour shifts, the relief workers were _____.

3. The environmental group _____ researched all sides of the issue.

Using the Word List

    exhaust   shard   swerve

B. DIRECTIONS: *For each pair of numbered words, choose the lettered pair of words that best expresses a similar relationship. Circle the letter of your choice.*

___ 1. SWERVE : OBSTACLE ::
    A. price : payment
    B. climb : mountain
    C. avoid : danger
    D. solution : problem

___ 2. VASE : SHARD ::
    A. part : whole
    B. object : fragment
    C. craft : skill
    D. beauty : utility

___ 3. EXHAUST : POLLUTION ::
    A. ocean : salty
    B. disaster : fatality
    C. airplane : propeller
    D. grass : vegetation

Name _____ Date _____

"Traveling Through the Dark" by William Stafford
"The Secret" by Denise Levertov **"The Gift"** by Li-Young Lee
Support for Writing

Prepare to write a comparison-and-contrast essay about the relationship between the title of two of these poems and the two poems' relationship to each other. As an aid in your preparation, use the chart below to make preliminary notes on the meaning of each poem's title and how that meaning compares or contrasts to the meaning of the other poems.

Poem Title	How Title Relates to Meaning of Poem	How Meaning of Poem Relates to Meaning of Other Poems
"Traveling Through the Dark"		
"The Secret"		
"The Gift"		

"Who Burns for the Perfection of Paper" by Martin Espada
"Camouflaging the Chimera" by Yusef Komunyakaa
"Streets" by Naomi Shihab Nye
Literary Analysis: Voice

A poem's unique **voice** comes from its style, its tone, and the individual personality of its speaker. Reading closely, you will find that every poem has a particular voice. Think about the different voices of the poems you have read. In what way does each poet express a unique style, tone, and personality?

DIRECTIONS: *As you read the three poems, make notes describing the style, tone, and personality of each speaker. Include details from the poems that emphasize or help create the speaker's voice.*

Poem	Voice
"Who Burns for the Perfection of Paper"	
"Camouflaging the Chimera"	
"Streets"	

Name _____ Date _____

"Who Burns for the Perfection of Paper" by Martin Espada
"Camouflaging the Chimera" by Yusef Komunyakaa
"Streets" by Naomi Shihab Nye

Reading Strategy: Analyze Author's Implicit Beliefs

Poems are almost always subjective—that is, they are based on the poet's own experiences, opinions, and beliefs. Sometimes, a poet will offer his or her beliefs in the hopes that the reader will adopt them and act on them, too. However, these beliefs may not be directly stated. Instead, they may be implied through poem details. Use a graphic organizer like this one to analyze each **author's implicit beliefs**.

Poem	Author's Implicit Beliefs	Details That Reveal Beliefs
"Who Burns for the Perfection of Paper"		
"Camouflaging the Chimera"		
"Streets"		

"Who Burns for the Perfection of Paper" by Martin Espada
"Camouflaging the Chimera" by Yusef Komunyakaa
"Streets" by Naomi Shihab Nye
Vocabulary Builder

Word List

terrain   refuge   crevices

A. DIRECTIONS: *Read the incomplete paragraph below. On each line, write one of the words from the Word List. You will use each word more than once. Think about the meaning of the word in the context of the paragraph.*

As the soldiers marched toward their next objective, a nearby village, they found themselves on unfamiliar (1) _____. They had to make their way through thick underbrush, but at least the ground seemed solid, so there was no danger of slipping into unseen (2) _____. If necessary, the soldiers could take (3) _____ in the thick surrounding vegetation if they found themselves under attack. Soon they found themselves approaching a farm, and the open (4) _____ promised to make for an easier advance. But there was no cover in those open fields that would provide ready or easy (5) _____ if they were spotted by the enemy, not even small (6) _____ in which they could hide temporarily.

B. DIRECTIONS: *Think about the meaning of the italicized Word List word in each item below. Then answer the question, and explain your answer.*

1. A geologist analyzes various types of <u>terrain</u>. Does he spend most of his working hours on land or in the air?

   _____

2. A villager being chased by a tiger found <u>refuge</u> in a small cabin. Was the villager safer than he was before?

   _____

3. The hiking guide alerted us to be on the lookout for <u>crevices</u>. Was the guide warning us of a potential danger?

   _____

C. DIRECTIONS: *On each line, write the letter of the word that is most nearly opposite in meaning to the Word List word.*

___ 1. terrain
    A. organism
    B. fatigue
    C. sky
    D. surroundings

___ 2. refuge
    A. exposure
    B. relief
    C. denial
    D. pretense

___ 3. crevices
    A. fires
    B. particles
    C. bumps
    D. appearances

"Who Burns for the Perfection of Paper" by Martin Espada
"Camouflaging the Chimera" by Yusef Komunyakaa
"Streets" by Naomi Shihab Nye
Support for Writing

Each of these poems expresses a belief about some fundamental aspect of life. Prepare to write an analytical essay on how each poem's theme, or central meaning, comments on the life of all humans. As part of your preparation, use the following chart as an aid in organizing your thoughts.

Key Question	"Who Burns for the Perfection of Paper"	"Camouflaging the Chimera"	"Streets"
What would you say each poem is "about"?			
What personal insight or experience is described in each poem?			
How does this experience relate to all people?			
What wish for humanity does each poem express?			

After reflecting on your answers to these questions, write a rough draft of your essay on a separate sheet of paper. Your draft should include a clear statement of your thesis, supporting details from the poems, and a conclusion.

"Halley's Comet" by Stanley Kunitz
Literary Analysis: Free Verse

Free verse is poetry without regular meter or rhyme. Nevertheless, free verse does contain many formal elements. The poet recreates the cadences of natural speech—or cadences that reflect meaning—by using line lengths crafted in one of the following ways.

- **End-stopped lines** are lines that end just where a speaker would pause:

    So mother scolded me
    and sent me early to my room.

    Such lines are used to create a conversational mood or to mimic a storytelling voice.

- **Enjambed** lines are lines that do not end with a grammatical break and that do not make full sense without the line that follows:

    At supper I felt sad to think
    that it was probably
    the last meal I'd share
    with my mother and sisters. . . .

Enjambed lines help the poet emphasize important words and hint at double meanings. In the lines above, for example, the poet emphasizes the key words and phrases *think, share*, and *mothers and sisters*, which call attention to what and whom he is thinking about.

Use the chart below to identify two examples of end-stopped lines and two examples of enjambed lines. In each case, briefly discuss the poet's purpose in using these devices.

End-stopped line 1:	Poet's Purpose:
End-stopped line 2:	Poet's Purpose:
Enjambed line 1:	Poet's Purpose:
Enjambed line 2:	Poet's Purpose:

Name _____ Date _____

Reading Strategy: Identify Changes in Tense and Tone

When writing in free verse, poets do not have the benefit of strong rhythm and rhyme to draw the reader's attention to important details. Instead, they must use more subtle techniques. As you read Halley's Comet, try to **identify changes in verb tenses and tone.** Then ask yourself whether these changes signal a shift in meaning, a shift in perspective, or both. Use a chart like the one shown to record your ideas.

Type of Change	
Where It Occurs	
Possible Meaning	
Type of Change	
Where It Occurs	
Possible Meaning	

Name _____ Date _____

"Halley's Comet" by Stanley Kunitz
Vocabulary Builder

Using the Prefix *pro-*

A. DIRECTIONS: *The Latin prefix* pro- *means "before" or "forward." The word* proclaim *literally means "to claim or announce before a group." Use the words below to answer the questions. Each one combines the prefix* pro- *with another Latin word part.*

produce   progress   projectile   propel

1. Which word means "make" or "bring forth" and comes from the Latin *ducere*, "to bring"?
   _____

2. Which word describes something thrown and comes from the Latin *jacere*, "to throw"?
   _____

3. Which word means "to advance" and comes from the Latin *gradi*, "to walk"?
   _____

4. Which word means "to drive forward" and comes from the Latin *pellere*, "to push"?
   _____

Word List

proclaiming   repent   steal

B. DIRECTIONS: *Circle the letter of the word or phrase that is closest in meaning to the Word List word.*

1. proclaiming
   A. whispering
   B. declaring
   C. lying
   D. questioning

2. repent
   A. confirm
   B. deny
   C. feel sorry
   D. think about

3. steal
   A. sneak
   B. tumble
   C. race
   D. soar

Name _____ Date _____

"Halley's Comet" by Stanley Kunitz
Support for Writing

The poem "Halley's Comet" evokes the confusions and distortions that a young boy's mind can bring to an event such as the arrival of Halley's Comet. As part of your preparation for writing a reflective essay about something you misunderstood or misinterpreted when you were a child, use the following chart to sketch out preliminary ideas and notes. Fill in each category of the chart as completely as you can.

Which childhood memory do I wish to write about? What did I misunderstand about it?	
Should I recount events in the past tense or the present tense? Why?	
What key words and images will help me to create a certain mood?	
Which details are most strongly related to my chosen memory?	

Using the notes you made in the chart, write a first draft of your essay on a separate page.

Name _____ Date _____

"The Latin Deli: An Ars Poetica" by Judith Ortiz Cofer
Literary Analysis: Imagery

Poets use **imagery** to give body to their ideas. Imagery is language that uses **images**—words or phrases that appeal to one or more of the five senses of sight, smell, touch, sound, or taste. Images can draw readers into a literary work by creating the sensations of actual experience—for example: "the heady mix of smells from the open bins / of dried codfish, the green plantains / hanging in stalks like votive offerings . . ." As they accumulate over the course of a poem, the images combine to express a central idea or feeling.

DIRECTIONS: *Use the chart below to give four examples of images from "The Latin Deli: An Ars Poetica." In the middle column, state the sense or senses to which the image appeals. Then, in the right column, briefly state how the image contributes to the meaning of the poem.*

Image	Sense to Which the Image Appeals	How the Image Contributes to the Meaning of the Poem

Name _____ Date _____

"The Latin Deli: An Ars Poetica" by Judith Ortiz Cofer
Reading: Analyze Sensory Details

Some poems present one main idea. Others present a large collection of concrete details from which you must infer the meaning. To read and understand this kind of poem, follow two steps:

- First, clearly picture in your mind each separate detail.

- Second, ask yourself what the details have in common and what overall feeling or idea they are trying to express.

Use a graphic organizer like this one to **analyze sensory details** as you read "The Latin Deli: An Ars Poetica." Choose four such details, tell what they have in common, and then state what overall feeling or idea they are trying to express.

Sensory Detail 1:	Sensory Detail 2:	Sensory Detail 3:	Sensory Detail 4:

What details have in common:

Overall feeling or idea expressed by details:

"The Latin Deli: An Ars Poetica" by Judith Ortiz Cofer
Vocabulary Builder

Word List

ample   disillusions   divine   heady

A. DIRECTIONS: *Write whether each statement is true of false. Then, explain your answer using the meaning of the word in italics.*

1. A *heady* mix of smells from open bins would be barely noticeable.

   _____

2. If you discovered that you had *ample* supplies in the refrigerator for the next week, you would need to make an urgent trip to the supermarket.

   _____

3. Experiencing a number of *disillusions* would leave you with fewer false notions about life.

   _____

4. If you had studied thoroughly for a test and had mastered all the material, there would be no need for you to *divine* the answers.

   _____

B. DIRECTIONS: *Circle the letter of the word that is closest in meaning to the word in CAPITAL LETTERS.*

1. HEADY
   A. egotistical
   B. smart
   C. cautious
   D. intoxicating

2. AMPLE
   A. sufficient
   B. excessive
   C. random
   D. luxurious

3. DISILLUSIONS
   A. disappointments
   B. realities
   C. difficulties
   D. memories

4. DIVINE
   A. pray
   B. restore
   C. guess
   D. accept

Name _____ Date _____

"The Latin Deli: An Ars Poetica" by Judith Ortiz Cofer
Support for Writing

A person in exile is someone who has been forced by circumstances to leave his or her homeland. Write an essay in which you explore the ideas of exile and home in this poem. As part of your preparation, answer the questions that appear below:

1. Who is exiled in this poem? From where? Why?

_____

_____

_____

_____

2. Which does the deli represent—exile, home, or both?

_____

_____

_____

_____

3. Why is the deli owner referred to as "the Patroness of Exiles"? What does she represent to the customers of the deli?

_____

_____

_____

_____

4. What larger, more universal kind of "exile" might be symbolized by the places and events of the poem?

_____

_____

_____

_____

After reflecting on your answer to these questions, write a rough draft of your essay. Be sure to include a clear thesis statement, details from the poem to support your assertions, and a conclusion.

"Onomatopoeia" by William Safire
Literary Analysis: Expository Essay

In an **expository essay,** the writer provides information about a topic, discusses ideas, or explains a process. In "Onomatopoeia," Safire explains the origin, meaning, pronunciation and uses of onomatopoeia.

Like other forms of nonfiction, expository essays can vary widely in tone, according to the nature of the subject and the author's purpose. Safire chooses to take a light, humorous approach to his subject, especially in his frequent use of idioms, expressions that have acquired meanings different from their literal meaning. For example, if you say that someone "has an axe to grind," that is an informal way of saying that he or she has a grievance or resentment. Or if you say that someone "gets your goat," it means that someone is able to annoy you easily.

A. DIRECTIONS: *Use the chart below to list four examples of idioms that Safire uses to establish an informal tone for his expository essay. In each case, provide a standard English definition of the idiomatic word or phrase you have identified.*

Safire's Idiom	Standard English Meaning

B. DIRECTIONS: *On the lines below or on a separate sheet of paper, write a brief explanation of some simple topic (for example, how to send an e-mail, how to record a DVD, how to hard-boil an egg, etc.). In your explanation, use at least two idioms to establish an informal, humorous tone.*

_____

_____

_____

_____

Name _____ Date _____

"Onomatopoeia" by William Safire
Reading Strategy: Paraphrase

To help you determine the main ideas in an essay, take time to **paraphrase,** or restate in your own words, any passages that require clarification. By helping you clarify meaning, paraphrasing allows you to identify and understand the author's main points.

A. DIRECTIONS: *Use the chart below to paraphrase passages from Safire's essay "Onomatopoeia."*

Original Passage	My Paraphrase
1. "He pointed out that one speculation about the origin of language was the *bow-wow theory,* holding that words originated in imitation of natural sounds of animals and thunder."	
2. "Thus we can see another way that the human mind creates new words: imitating what can be heard only in the mind's ear."	
3. "The coinage filled a need for an unheard sound and—*pow!*—slammed the vocabulary right in the kisser."	

B. Directions: *On the lines below, briefly paraphrase the main points of "Onomatopoeia" in no more than four sentences.*

_____

_____

_____

_____

Name _____ Date _____

"**Onomatopoeia**" by William Safire
Vocabulary Builder

Word List

coinage   derive   speculation   synonymous

A. DIRECTIONS: *Think about the meaning of the underlined Word List word in each sentence. Then, answer the question.*

1. The teacher asked us to think of a word that is <u>synonymous</u> with the word *stubborn*. Does that mean she was asking for a word that means the opposite of *stubborn*? How do you know?

   _____

   _____

2. Safire writes that you can <u>derive</u> the meaning of the word *onomatopoeia* from a Greek word meaning "word making." Does that mean that Safire is discussing the origin of *onomatopoeia*? How do you know?

   _____

   _____

3. Safire writes that the bow-wow theory of language is <u>speculation</u>. Does that mean that the theory is well grounded in facts? How do you know?

   _____

   _____

4. Safire speaks of the <u>coinage</u> of the word *zap*. Is he talking about the way the word came into being? How do you know?

   _____

   _____

B. DIRECTIONS: *On each line, write the letter of the word or phrase that is* closest *in meaning to the Word List word.*

1. synonymous
   A. original
   B. imaginary
   C. linguistic
   D. similar

2. derive
   A. trace
   B. steer
   C. theorize
   D. question

3. speculation
   A. conjecture
   B. significance
   C. attempt
   D. conclusion

4. coinage
   A. pronunciation
   B. trial
   C. invention
   D. novelty

Name _____ Date _____

"Onomatopoeia" by William Safire
Support for Writing

Use the chart below to help you prepare to write an essay on a word or phrase in English that you find interesting, odd or funny. Fill in the blanks in the chart to help you organize the results of your research on the word you have chosen.

The word I have chosen to write about is _____.

Why I find the word odd, interesting, or funny	
Origins of the word	
Earliest known appearance or usage in English	
Changes in meaning over the years	

Now, on a separate piece of paper, use the results of your research to write a rough draft of your essay on the origin and evolution of the word you have chosen. Try to use idiomatic language to help to create an informal tone of the kind Safire uses in his essay.

Name _____ Date _____

"**Coyote v. Acme**" by Ian Frazier
Literary Analysis: Parody

A **parody** is a humorous piece of writing that mocks the characteristics of a literary form, a specific work, or the style of a certain writer. Through the use of exaggeration, a parody calls attention to ridiculous elements of the original, particularly those that have become clichés.

DIRECTIONS: *On the lines following each of the passages from "Coyote v. Acme," explain what is exaggerated and/or ridiculous in the passage and how those elements add to the humor of the parody.*

1. My client, Mr. Wile E. Coyote, a resident of Arizona and contiguous states, does hereby bring suit for damages against the Acme Company. . . ."

   _____

   _____

   _____

2. "Such injuries sustained by Mr. Coyote have temporarily restricted his ability to make a living in his profession of predator. Mr. Coyote is self-employed and thus not eligible for Workmen's Compensation."

   _____

   _____

   _____

3. "As Mr. Coyote gripped the handlebars, the Rocket Sled accelerated with such sudden and precipitate force as to stretch Mr. Coyote's forelimbs to a length of fifty feet."

   _____

   _____

   _____

4. "The sequence of collisions resulted in systemic physical damage to Mr. Coyote, viz., flattening of the cranium, sideways displacement of the tongue, reduction of length of the legs and upper body, and compression of vertebrae from base of tail to head."

   _____

   _____

   _____

5. "Mr. Coyote respectfully requests that the Court regard these larger economic implications and assess punitive damages in the amount of seventeen million dollars. In addition, Mr. Coyote seeks actual damages (missed meals, medical expenses, days lost from professional occupation) of one million dollars. . . ."

   _____

   _____

   _____

"Coyote v. Acme" by Ian Frazier

Reading Strategy: Cause and Effect

As a parody of a legal argument, this essay is organized using **cause-and-effect text structure.** To analyze cause and effect, look for words and phrases that signal those relationships, such as *subsequently, as a result,* and *resulted in.*

DIRECTIONS: *Use the chart below to analyze examples of cause-and-effect text structure in "Coyote v. Acme." For each example given, identify the key word or phrase that signals the cause/effect relationship, the cause(s), and the effect(s).*

Example	Key Word or Phrase	Cause(s)	Effect(s)
1. "Mr. Coyote is self-employed and thus not eligible for Workmen's Compensation."			
2. "Mr. Coyote vigorously attempted to follow this maneuver but was unable to, due to poorly designed steering on the Rocket Sled and a faulty or nonexistent braking system."			
3. "The force of this impact then caused the springs to rebound, whereupon Mr. Coyote was thrust skyward."			
4. "The sequence of collisions resulted in systemic physical damage to Mr. Coyote, viz., flattening of the cranium, sideways displacement of the tongue. . . ."			

"Coyote v. Acme" by Ian Frazier
Vocabulary Builder

Using the Latin Root -corpus-

A. DIRECTIONS: *Knowing that the Latin root -corpus- means "body," circle the letter of the best synonym for each word*

1. *corpulent*   **A.** official   **B.** competent   **C.** fat   **D.** distant
2. *corpse*   **A.** cadaver   **B.** officer   **C.** precedent   **D.** ground
3. *corporate*   **A.** combined   **B.** light   **C.** profitable   **D.** risky

Using the Word List

contiguous   emit   incorporated   vigorously   punitive   systemic

B. DIRECTIONS: *For each of the following items, choose the Word List word that best completes the meaning of the sentence. Circle the letter of your choice.*

1. The United States has a large _____ border with Canada.
   A. incorporated   **B.** contiguous   **C.** precipitate   **D.** punitive

2. In addition to compensation for the flaws in the product, the plaintiff sought _____ damages as well to deter the company from making shoddy products in the future.
   A. incorporated   **B.** contiguous   **C.** precipitate   **D.** punitive

3. I was so angry with my boss that I needed to burn off some energy by _____ exercising at the gym later that day.
   A. incorporated   **B.** contiguous   **C.** vigorously   **D.** punitive

4. The electric-generating plant seemed to _____ a strange odor at night.
   A. incorporated   **B.** contiguous   **C.** systemic   **D.** emit

5. After receiving my rough draft back from the teacher, I _____ all her suggestions in my final draft.
   A. incorporated   **B.** contiguous   **C.** systemic   **D.** emit

6. My doctor advised me that my symptoms were not serious and were not due to any _____ disorder.
   A. incorporated   **B.** contiguous   **C.** systemic   **D.** emit

Name _____ Date _____

"Coyote v. Acme" by Ian Frazier
Support for Writing

In his satirical essay "Coyote v. Acme," Frazier parodies aspects of the legal profession. Working in groups as teams of attorneys defending the Acme Company, develop a response to the arguments presented in "Coyote v. Acme."

Prewriting   Work together to come up with effective responses to the main arguments presented in the essay. Use the following suggested starting points as an aid in organizing your thoughts.

1. The plaintiff Coyote misused Acme's products in the following ways:

_____

_____

_____

_____

2. Acme's products are reliable when used as recommended because . . .

_____

_____

_____

_____

_____

3. Acme's products have a record of being used safely and effectively by . . .

_____

_____

_____

_____

_____

After you have gathered and thought out your best counterarguments to Coyote's brief, Prepare an **opening statement** for the defense. Use your most convincing response to address each of the essay's main arguments. Mimic the exaggerated style of the original piece to add humor and irony.

"Urban Renewal" by Sean Ramsay
"Playing for the Fighting Sixty-Ninth" by William Harvey
Primary Sources: Oral History and E-mail

An **oral history** is a spoken account of an event by an eyewitness. It is usually unrehearsed, and combines factual information with impressions, feelings, and memories. An oral history can help bring a major event to life for those who were not present. An e-mail (short for "electronic mail") is a message sent through a computer network. Though **e-mails** often contain informal, unimportant messages, they have also proved to be an important source of communication during times of crisis.

As you read these primary sources, you might find it useful to **apply background knowledge** based on what you have already read, learned, or witnessed about the events of 9–11. You might also wish to **draw conclusions** about the speakers: their thoughts and feelings, and their relationship to larger events.

DIRECTIONS: *Read each question about the primary sources presented in this group and answer the questions.*

1. Based on your own reactions to the events of 9–11 or the reactions of people you know, what conclusions can you draw about Sean Ramsay's motivation in walking along the promenade in Brooklyn Heights, across from the scene of the collapse of the Twin Towers in "Urban Renewal"?

   _____

   _____

2. Based on the actions of the sanitation workers as recounted in "Urban Renewal," what can you conclude about the feelings and attitudes of all New Yorkers in the immediate aftermath of the events of 9–11?

   _____

   _____

3. What advantages of an oral history as a primary source—as opposed to other sources such as print and broadcast journalism accounts, photographs, and so on—are evident in "Urban Renewal"?

   _____

   _____

4. Using your background knowledge of the events of 9–11, what can you conclude about how humans react to emergencies based on Harvey's account of his own extraordinary services and those of the soldiers he played for in "Playing for the Fighting Sixty-Ninth"?

   _____

   _____

5. What aspect of Harvey's written account in "Playing for the Fighting Sixty-Ninth" shows a possible advantage of an e-mail as a primary source as opposed to an oral account of the kind provided in "Urban Renewal"?

   _____

   _____

Name _____ Date _____

"**Urban Renewal**" by Sean Ramsay
"**Playing for the Fighting Sixty-Ninth**" by William Harvey
Vocabulary Builder

Word List

accosted   cadence   casualties   condolences   fatigues
homages   intently   intonation   memorials   regiment

A. DIRECTIONS: *For each of the following items, choose the Word List word that best completes the meaning of the sentence.*

1. The city of Washington, D.C., is notable for its many prominent ——————— that honor the achievements of past great presidents of the United States.
   A. memorials   B. condolences   C. casualties   D. fatigues

2. Judging by the low, simmering ——————— of my teacher's voice, she was none too pleased with the effort I had made on my oral report.
   A. regiment   B. cadence   C. intonation   D. homages

3. At the town ceremony on Memorial Day, many of the speakers delivered moving ——————— to the brave men and women who had made the ultimate sacrifice for their country in wartime.
   A. regiment   B. cadence   C. intonation   D. homages

4. I was nervous and wary as a strange man ——————— me on a dark, deserted street late at night.
   A. intently   B. accosted   C. intonation   D. intently

5. Everyone in the audience listened ——————— as the speaker told of his experiences flying on the space shuttle.
   A. casualties   B. intonation   C. regiment   D. intently

6. After the tornado devastated the town, a ——————— of the National Guard quickly appeared to help survivors and restore order.
   A. memorials   B. intonation   C. regiment   D. intently

7. Many of the officers kindly offered their ——————— to grieving residents who had lost family members to the tornado.
   A. memorials   B. condolences   C. casualties   D. fatigues

8. Dressed in their battle ———————, the soldiers set about giving first aid to survivors, clearing debris, and restoring essential services.
   A. cadence   B. condolences   C. casualties   D. fatigues

9. Speaking in a slow, mournful ———————, the minister paid tribute to the memory of those who had fallen victim to the tornado.
   A. cadence   B. condolences   C. casualties   D. fatigues

10. Despite the terrible toll taken by the tornado, the ——————— could have been much worse if the twister had taken a more direct path through the residential area of the town.
    A. memorials   B. condolences   C. casualties   D. fatigues

Name _____ Date _____

"One Day, Broken in Two" by Anna Quindlen
Literary Analysis: Comparison-and-Contrast Essay

A **comparison-and-contrast essay** presents differences and similarities between two or more people, topics or events. In this essay, Quindlen compares the thoughts and behaviors of Americans in the days following the events of September 11, 2001, to those one year later.

DIRECTIONS: *Use the chart below to compare and contrast various aspects of American life before and after the events of 9-11 as discussed in "One Day, Broken in Two." Briefly cite details from the essay to support your answers.*

Aspect of Life	Before 9-11	After 9-11
Personal Feelings		
Daily Routines		
Travel		
What Kind of People Are We		
What Kind of World Do We Live In		

Name _____ Date _____

Reading Strategy: Relate a Literary Work to Primary Source Documents

Primary source documents are nonfiction works that comment upon events taking place at the time the works were written. Some primary source documents, like the Declaration of Independence, speak solely of issues of public concern. Others reveal information about the private life of the writer. By providing personal reflections and first-hand accounts, primary source documents can offer insights into a literary work that would otherwise be unavailable.

DIRECTIONS: *There is a wide variety of primary source documents available on the subject of the events of 9-11. Use the chart below to list five such possible sources. In the middle column, state where such a source is likely to be found. In the right-hand column explain the advantage of that source to someone researching the events of 9-11.*

Primary Source	Where It to Find It	Advantage of Source

Name _____ Date _____

"One Day, Broken in Two" by Anna Quindlen
Vocabulary Builder

Word List

induce   mundane   prosperity   revelations   savagery

A. DIRECTIONS: *Read the incomplete paragraph below. On each line, write one of the words from the Word List. Think about the meaning of each word in the context of the paragraph.*

On the morning of September 11, 2001, most Americans began their day in an ordinary fashion, getting ready for another (1) _____ round of work or school. Then, as the (2) _____ of the terrible events at the World Trade Center began to hit the airwaves, they reacted with shock and disbelief. Few could believe the (3) _____ of the violent acts that were unfolding right before their very eyes on televisions across the country. Some believed that the seemingly invincible military strength of the United States, built on the foundations of a long term (4) _____, had managed to (5) _____ a false sense of security among its citizens.

B. DIRECTIONS: *On each line, write the letter of the word whose meaning is most nearly* opposite *in meaning to the Word List word.*

1. mundane
   A. worldly
   B. extraordinary
   C. temporary
   D. compassionate

2. induce
   A. dissuade
   B. surrender
   C. affirm
   D. question

3. savagery
   A. originality
   B. renewal
   C. gentleness
   D. intelligence

4. revelations
   A. cover-ups
   B. writings
   C. failures
   D. emancipations

5. prosperity
   A. sturdiness
   B. generosity
   C. elevation
   D. poverty

"One Day, Broken in Two" by Anna Quindlen
Support for Writing

Prepare to write a letter to Anna Quindlen in which you share your thoughts about her essay "One Day, Broken in Two." As part of your preparation, think of questions that occurred to you as you read her essay. Use the suggested questions below to get started, and add others of your own before you write a rough draft of your letter.

1. America had unprecedented sympathy throughout the world right after 9-11. Does America command the same sympathy from other countries today? Why or why not?

   _____

   _____

   _____

   _____

2. Have Americans completely resumed all of their normal routines since 9-11, or have some aspects of American life changed permanently since then? If so, which ones?

   _____

   _____

   _____

   _____

3. Have Americans regained their pre-9-11 sense of optimism and security about this country's place in the world? Why or why not?

   _____

   _____

   _____

   _____

4. Do Americans feel safer from terrorist attack now than they did in first year after 9-11? Why or why not?

   _____

   _____

   _____

   _____

5. What lessons can we as a country learn from the events of 9-11?

   _____

   _____

   _____

   _____

After you have sketched out answers to these questions and others you may have posed, begin to assemble your material into a rough draft of a letter to Anna Quindlen.

"For the Love of Books" by Rita Dove
"Mother Tongue" by Amy Tan
Literary Analysis: Reflective Essay

In a **reflective essay,** the writer uses an informal tone to explore and identify the meaning of personal experience or pivotal event. This type of essay can reveal the writer's feeling about these experiences as well as his or her values and personality.

DIRECTIONS: *Write your answers to the following questions.*

1. What books and writers does Dove remember reading as a child?

   _____

   _____

2. What do Dove's reading tastes reveal about her values?

   _____

   _____

3. What do Dove's recollections about reading reveal about her childhood?

   _____

   _____

4. What was significant about Dove's meeting with the professional writer/poet John Ciardi when she was a high school student?

   _____

   _____

5. What do Tan's experiences with her mother reveal about her personality?

   _____

   _____

6. What do Tan's experiences with her mother reveal about her values?

   _____

   _____

7. What is the reason that Tan believes she did not do as well on standardized English tests as she did on standardized math tests?

   _____

   _____

8. How did Tan's perception of her mother's imperfect, "broken" English change from her adolescence to her adulthood?

   _____

   _____

"For the Love of Books" by Rita Dove
"Mother Tongue" by Amy Tan
Reading Strategy: Outlining

To clarify your understanding of each essay, it may be useful to create an **outline** of the author's main points. Outlining can also help you make comparisons between the essays. A key to mastering outlining skills is practicing your ability to identify an author's main ideas and the details—facts, examples, or reasons—that support those ideas. The graphic organizer below will help you to work on identifying main ideas and supporting details.

DIRECTIONS: *Identify a main idea from each of the essays in this section: "For the Love of Books" by Rita Dove and "Mother Tongue" by Amy Tan. Then identify the supporting details that support each main idea.*

"For the Love of Books"

Main Idea:	
Supporting Details:	

"Mother Tongue"

Main Idea:	
Supporting Details:	

"For the Love of Books" by Rita Dove

"Mother Tongue" by Amy Tan

Grammar and Style: Parallel Structure

Parallel structure is the expression of similar ideas in similar grammatical forms. Writers often use parallel structure to emphasize important ideas. One of the most famous examples is Julius Caesar's declaration, "I came, I saw, I conquered." Here's an example from "The Love of Books" by Rita Dove: "I loved to feel their heft in my hand . . .; I loved the crisp whisper of a page turning. . . ."

When the items in a sentence are joined by coordinating conjunctions *(and, but, yet, or)* or correlative conjunctions *(either/or, neither/nor)*, the items must be parallel. Read the following examples:

Faulty: People in the classroom were talking of poetry, hauling books, and they read aloud.

Parallel: People in the classroom were talking of poetry, hauling books, and reading aloud.

Faulty: They were either reading aloud or they listened.

Parallel: They were either reading aloud or listening.

A. PRACTICE: *Find and list four examples of parallel structure in "For the Love of Books" and/or "Mother Tongue." Underline the parallel elements in each example.*

_____

_____

_____

_____

B. WRITING APPLICATION: *Rewrite the following sentences, making the structure parallel in each*

1. Tan's mother is shown getting rebuffed and she endures rude behavior.

_____

_____

2. The writer hopes for achieving a sense of truth and to reach a receptive audience.

_____

_____

3. Amy Tan is recognized for seeing a world in which various cultures are of equal value and as an astute portrayer of family relationships.

_____

_____

"For the Love of Books" by Rita Dove
"Mother Tongue" by Amy Tan
Vocabulary Builder

Using the Roots *-scrib-* and *-script-*

A. DIRECTIONS: *Knowing that -scrib- and -script- mean "write," use each of the following words in an original sentence that demonstrates the root's meaning.*

1. inscribe _____

2. manuscript _____

Using the Word List

aspirations   benign   daunting   ecstasy   transcribed

B. DIRECTIONS: *For each of the following items, choose the Word List word that best completes the meaning of the sentence. Circle the letter of your choice.*

1. Juanita was in _____ after she received a letter of acceptance from the college that was her first choice.
   A. benign   B. ecstasy   C. daunting   D. transcribed

2. The _____ expression on the man's face was reassuring, so I stopped my car to see if he needed help.
   A. benign   B. ecstasy   C. daunting   D. transcribed

3. During the hearing, every word that the witness spoke was carefully _____ by the court reporter to preserve a permanent, official record of the proceedings.
   A. aspirations   B. benign   C. daunting   D. transcribed

4. Because of my love of animals, I have always had _____ to become a veterinarian.
   A. benign   B. transcribed   C. aspirations   D. daunting

5. Training for the triathlon while studying for finals seemed like too _____ a task, so I reluctantly decided to resign from the track team.
   A. transcribed   B. ecstasy   C. daunting   D. benign

"For the Love of Books" by Rita Dove

"Mother Tongue" by Amy Tan

Support for Writing

As you prepare to write an e-mail or a regular letter to one of the authors of these two essays, collect information on the essay you like better in the graphic organizer below. Reread the essay before you begin.

e-mail to _____

Ideas, images, characters that I liked in the essay:	Reasons that I liked them:
_____	_____
_____	_____
_____	_____
_____	_____
Ideas, images, characters that concerned me in the essay:	**Reasons for my concern:**
_____	_____
_____	_____
_____	_____
_____	_____

On a separate page, write a draft of your e-mail or other letter. Begin by telling the author why you liked her essay. Then, provide more details of your opinion in the following paragraphs. When you revise, replace vague words with those that are specific.

from **The Woman Warrior** by Maxine Hong Kingston
from **The Names** by N. Scott Momaday
Literary Analysis: Memoirs

Most **memoirs** are similar to autobiographies. They are usually first-person nonfiction narratives describing significant experiences and events in the life of the writer. Maxine Hong Kingston's *The Woman Warrior*, subtitled *Memoirs of a Girlhood Among Ghosts*, has features that are both similar to and different from those of typical memoirs. The excerpt from *The Names* by N. Scott Momaday has a format that is more typical of most memoirs.

DIRECTIONS: *Answer the following questions.*

1. What is the narrative point of view of the excerpt from *The Names*? Is this point of view typically used in memoirs? Explain.

   _____

   _____

   _____

   _____

2. What are two significant experiences, moments, or events described in the excerpt from *The Names*? Why are they significant?

   _____

   _____

   _____

   _____

3. On whose personal impressions of events does the excerpt from *The Woman Warrior* focus? Describe two passages in the selection that reveal this person's unique perspective.

   _____

   _____

   _____

   _____

4. Explain why features of *The Woman Warrior* are different from those of standard memoirs. Why do you think Maxine Hong Kingston chose this unique style for her memoirs? In what way does this style help to convey her central message?

   _____

   _____

   _____

   _____

All-in-One Workbook
405

from **The Woman Warrior** by Maxine Hong Kingston

from **The Names** by N. Scott Momaday

Reading Strategy: Relate to Your Own Experiences

The writers of these essays describe experience that have great personal significance. You can better understand the writers and their ideas if you look for ways in which the essays relate to your own experiences.

DIRECTIONS: *Write your answers to the following questions.*

1. At age thirteen, Momaday received a horse from his parents. What event from your own experience can you relate to Momaday's experience?

   _____

   _____

   _____

2. What significance did your experience have?

   _____

   _____

   _____

3. How does recalling your experience help you understand Momaday's?

   _____

   _____

   _____

4. The excerpt from *The Woman Warrior* describes Brave Orchid as having some superstitious beliefs: that she can help to keep an airplane in the air or a ship afloat through sheer will-power. Do you—or does anyone you know—have or practice any superstitions, such as not walking on the cracks of the pavement? Briefly describe any of your own superstitions or those of your friends or family members.

   _____

   _____

   _____

5. In the excerpt from *The Woman Warrior,* Brave Orchid shows impatience with some of the personal habits and tastes of her children, who have grown up in the United States. Have your parents or grandparents ever disapproved of any of your tastes in food, music, or other areas? Briefly describe any such "conflict of generations" that you may have experienced.

   _____

   _____

   _____

from **The Woman Warrior** by Maxine Hong Kingston
from **The Names** by N. Scott Momaday

Vocabulary Builder

Using the Root -aud-

The root -*aud*- comes from the Latin word *audire*, which means "to hear." Most words containing the root -*aud*- are related to sound and hearing.

   audible   audience   audiology   audiovisual

A. DIRECTIONS: *Read each of the following descriptions. On the line provided, write the correct word with the root -aud- that appears on the list above.*

1. a kind of presentation that involves both hearing and sight _____

2. a branch of science that deals with hearing _____

3. a group of people gathered to hear a concert, speech, or play _____

4. loud and clear enough to be heard _____

Using the Word List

gravity   inaudibly   oblivious   pastoral   supple

B. DIRECTIONS: *Choose a lettered word pair that best expresses a relationship similar to that expressed in the numbered pair. Circle the letter of your choice.*

1. PASTORAL : COUNTRY ::
   A. priest : parish
   B. shepherd : flock
   C. literal : actual
   D. urban : city

2. SUPPLE : FLEXIBLE ::
   A. buyer : regret
   B. problem : solution
   C. strange : alien
   D. softness : texture

3. INAUDIBLY : FAINTLY ::
   A. sincerely : frankly
   B. swift : slow
   C. gradual : movement
   D. lively : animate

4. GRAVITY : PROBLEM ::
   A. friendly : relationship
   B. excitement : surprise
   C. clearly : transparent
   D. complicated : problem

5. OBLIVIOUS : UNAWARE ::
   A. gigantic : impressive
   B. attentive : neglectful
   C. abundant : plentiful
   D. hopelessness : sorrow

from **The Woman Warrior** by Maxine Hong Kingston

from **The Names** by N. Scott Momaday

Grammar and Style: Creating Sentence Variety

A healthy variety of sentence structures can make your writing vital and engaging. Simple sentences contain one independent clause and convey ideas concisely and directly. Compound sentences, which contain two or more independent clauses, and complex sentences, which contain an independent clause and one or more subordinate clauses, can enhance the flow of ideas.

A. UNDERSTANDING STYLE: *Write the types of sentence structures used in each of the following quotations. Then explain how each writer's sentence structure affects his or her prose.*

1. When she was about sixty-eight years old, Brave Orchid took a day off to wait at San Francisco International Airport for the plane that was bringing her sister to the United States. She had not seen her sister for thirty years. —Maxine Hong Kingston

   _____

   _____

2. They had said he was in Japan, and then they said he was in the Philippines. But when she sent him her help, she could feel that he was on a ship in Da Nang. — Maxine Hong Kingston

   _____

   _____

3. When the song, which was a song of riding, was finished, I had Pecos pick up the pace. Far down on the road to San Ysidro I overtook my friend Pasqual Fragua. — N. Scott Momaday

   _____

   _____

B. Writing Application: Varying your sentence structure, write a paragraph in which you describe a memorable experience.

   _____

   _____

   _____

   _____

   _____

   _____

   _____

   _____

   _____

Name _____ Date _____

from **The Woman Warrior** by Maxine Hong Kingston

from **The Names** by N. Scott Momaday
Support for Writing

Write a **memoir** on an event that changed your life. Prepare to write a reflective essay. In the diagram below, enter three important events from your past, and describe how they affected you.

Events That Affected or Changed My Life

Event:

_____

Effects it has had on my life:

_____

_____

_____

Event:

_____

Effects it has had on my life:

_____

_____

_____

Event:

_____

Effects it has had on my life:

_____

_____

On a separate page, draft your memoir. Choose one event from your organizer, and explain the insight it provided to you. Describe how the event affects your life today. Add additional information, if necessary, to make your essay clear to your readers.

Essential Questions Workshop—Unit 6

In their stories, poems, and nonfiction, the writers in Unit Six express ideas that relate to the three Essential Questions framing this book. Review the literature in the unit. Then, for each Essential Question, choose an author and at least one passage from his or her writing that expresses a related idea. Use this chart to complete your work.

Essential Question	Author/Selection	Literary Passage
How does literature shape or reflect society?		
What is the relationship between place and literature?		
What makes American literature American?		

Screening Test

Directions: Read the following sentences. Choose the *best* meaning of the underlined word. On the answer sheet, fill in the bubble for the answer that you think is correct.

1 Nowhere, wrote T. S. Eliot, was there a cat as <u>deceitful</u> as Macavity, the "Hidden Paw."
  A arrogant
  B lazy
  C dishonest
  D beautiful

2 In "A Dream Deferred," Langston Hughes examines the <u>disastrous</u> effects of frustrated hopes.
  F common
  G permanent
  H catastrophic
  J unending

Directions: Read the following passages. Then answer the questions. On the answer sheet, fill in the bubble for the answer that you think is correct.

> The hair on her head was dark brown streaked with gray. Her old fur hat was gray . . . her blue raincoat hung nearly to the ground in front and was several inches shorter in the back. She carried a shopping bag in each hand. In that city neighborhood, she was a sign of spring. Like a battered crocus or a soot-sprinkled daffodil planted too near the sidewalk, she shrugged off the dirt and burst forth each year. But she was a thorny flower. And none ventured too near, for she mumbled as she <u>trudged</u> from trash basket to trash basket, and anyone—child or adult—who got too close was liable to be jabbed with words that stung like sharp, prickly spines.

3 Using the information presented about the woman, what can you infer about her social status?
  A She lives on the streets and collects items from trash baskets.
  B She is an irritable person who has inadvertently thrown something important away.
  C She is antisocial, preferring squirrels and flowers to people.
  D She enjoys shopping but not socializing.

4 On the basis of the information in the passage, evaluate the author's opinion of the woman.
  F Because the author calls her "a sign of spring" and compares her to a flower, the author thinks the woman has her own beauty.
  G The author is prejudiced against the woman because she looks shabby, searches through trash baskets, and scares people away.
  H Because the author focuses on the woman's charm behind the ragged clothes and cantankerous attitude, the woman is seen in a positive light.
  J both F and H

5 What is the denotation of the word <u>trudged</u>?
A walked quietly
B skipped lightly
C marched steadily
D ran quickly

6 The connotation for the word <u>trudged</u> is —
F positive
G negative
H neutral
J none of the above

---

1   "And I . . . I suppose you'll want to get that can off him."

2   "Oh, yes, yes, please!"

3   It took all my strength to lift him onto the table. He was heavier now than before his illness. I reached for those familiar forceps and began to turn the jagged edges of the can outwards from the nose and mouth. Tomato soup must have been one of his favorites because he was really deeply embedded, and it took some time before I was able to slide the can from his face.

4   I fought off his slobbering attack. "He's back in the dustbins, I see," I said.

5   "Yes, he is quite regularly. I've pulled several cans off him myself. And he goes sliding with the children, too." She smiled.

6   I took my stethoscope from the pocket of my white coat and listened to his lungs. They were wonderfully clear. . . .

7   "But Mr. Herriot." Mrs. Westby's eyes were wide. "How on earth has this happened? How has he gotten better?"

8   . . . "The healing power of nature. Something no veterinary surgeon can compete with when it decides to act."

9   "I see. And you can never tell when this is going to happen?"

10   "No."

---

7 Which statement *best* expresses the implied main idea of the passage?
A The dog's needing medical attention for another problem revealed his return to health.
B Using forceps is the only way to remove a tomato soup can from a dog's muzzle.
C Tomato is the dog's favorite kind of soup.
D Mrs. Westby has pulled several tomato soup cans off the dog's nose and mouth.

8 Select the statement below that *best* supports the main idea of the passage.
F Mr. Herriot finds the dog's lungs to be "wonderfully clear."
G Mr. Herriot puts the dog on a table before he examines it.
H Mr. Herriot uses forceps to loosen the can from the dog's nose and mouth.
J Mrs. Westby has pulled several tomato soup cans off the dog's nose and mouth.

Where did the idea of a park come from? In the early 1800s New York was already a "tumultuous and brutal city," packed into the lower part of the island of Manhattan. Businessmen were bent on buying up and making a profit from every square foot of the city's tight space. If this kept on, some feared, masses of New Yorkers would be crowded to death. It was a few thoughtful people, led by the poet and newspaper editor William Cullen Bryant and the writer Washington Irving who imagined what a great open space could do to bring light and air and peace and quiet to the harried souls of the great city.

9 Which of the following statements *best* expresses the author's strong feelings about New York?

A The author considers the city noisy and violent, and the population explosive and tormented.

B The author regards the city as busy, exciting, and full of energetic, interesting people.

C The author believes that the city is a great place for adults and children.

D The author despises New York and concludes that the only answer is to move to a quiet, peaceful part of the country.

10 Which of the following statements is supported by the information given in the passage?

F Land was hard to come by in Manhattan.

G William Cullen Bryant knew the value of open space.

H Light, air, peace, and quiet are of some benefit to individuals.

J all of the above

11 William Cullen Bryant and Washington Irving were both —

A writers

B businessmen

C real estate brokers

D landscapers

12 Which of the following statements *best* summarizes the passage?

F Businessmen in Manhattan were extremely greedy.

G New York was a "tumultuous and brutal city," packed into the lower part of the island of Manhattan.

H In the early 1800s, some feared that masses of New Yorkers would be crowded to death.

J William Cullen Bryant and Washington Irving were integral in creating the idea of a public park.

> **Watson:** But, Holmes—if she's correct in saying the door and window of her sister's room were locked, then the girl must have been absolutely alone when she met her death.
>
> **Holmes:** Death in a sealed room, in fact?
>
> **Watson:** Natural causes. No other explanation. [Scratching his head] But then, what about that whistling in the night—and that speckled band business.
>
> **Holmes:** I was hoping *you* were going to provide me with those answers, my dear Watson.
>
> **Watson:** Well, you'll have to hope again!
>
> **Holmes:** [Mock dismay] Dear me!
>
> **Watson:** Have you any ideas?
>
> **Holmes:** We have whistles at night, a group of gypsies . . .
>
> **Watson:** Yes.
>
> **Holmes:** . . . And we have a dying reference to a speckled band. Now, if we combine all these elements, I think there is good ground to believe that the mystery may be cleared up.

13 **All of the following comparisons of Watson and Holmes are true EXCEPT —**
  A They are very slow to draw conclusions about the death in the locked room.
  B They listen to each other's opinions.
  C They do not ridicule each other's reasoning.
  D They both have an appetite for solving mysteries.

14 **What conclusion about the girl's death can be drawn from Holmes and Watson's conversation?**
  F She died of natural causes.
  G She was murdered.
  H Her death is definitely related to a group of gypsies, a whistle in the night, and a speckled band.
  J The girl's sister knows the truth about the girl's death.

> As we were thus conversing in a low tone while Old Barley's sustained growl vibrated in the beam that crossed the ceiling, the room door opened, and a very pretty, slight, dark-eyed girl of twenty or so came in with a basket in her hand and whom Herbert tenderly relieved of the basket, and presented blushingly as "Clara." She really was a most charming girl, and might have passed for a captive fairy whom the truculent ogre, Old Barley, had pressed into his service.

15 **Which of the following statements is a *fact* presented in the passage?**
  A Clara has dark eyes.
  B Clara resembles a fairy.
  C Clara is very pretty.
  D Clara's looks resemble those of her father.

16 **Which of the following statements is an *opinion* presented in the passage?**
  F Clara is in her early twenties.
  G A girl named Clara entered the room carrying a basket.
  H Clara is a charming girl.
  J The narrator is conversing with a man named Herbert.

At breakfast on our chosen day, when Mama, Daddy, and Aunt Nicey were in the dining room, I brought Doodle to the door in the go-cart just as usual and had them turn their backs, making them cross their hearts and hope to die if they peeked. I helped Doodle up, and when he was standing alone I let them look. There wasn't a sound as Doodle walked slowly across the room and sat down at his place at the table. Then Mama began to cry and ran over to him, hugging him and kissing him. Daddy hugged him too, so I went to Aunt Nicey, who was praying thanks in the doorway, and began to waltz her around. We danced together quite well until she came down on my big toe with her brogans, hurting me so badly I thought I was crippled for life.

17 Which of the following statements is the *best* summary of the passage?
- **A** A family that frequently eats breakfast together is surprised to find one of its members sitting at the table.
- **B** A happy occasion ends in pain when two family members show off by dancing.
- **C** A family witnesses one of its members accomplish something difficult and then celebrates together.
- **D** There wasn't a sound as Doodle walked slowly across the floor and sat down at his place at the table.

18 Which of the following is the *best* paraphrase of the last sentence?
- **F** I enjoyed dancing with Aunt Nicey until she injured me by stepping on my foot.
- **G** We danced together quite well until she came down on my big toe with her brogans, hurting me so badly I thought I was crippled for life.
- **H** Aunt Nicey and Daddy danced together, until Daddy stepped on her foot with his big boots.
- **J** Aunt Nicey enjoyed dancing with me, but then she came down on my big toe with her brogans, hurting me so badly I thought I was crippled for life.

19 From the passage, what generalization can you make about Mama, Daddy, and Aunt Nicey?
- **A** They are conniving and jealous.
- **B** They are cold and reserved.
- **C** They are emotional and loving.
- **D** They are bitter and indignant.

20 What was the effect of Doodle's walking to his chair without assistance?
- **F** Mama and Daddy hug him.
- **G** The narrator pushes the go-cart across the dining room floor.
- **H** Aunt Nicey and the narrator dance.
- **J** both F and H

21 Which of the following is the *best* paraphrase of the first sentence?

A I had Mama, Daddy, Aunt Nicey, and Doodle turn their backs and promise not to peek while I entered the dining room.

B I had Mama, Daddy, and Aunt Nicey look away when I brought Doodle into the dining room in his go-cart.

C I brought Doodle to the dining room door in the go-cart just as usual during breakfast on our chosen day, making Mama, Daddy, and Aunt Nicey turn their backs, cross their hearts and hope to die if they peeked.

D Doodle stood by himself as Mama, Daddy, and Aunt Nicey hid their eyes.

The latest blight to afflict the spoken word in the United States is the rapidly spreading reiteration of the phrase "you know." I don't know just when it began moving like a rainstorm through the language, but I tremble at its increasing garbling of meaning, ruining of rhythm, and drumming upon my hapless ears. One man, in a phone conversation with me last summer, used the phrase thirty-four times in about five minutes, by his own count; a young matron in Chicago got seven "you knows" into one wavy sentence, and I have also heard it as far west as Denver, where an otherwise charming woman at a garden party in August said it almost as often as a whippoorwill says, "Whippoorwill."

---

22 What *probably* caused the author to write this passage?

F The author noticed more and more people saying "you know."

G The author uses "you know" frequently.

H The author likes whippoorwills.

J The author works to explore the origins of "you know."

23 From the passage, what generalization can you make about Americans?

A They will be reprimanded for annoying habits.

B They like to ruin language by saying "you know."

C They are developing similar speech patterns.

D They can be as annoying as birds.

24 From the passage, what conclusion can you draw about the author?

F The author never makes mistakes.

G The author cares deeply about language and how it is used.

H The author believes that people from the East Coast speak better than others.

J The author does not like birds.

Practice Test 1

Suppose you have been asked to give a speech about why eleventh-grade students should be placed in charge of planning the lunch menu at your school. Answer the following questions.

1. Which of the following is the **least** useful strategy for organizing your ideas before you begin writing?
   A. talking to other students about their opinions of the current lunch menu
   B. conducting research to see whether any schools have succeeded in allowing students to plan lunch menus
   C. talking to school administrators to learn what their objections might be
   D. finding research that explains the principles of nutrition

2. What should you do in order to convince your audience that your proposal is worthwhile?
   A. Include evidence that supports it.
   B. Quote students who like the idea.
   C. Talk about the kinds of food you like.
   D. Read the current lunch menu aloud.

3. During the question-and-answer session, the principal states that a licensed dietician must plan lunch menus in order for the school to qualify for certain food programs. What should you do?
   A. Imply that the principal is mistaken.
   B. Walk off the stage.
   C. Ask how students can offer ideas about the planning of school lunches.
   D. Take another question from the audience.

4. What vocabulary and tone should you use during your presentation?
   A. lighthearted
   B. professional
   C. confrontational
   D. casual

5. Which of the following is true about the strategy of referring to a book, television show, or movie in which students seem to have better lunch choices than you have at your school?
   A. It is a good idea because it shows that some students have more options.
   B. It is a good idea because it shows you did some research.
   C. It is a bad idea because it suggests that fiction and reality are the same thing.
   D. It is a bad idea because not everyone may like that book, show, or movie.

6. Which of the following is an effective technique when delivering an oral presentation?
   A. making eye contact
   B. speaking clearly
   C. emphasizing important words
   D. all of the above

Read the following passages. Then answer the questions that follow.

from *The Navajo Origin Legend*

On the morning of the twelfth day the people washed themselves well. The women dried themselves with yellow cornmeal; the men with white cornmeal. Soon after the ablutions were completed they heard the distant call of the approaching gods. It was shouted, as before, four times—nearer and louder at each repetition—and, after the fourth call, the gods appeared. Blue Body and Black Body each carried a sacred buckskin. White Body carried two ears of corn, one yellow, one white, each covered at the end completely with grains.

7. Which of the following subjects is **unrelated** to the subject of this excerpt from *The Navajo Origin Legend*?
   A. the spirituality of the Navajo
   B. hardships endured by colonial settlers
   C. one of the many cultures that is a part of the American literary tradition
   D. how the Navajos saw themselves in relation to the gods

8. Which of the following gives the **best** description of the author's style?
   A. flowery and poetic
   B. complex and literary
   C. plain and straightforward
   D. dry and technical

from *Poor Richard's Almanack* by Benjamin Franklin

Have you something to do tomorrow, do it today.

A true friend is the best possession.

'Tis easier to prevent bad habits than to break them.

Well done is better than well said.

Dost thou love life? Then do not squander time; for that's the stuff life is made of.

9. Which of the following gives the **best** description of the structure of the excerpt from *Poor Richard's Almanack*?
   A. a paragraph
   B. a series of paragraphs
   C. a poetic stanza
   D. a series of aphorisms

10. This excerpt from Franklin's writing confirms which of the following statements about the early days of America?
   A. People had to work hard.
   B. Self-discipline was valued.
   C. Time was a precious commodity.
   D. all of the above

11. Based on the Franklin passage, what might one conclude about other literature being written in American in the 1770s?
   A. It included long and intricate novels.
   B. It included stories about very wealthy people who did not have to work.
   C. It included poetry about the beauty of many colonists' homeland, England.
   D. It included straightforward writing that gave advice.

12. The two excerpts above come from very different cultures. In comparison to Franklin's culture, what seems to be true about the culture from which the Navajo legend comes?
    A. It seems to be more concerned with material possessions.
    B. It seems to be not worried about using time wisely.
    C. It seems to be more family-oriented.
    D. It seems to be more focused on spirituality.

from "An Account of an Experience with Discrimination" by Sojourner Truth

A few weeks ago I was in company with my friend Josephine S. Griffing, when the conductor of a streetcar refused to stop his car for me, although [I was] closely following Josephine and holding on to the iron rail. They dragged me a number of yards before she succeeded in stopping them. She reported the conductor to the president of the City Railway, who dismissed him at once, and told me to take the number of the car whenever I was mistreated by a conductor cr driver. On the 13th, I had occasion to go for necessities for the patients in the Freedmen's Hospital where I have been doing and advising for a number of months. I thought now I would get a ride without trouble as I was in company with another friend, Laura S. Haviland of Michigan. As I ascended the platform of the car, the conductor pushed me, saying, "Go back—get off here." I told him I was not going off, then "I'll put you off," said he furiously, clenching my right arm with both hands, using such violence that he seemed about to succeed, when Mrs. Haviland told him he was not going to put me off. "Does she belong to you?" said he in a hurried, angry tone. She replied, "She does not belong to me, but she belongs to humanity." The number of the car was noted, and the conductor dismissed at once upon the report to the president, who advised his arrest for assault and battery as my shoulder was sprained by his effort to put me off. Accordingly I had him arrested and the case tried before Justice Thompson. My shoulder was very lame and swollen, but it is better. It is hard for the old slaveholding spirit to die. But die it must....

13. This passage addresses which theme found repeatedly in American literature?
    A. People use public transportation.
    B. Women must run family errands.
    C. Respect is important to each individual.
    D. Conductors often do not follow the rules.

14. Based on the information in this passage, what can you conclude?
    A. Racism was unacceptable, although some people resisted changing their ways.
    B. Racism was acceptable among railway conductors.
    C. Racism was acceptable to Mrs. Haviland.
    D. Racism was unacceptable but went unpunished.

15. Truth ends her essay with "It is hard for the old slaveholding spirit to die. But die it must." Which of the following statements **best** expresses what she means?
    A. She is uncomfortable expressing her opinion.
    B. Some people struggle to let go of the past.
    C. She wants people to know how much she suffered as a slave.
    D. Slavery is going to make a comeback.

from John F. Kennedy's 1961 Inaugural Address

...The world is very different now. For man holds in his mortal hand the power to abolish all forms of human poverty and all forms of human life. And yet the same revolutionary beliefs for which our forebears fought are still at issue around the globe—the belief that the rights of man come not from the generosity of the state, but from the hand of God.

We dare not forget today that we are the heirs of that first revolution. Let the word go forth from this time and place, to friend and foe alike, that the torch has been passed to a new generation of Americans—born in this century, tempered by war, disciplined by a hard and bitter peace, proud of our ancient heritage—and unwilling to permit or witness the slow undoing of those human rights to which this Nation has always been committed, and to which we are committed today at home and around the world....

16. Which of the following passages demonstrates President Kennedy's intent to show respect for both younger and older Americans?
    A. "the torch has been passed to a new generation of Americans"
    B. "We dare not forget today that we are the heirs of that first revolution."
    C. "born in this century, tempered by war, disciplined by a hard and bitter peace"
    D. all of the above

17. In the first paragraph of the passage, what concept does the author address?
    A. justifiable war
    B. economics
    C. social classes
    D. democracy

Steps for Applying for Summer Work at Ellen's Day Care Center

1. Complete and return application form to Ellen's Day Care Center weekdays between noon and 5:00 P.M.

2. If you are called for an interview, bring proof that you are at least eighteen years old and two letters of recommendation from non-relatives.

3. If you are called back for a second interview, you must submit a medical form completed by your family doctor that shows you have had a recent physical examination.

4. If hired, you must be able to work every weekday between June 1 and August 20.

18. Riley has been called for a first interview. In addition to the two letters, what should she bring?
    A. her Social Security card
    B. her most recent report card
    C. her driver's license
    D. her completed medical form

19. Aiden would like to apply for a job at Ellen's for the summer. However, he and his family will travel to California for five days in July. What should he do?
    A. Tell his supervisor about his vacation on the first day of work.
    B. State in his application that if hired, he will need to be excused for a few days in July.
    C. Say nothing about his vacation because it is too early to mention it.
    D. Wait until he is called for an interview before mentioning the vacation.

"A Winter Idyll," from "Snowbound" by John Greenleaf Whittier

The sun that brief December day
Rose cheerless over hills of gray,
And, darkly circled, gave at noon
A sadder light than waning moon.
5 Slow tracing down the thickening sky
Its mute and ominous prophecy,

A portent seeming less than threat,
It sank from sight before it set.
A chill no coat, however stout,
10 Of homespun stuff could quite shut out,
A hard, dull bitterness of cold,
That checked, mid-vein, the circling race
Of lifeblood in the sharpened face,
The coming of the snowstorm told.
15 The wind blew east; we heard the roar
Of Ocean on his wintry shore,
And felt the strong pulse throbbing there
Beat with low rhythm our inland air.

20. The first two lines of the second stanza contain which of the following?

  A. iambic tetrameter   **C.** assonance

  B. alliteration   **D.** all of the above

21. Which of the following literary devices is *absent* from this excerpt from "Snowbound"?

  A. rhyme scheme   **C.** enjambment

  B. narrative   **D.** simile

Sympathy *by Paul Laurence Dunbar*

I know what the caged bird feels, alas!
When the sun is bright on the upland slopes;
When the wind stirs soft through the springing grass,
And the river flows like a stream of glass;
5 When the first bird sings and the first bud opens,
And the faint perfume from its chalice steals—
I know what the caged bird feels!
I know why the caged bird beats his wing
Till its blood is red on the cruel bars;
10 For he must fly back to his perch and cling
When he fain would be on the bough a-swing;
And a pain still throbs in the old, old scars
And they pulse again with a keener sting—
I know why he beats his wing!
15 I know why the caged bird sings, ah me,
When his wing is bruised and his bosom sore,—
When he beats his bars and he would be free;
It is not a carol of joy or glee,

But a prayer that he sends from his heart's deep core,
20 But a plea, that upward to Heaven he flings—
I know why the caged bird sings!

22. What is the poet describing in line 5, "When the first bird sings and the first bud opens"?
   A. the first birds and flowers in existence
   B. the sounds and sights of morning
   C. the other birds in the cages
   D. the first signs of spring

23. What is the main idea of this poem?
   A. All creatures want to be free.
   B. Birds are often injured while in their cages.
   C. Birds should not be kept in cages.
   D. Birds should be let out of their cages for a short time every day.

24. What is the speaker feeling?
   A. He is happy because spring is coming.
   B. He wants more freedom.
   C. He is upset because the bird is injured.
   D. He feels smart because he understands the bird.

25. Which of the following relationships is most similar to the following relationship?
   Bird : Cage

   A. Driver : Car
   B. Customer : Restaurant
   C. Swimmer : Pool
   D. Prisoner : Jail

26. How is the Whittier poem similar to the Laurence poem?
   A. Both describe images found in nature.
   B. Both use the same rhyme scheme.
   C. Both use dialogue.
   D. Both use hyperbole.

from *My Bondage and My Freedom* by Frederick Douglass

Mrs. Auld was an apt woman, and the advice of her husband, and her own experience, soon demonstrated, to her entire satisfaction, that education and slavery are **incompatible** with each other. When this **conviction** was thoroughly established, I was most **narrowly** watched in all my movements. If I remained in a separate room from the family for any **considerable** length of time, I was sure to be suspected of having a book, and was at once called upon to give an account of myself. All this, however, was entirely too late. The first, and never to be **retraced**, step had been taken.

27. In this passage, what does the word *incompatible* mean?

    A. intertwined

    B. comfortable

    C. in conflict

    D. unreliable

28. In this passage, what is the part of speech and meaning of the word *narrowly*?

    A. an adverb meaning closely

    B. an adjective meaning violently

    C. a verb meaning examined

    D. an adverb meaning enviously

29. What is the meaning of the word *retraced*?

    A. refused

    B. drawn again

    C. drawn before

    D. annexed

30. According to the meanings of the words in this passage, which of the following words **best** completes this analogy?

    conviction is to _____ as *considerable* is to *extended*

    A. punishment

    B. history

    C. persuasive

    D. belief

Practice Test 2

Read the following passages. Then answer the questions that follow.

from Act 1 of *The Crucible* by Arthur Miller

Enter MERCY LEWIS, *the Putnams' servant, a fat, sly, merciless girl of eighteen.*
MERCY: Your pardons. I only thought to see how Betty is.
PUTNAM: Why aren't you home? Who's with Ruth?
MERCY: Her grandma come. She's improved a little, I think—she give a powerful sneeze before.
MRS. PUTNAM: Ah, there's a sign of life!
MERCY: I'd fear no more, Goody Putnam. It were a grand sneeze; another like it will shake her wits
together, I'm sure. *She goes to the bed to look.*
PARRIS: Will you leave me now, Thomas? I would pray a while alone.

1. How does Miller show that Mercy is a servant?
   - A. Directions tell her where to move on the stage.
   - B. Her language is less refined than the others' language.
   - C. She enters the room while others are already there.
   - D. The others ask her questions.

Enter MERCY LEWIS, *the Putnams' servant, a fat, sly eighteen-year-old.*
MERCY: I'm sorry to interrupt. I just wanted to check on Betty.
PUTNAM: Why aren't you home? Who's with Ruth?
MERCY: Her grandma. She's improved a little, I think. She sneezed violently before.
MRS. PUTNAM: That's a good sign.
MERCY: I wouldn't worry about her anymore, Mrs. Putnam. I don't know if she can handle another
sneeze like that. *She goes to the bed to look.*
PARRIS: Will you leave me now, Thomas? I'd like to be alone and pray for a while.

2. Which of the following **best** describes the effect of this revised version of the Miller passage?
   - A. It seems more old-fashioned.
   - B. It seems more brutal.
   - C. It seems more contemporary.
   - D. It seems more serious.

3. Which of the following is true about this revision?
   - A. Putnam seems more demanding.
   - B. Parris seems more religious.
   - C. Mrs. Putnam seems more worried.
   - D. Mercy seems more refined.

Suppose that you have been assigned to write a persuasive essay about why you think students should
be allowed to send and receive e-mail from the computers in the school's computer lab. Answer the
following questions.

4. Before you begin writing, you should do which of the following?
   - A. Brainstorm ideas.

    B. Compile a works cited list.

    C. Figure out what will appear in your conclusion.

    D. Ask your friends what their essay topics are.

5. What should be the focus of your essay?

    A. Students should be allowed to talk on cell phones during class.

    B. Students should be allowed to listen to headphones in school.

    C. Students should be allowed to access e-mail during the school day.

    D. Students should be allowed to download music on school computers.

6. Which of the following would be the **least** helpful information for writing this essay?

    A. current school rules for the computer lab

    B. quotes from administrators in other schools that allow students e-mail access

    C. statistics about students' reasons for using e-mail

    D. the amount the average family spends each year on computers and Internet access

7. How should your essay be organized?

    A. according to the order in which the ideas came to you during brainstorming sessions

    B. introduction, body, conclusion

    C. a progression from minor details to more important details

    D. conclusion, body, introduction

8. Which of the following would be the **most** clear and accurate main idea for the essay?

    A. Students should be able to study in school computer labs.

    B. It is important to be able to receive e-mail each school day.

    C. Students should be able to check their e-mail from school computer labs.

    D. Students should have access to word-processing programs during the school day.

9. Which of the following describes the **most** appropriate content, vocabulary, and tone for your essay?

    A. convincing and knowledgeable

    B. informal and humorous

    C. forceful and demanding

    D. vague and disinterested

10. After you have completed your draft, you should do which of the following?

    A. Make sure that all details support your main idea.

    B. Revise unclear or inaccurate passages.

    C. Check that you have used the correct format (spacing, margins, title, etc.).

    D. all of the above

Answer the following questions.

11. What is the purpose of proofreading?

    A. to show readers that you really wrote the essay

    B. to catch and correct any spelling or grammatical errors

    C. to make sure that your argument is correct

    D. to prove that you have read all research sources cited in the essay

12. Which of the following parenthetical citations adheres to MLA style?

    A. "Asserting one's identity is an important theme in American literature." (Savage 19).

    B. "Asserting one's identity is an important theme in American literature (Savage 19)."

    C. "Asserting one's identity is an important theme in American literature." (Savage 19)."

    D. "Asserting one's identity is an important theme in American literature" (Savage 19).

13. Which of the following statements is worded **most** clearly?

    A. When a person runs, he or she burns more calories than when a person sits on a couch.

    B. When a person runs, he or she burns more calories than a person who is sitting on a couch.

    C. Running burns more calories than sitting on a couch.

    D. A person sitting on a couch does not burn as many calories as a runner.

14. When you adapt a research essay you have written in order to present it as a speech, which of the following is it **unnecessary** to do?

    A. Write your most important points on note cards.

    B. Adjust vocabulary and tone, if necessary, for your audience.

    C. Print the essay in a larger type size so that you can read it aloud more easily.

    D. Plan to review ideas as you speak to help the audience remember your points.

Suppose that Ruth, a college sophomore who studies art history, would like to be considered for a summer internship in Paris. She must write a letter to accompany her application. Answer the following questions.

15. Before Ruth begins writing her letter, she should do which of the following?

    A. Jot down a list of points she would like to make in the letter.

    B. Call to find out exactly what the purpose of the letter should be.

    C. Review her application so she knows what points she should emphasize.

    D. all of the above

16. Ruth should make sure that her letter includes which of the following?

    A. her name, address, and phone number

    B. the name of her favorite artist

    C. a list of places in Paris she intends to visit

    D. all of the information found in her application

17. How should Ruth organize the information in her letter?

    A. from most to least important because the recipient may have time only to skim it

    B. from least to most important because this will build interest

    C. in no particular order so that the writing appears natural

    D. in chronological order

18. Choose the statement that is worded **most** clearly.

    A. I hope to be accepted to the program that offers internships in Paris.

    B. I hope the program that offers internships in Paris accepts my application.

    C. I hope to be accepted into the Paris internship program.

    D. In Paris, I hope to be accepted into the internship program.

19. In what final form should Ruth's letter appear?

    A. handwritten to appear more personal

    B. word-processed to appear more professional

    C. word-processed in a font that looks like handwriting

    D. handwritten to show Ruth's confidence in her penmanship and spelling skills

Suppose that you have been assigned to write a research essay about why you believe drivers below the age of eighteen should be allowed to operate vehicles between midnight and 4:00 A.M. with no restrictions. Answer the following questions.

20. In conducting your research, which of the following should be the **primary** focus?

    A. information about the history of traffic laws

    B. information that explains how to get a driver's license in North Carolina

    C. information about young drivers

    D. information that shows how other states' laws are the same as or different from North Carolina's

21. Which of the following sources would provide reliable information?

    A. books   C. government Web sites

    B. articles in periodicals   D. all of the above

22. After you have found a sufficient number of research sources, you should compose a thesis. Which of the following **best** describes a good thesis?

    A. It is one that echoes the ideas of your best source.

    B. It is one with which your teacher will agree.

    C. It is one that will take you the least amount of space to develop.

    D. It is one that can be supported by several sources.

23. Who are **most** likely to be the writers of worthwhile sources for your topic?

    A. teens who are mature enough to drive after midnight

    B. experts on motor vehicle safety

    C. people who work for automobile manufacturers

    D. people who have been in car accidents involving teenage drivers

24. For what reason should you use information from sources?

    A. to fill space

    B. to present a viewpoint that contradicts your own

    C. to support your points

    D. to help create the structure of your essay

25. Choose the correct format for a book that appears on the Works Cited page of your essay.

    A. David Kendall. *Responsible Teen Drivers*. New York: Goode Publishing Company, 2004.

B. Kendall, David. *Responsible Teen Drivers*. New York: Goode Publishing Company, 2004.

C. *Responsible Teen Drivers*. Kendall, David. New York: Goode Publishing Company, 2004.

D. *Responsible Teen Drivers* by David Kendall. New York: Goode Publishing Company, 2004.

26. Choose the statement that demonstrates the ***most*** clear and effective wording.
   A. People, below the age of eighteen, who are drivers, are responsible.
   B. People who are below eighteen years old drive and are responsible.
   C. Drivers below the age of eighteen are responsible.
   D. Drivers, responsible, are below the age of eighteen.

27. Choose the sentence that is grammatically correct.
   A. Accidents happen at all hours of the day or night, keeping young drivers off the road at night does not help them.
   B. Accidents happen at all hours of the day or night; keeping young drivers off the road at night does not help them.
   C. Accidents happen at all hours of the day or night keeping young drivers off the road at night does not help them.
   D. Accidents happen at all hours of the day or night. Keeping young drivers off the road at night. Does not help them.

Writing Prompt 1

What is the most important thing about the young people who live in your community that you would like people from other parts of North Carolina to know? Identify an experience or event from the past that involved young people in your community in some significant way. Write an essay in which you relate and discuss this experience so that people in another part of the state may understand an important quality or characteristic of your community's young people. Be sure that your descriptions and details support your main idea.

Writing Prompt 2

Think about a piece of writing that is special to you. It could be a novel, a short story, a play, a poem, a biography, or another work of nonfiction. Why is this literary work important to you? In what ways does the text relate to your own experiences in life? What cultural or historical significance does this piece of writing possess? Write an essay in which you explain the importance of the work to your life and suggest how it might relate to others' lives. Use examples and details from the text to support your ideas.

SAT/ACT PRACTICE TEST

CRITICAL READING
Section 1: Sentence Completion

Each sentence below has one or two blanks, each blank indicating that something has been omitted. Beneath the sentence are five words or sets of words labeled A through E. Choose the word or set of words that, when inserted in the sentence, best fits the meaning of the sentence as a whole.

Example:

My sister and I ---- and then didn't speak for days.

(A) reconciled

(B) quarreled

(C) scourged

(D) reiterated

(E) submitted

1. She hoped that her decision not to vote for Roberto would not ---- her friends.

(A) enchant

(B) entice

(C) allude

(D) alienate

(E) relieve

2. The children held a ---- meeting to plan their parents' anniversary party.

(A) clandestine

(B) national

(C) boisterous

(D) fastidious

(E) extenuating

3. Jim is the ---- one, always concerned with what is ----.

(A) pragmatic. .practical

(B) irresponsible. .meaningful

(C) extravagant. .affordable

(D) ostentatious. .worthwhile

(E) careful. .thrilling

4. My dignified grandmother taught me to be ---- to my elders.

(A) repugnant

(B) cheerful

(C) respectful

(D) somber

(E) sympathetic

5. Although staying in the hospital is not ----, visits from friends and family make it ----.

(A) understandable. .enjoyable

(B) reproachful. .endurable

(C) whimsical. .encouraging

(D) pleasant. .tolerable

(E) enjoyable. .superficial

6. Much to my ----, my daughter traveled to Italy alone.

(A) desire

(B) fascination

(C) hindrance

(D) chagrin

(E) harangue

7. Tyler is a very ---- child who never seems to stop talking.

(A) gregarious

(B) serene

(C) tranquil

(D) hypocritical

(E) timid

8. Without its shell, a turtle is very ----.

(A) brawny

(B) vulnerable

(C) irate

(D) visible

(E) shielded

9. His bills in ---- were more than he could pay.

(A) circumspection

(B) classification

(C) generalization

(D) aggregate

(E) forbearance

10. Even though I dislike most seafood, I found lobster to be quite ----.

(A) revolting

(B) atrocious

(C) opportune

(D) mediocre

(E) palatable

11. Rachel thought the online history course was a(n) ----, a solution to all her problems.

(A) allegiance

(B) panacea

(C) complexity

(D) opportunity

(E) amendment

12. Because the sidewalks were icy, the police report said the building's owner had been ----.

(A) negligent

(B) virtuous

(C) agreeable

(D) salacious

(E) parsimonious

13. I ---- my niece Kelly, the most ---- little girl in the world.

(A) detest. .kind

(B) chastise. .conscientious

(C) adore. .amiable

(D) abhor. .comely

(E) dislike. .enchanting

Name _____ Date _____

Section 2 : Reading Comprehesion

Questions 14–19 are based on the following passage.

In "The Diamond Lens," Fitz-James O'Brien describes a memorable event from his youth. He is given a hand-made microscope which is soon replaced by a real one. O'Brien recalls how this microscope helped him to pick his profession.

1. From a very early period of my life the entire bent of my inclinations had been toward microscopic investigations. When I was not more than ten years old, a distant relative of our family, hoping to astonish my inexperience, constructed a simple microscope for me by drilling in a disk of copper a small hole in which a drop of pure water was sustained by capillary attraction. This very primitive apparatus, magnifying some fifty diameters, presented, it is true, only indistinct and imperfect forms, but still sufficiently wonderful to work up my imagination to a preternatural state of excitement.

2. Seeing me so interested in this rude instrument, my cousin explained to me all that he knew about the principles of the microscope, related to me a few of the wonders which had been accomplished through its agency, and ended by promising to send me one regularly constructed, immediately on his return to the city. I counted the days, the hours, the minutes` that intervened between that promise and his departure.

3. At last the promised instrument came. It was of that order known as Field's simple microscope, and had cost perhaps about fifteen dollars. As far as educational purposes went, a better apparatus could not have been selected. Accompanying it was a small treatise on the microscope—its history, uses, and discoveries. The dull veil of ordinary existence that hung across the world seemed suddenly to roll away, and to lay bare a land of enchantments. I felt toward my companions as the seer might feel toward the ordinary masses of men. I held conversations with nature in a tongue which

they could not understand. I was in daily communication with living wonders such as they never imagined in their wildest visions, I penetrated beyond the external portal of things, and roamed through the sanctuaries. Where they beheld only a drop of rain slowly rolling down the window-glass, I saw a universe of beings animated with all the passions common to physical life, and convulsing their minute sphere with struggles as fierce and protracted as those of men.

4. It was no scientific thirst that at this time filled my mind. It was the pure enjoyment of a poet to whom a world of wonders has been disclosed. I talked of my solitary pleasures to none. Alone with my microscope, I dimmed my sight, day after day and night after night, poring over the marvels which it unfolded to me.

5. As I grew up, my parents, who saw but little likelihood of anything practical resulting from the examination of bits of moss and drops of water through a brass tube and a piece of glass, were anxious that I should choose a profession.

6. After much cogitation, I complied with the wishes of my family, and selected a profession. I determined to study medicine at the New York Academy. It was with the most buoyant hope that I left my New England home and established myself in New York.

14. Why did a distant relative give the author a microscope?

A. The author asks for a microscope.

B. The relative does not want the microscope any more.

C. The relative feels sorry for the author.

D. The relative wants to amaze the author.

E. The author's parents asked the relative to get the microscope.

15. Based on the context, which of the following does not describe what the author thinks about the microscope?

A. Wonderful

B. Brought much enjoyment

C. Very educational

D. Allowed him to see more of nature

E. Difficult to use

16. In paragraph 5, what does the author mean when he says "It was the pure enjoyment of a poet to whom a world of wonders has been disclosed"?

A. Like a poet, the author sees beyond the ordinary when he uses the microscope.

B. He enjoys poetry.

C. When he writes poetry, the author speaks of what he has seen under the microscope.

D. Poetry that the author reads helps him understand more fully the wonders under the microscope.

E. All of the above.

17. Which of the following best describes the author's way of expressing himself?

A. He uses exaggeration to let the reader know that he is relating a fantasy

B. He relates events without using emotion

C. He uses persuasive language to convince the reader of the importance of owning a microscope.

D. He uses a simple childhood event to illustrate how it helped him make an important decision.

E. He informs the reader of how to use a microscope.

18. The author's parents saw little value in their son's use of the microscope. Which of the following statements best describes what the author does to please both himself and his parents?

A. He chooses to study medicine at New York Academy.

B. He stops writing poetry, but continues to work with the microscope.

C. He gives up using the microscope and goes to college.

D. He continues microscopic investigations, and does not go to college.

E. A and C

19. Based on the context of paragraph 6, what does the word "cogitation" mean?

A. arguing

B. conversation

C. serious thought

D. daydreaming

E. resting

Questions 20–26 are based on the following passage.

This selection is from the inaugural address of the 35th president of the United States, John F. Kennedy.

The world is very different now. For man holds in his mortal hands the power to abolish all forms of human
Line poverty and all forms of human life.
(5) And yet the same revolutionary beliefs for which our forebears fought are still at issue around the globe—the belief that the rights of man come not from the generosity of the state, but
(10) from the hand of God.

We dare not forget today that we are the heirs of that first revolution. Let the word go forth from this time and place, to friend and foe alike, that
(15) the torch has been passed to a new generation of Americans—born in this century, tempered by war, disciplined by a hard and bitter peace, proud of our ancient heritage—and unwilling
(20) to witness or permit the slow undoing of those human rights to which . . . we are committed today at home and around the world.

Let every nation know, whether it
(25) wishes us well or ill, that we shall pay any price, bear any burden, meet any hardship, support any friend, oppose any foe, in order to assure the survival and the success of liberty.

(30) This much we pledge—and more.

To those old allies whose cultural and spiritual origins we share, we pledge the loyalty of faithful friends. United, there is little we cannot do in
(35) a host of cooperative ventures. Divided, there is little we can do—for we dare not meet a powerful challenge at odds and split asunder.

To those new States whom we
(40) welcome to the ranks of the free, we pledge our word that one form of colonial control shall not have passed away merely to be replaced by a far

more iron tyranny. We shall not
(45) always expect to find them supporting our view. But we shall always hope to find them strongly supporting their own freedom—and to remember that, in the past, those who foolishly
(50) sought power by riding the back of the tiger ended up inside.

To those people in the huts and villages across the globe struggling to break the bonds of mass misery, we
(55) pledge our best efforts to help them help themselves, for whatever period is required—not because the Communists may be doing it, not because we seek their votes, but
(60) because it is right. If a free society cannot help the many who are poor, it cannot save the few who are rich.

To our sister republics south of our border, we offer a special pledge—to
(65) convert our good words into good deeds—in a new alliance for progress—to assist free men and free governments in casting off the chains of poverty. But this peaceful
(70) revolution of hope cannot become the prey of hostile powers. Let all our neighbors know that we shall join with them to oppose aggression or subversion anywhere in the Americas.
(75) And let every other power know that this Hemisphere intends to remain the master of its own house.

20. According to the passage, the rights of man ultimately come from

(A) the generosity of the state

(B) our home and work place

(C) the Americas

(D) the hand of God

(E) our forbears

21. You can tell from the context of this passage that "tyranny" (line 44) *probably* means

(A) democracy

(B) oppressive government

(C) kingdom

(D) underworld nation

(E) business

22. Which of the following *best* paraphrases the statement ". . . those who foolishly sought power by riding the back of the tiger ended up inside" in lines 49–51?

(A) Those who are not strong and independent may be conquered.

(B) Kindness never prevails.

(C) Kindness usually prevails over cruelty.

(D) The educated usually dominate the uneducated.

(E) Those who take advantage of others are often destroyed.

23. The phrase "remain the master of its own house" in lines 76–77 *probably* means

(A) submit to dominance

(B) be independent

(C) conquer by war

(D) become powerful and dominant

(E) rule by force

24. The author addresses all of the following directly in this passage EXCEPT

(A) old allies

(B) new States

(C) sister republics

(D) wealthy Americans

(E) friends and foes

25. Which of the following *best* paraphrases the main idea of the third paragraph?

(A) We will do what it takes to ensure liberty.

(B) We will support all friends.

(C) We will oppose all foes.

(D) We can accomplish anything if we stand united.

(E) We will try to understand our enemies.

26. You can tell from the context that "subversion" (line 74) *probably* means

(A) impression

(B) submission

(C) sabotage

(D) confinement

(E) diversification

Questions 27–31 are based on the following passage.

This selection is from Journal of the First Voyage to America *by Christopher Columbus. Columbus's purpose in writing the journal was to impress Spain's king and queen, who were financing his expedition and expecting a return on their investment.*

Sunday, Oct. 21st [1492]. At 10 o'clock, we arrived at a cape of the island, and anchored, the other vessels
Line in company. After having dispatched a
(5) meal, I went ashore, and found no habitation save a single house, and that without an occupant; we had no doubt that the people had fled in terror at our approach, as the house was
(10) completely furnished. I suffered nothing to be touched, and went with my captains and some of the crew to view the country. This island even exceeds the others in beauty and
(15) fertility. Groves of lofty and flourishing trees are abundant, as also large lakes, surrounded and overhung by the foliage, in a most enchanting manner. Everything looked as green as in April
(20) in Andalusia. The melody of the birds was so exquisite that one was never willing to part from the spot, and the flocks of parrots obscured the heavens. The diversity in the appearance of the
(25) feathered tribe from those of our country is extremely curious. A thousand different sorts of trees, with their fruit were to be met with, and of a wonderfully delicious odor. It was a
(30) great affliction to me to be ignorant of their natures, for I am very certain they are all valuable; specimens of them and of the plants I have preserved. Going round one of these lakes, I saw a
(35) snake, which we killed, and I have kept the skin for your Highnesses; upon being discovered he took to the water, whither we followed him, as it was not deep, and dispatched him with our
(40) lances; he was seven spans in length; I think there are many more such about here. I discovered also the aloe tree, and am determined to take on board the ship tomorrow, ten quintals of it, as

(45) I am told it is valuable. While we were in search of some good water we came upon a village of the natives about half a league from the place where the ships lay; the inhabitants on discovering us
(50) abandoned their houses, and took to flight, carrying off their goods to the mountain. I ordered that nothing which they had left should be taken, not even the value of a pin. Presently we saw
(55) several of the natives advancing towards our party, and one of them came up to us, to whom we gave some hawk's bells and glass beads, with which he was delighted. We asked him
(60) in return, for water, and after I had gone on board the ship, the natives came down to the shore with their calabashes full, and showed great pleasure in presenting us with it. I
(65) ordered more glass beads to be given them, and they promised to return the next day. It is my wish to fill all the water casks of the ships at this place, which being executed, I shall depart
(70) immediately, if the weather serve, and sail round the island, till I succeed in meeting with the king, in order to see if I can acquire any of the gold, which I hear he possesses. Afterwards I shall
(75) set sail for another very large island which I believe to be *Cipango*, according to the indications I receive from the Indians on board. They call the Island *Colba*, and say there are
(80) many large ships, and sailors there. This other island they name *Bosio* and inform me that it is very large; the others which lie in our course, I shall examine on the passage, and according
(85) as I find gold or spices in abundance, I shall determine what to do; at all events I am determined to proceed on to the continent, and visit the city of Guisay where I shall deliver the letters
(90) of your Highnesses to the *Great Can*, and demand an answer, with which I shall return.

27. You can tell from the context of the passage that "exquisite" (line 21) means

(A) painful

(B) beautiful

(C) quiet

(D) obnoxious

(E) fleeting

28. Columbus *probably* relates the story of capturing and skinning the snake (lines 34–42) to

(A) increase general interest in the area

(B) encourage his financers to give him more money

(C) record possible threats for others who might explore the area

(D) make his journey seem dangerous and exciting

(E) discourage future explorations of the area

29. On the basis of the passage's details, you can tell that Columbus finds the area to be

(A) interesting yet of little value

(B) unusual and troubling

(C) barren and difficult to navigate

(D) intriguing yet full of danger

(E) beautiful and potentially valuable

30. The actions of Columbus and his men in lines 10–11 and 52–54 indicate that they

(A) respect the natives

(B) are afraid of the natives

(C) dislike the natives

(D) have little interest in the natives

(E) believe that the natives will hurt them

31. Which of the following is the *best* explanation for Columbus referencing the value of things?

(A) He wants to show the breadth of knowledge that he possesses.

(B) He wants to convince the king and queen that he is a capable leader.

(C) He wants his investors to send him to a different part of the world.

(D) He wants to inspire other explorers to come to the area.

(E) He wants to keep the interest of his financial supporters.

Direction: *The two passages below is followed by questions based on its content Answer the questions on the basis of what is stated or implied in each passage and in any introduction material that may be provided*

Questions 32–38 are based on the following passage.

In the following passage, John, the son of a farmer in Wisconsin, is describing how farming is so difficult and how at young age he was plowing the fields.

Passage 1

Many of our old neighbors toiled and sweated and grubbed themselves into their graves years before their natural dying days, in getting a living on a quarter-section of land and vaguely trying to get rich.

I was put to the plough at the age of twelve, when my head reached but little above the handles, and for many years I had to do the greater part of the ploughing. It was hard work for so small a boy; nevertheless, as good ploughing was exacted from me as if I were a man, and very soon I had to become a good ploughman, or rather ploughboy. None could draw a straighter furrow. For the first few years the work was particularly hard on account of the tree-stumps that had to be dodged. Later the stumps were all dug and chopped out to make way for the McCormick reaper, and because I proved to be the best chopper and stump-digger I had nearly all of it to myself. It was dull, hard work leaning over on my knees all day, chopping out those tough oak and hickory stumps, deep down below the crowns of the big roots. Some, though fortunately not many, were two feet or more in diameter.

Passage 2

from *Up From Slavery: An Autobiography* by Booker T. Washington

The opening of the school in the Kanawha Valley, however, brought to me one of the keenest disappointments that I ever experienced. I had been working in a salt-furnace for several months, and my stepfather had discovered that I had a financial value, and so, when the school opened, he decided that he could not spare me from my work. This decision seemed to cloud my every ambition. The disappointment was made all the more severe by reason of the fact that my place of work was where I could see the happy children passing to and from school mornings and afternoons. Despite this disappointment, however, I determined that I would learn something, anyway. I applied myself with greater earnestness than ever to the mastering of what was in the "blue-back" speller.

My mother sympathized with me in my disappointment, and sought to comfort me in all the ways she could, and to help me find a way to learn. After a while I succeeded in making arrangements with the teacher to give me some lessons at night, after the day's work was done. These night lessons were so welcome that I think I learned more at night than the other children did during the day. My own experiences in the night-school gave me faith in the night-school idea, with which, in after years, I had to do both at Hampton and Tuskegee. But my boyish heart was still set upon going to the day-school, and I let no opportunity slip to push my case. Finally I won, and was permitted to go to the school in the day for a few months, with the understanding that I was to rise early in the morning and work in the furnace till nine o'clock, and return immediately after school closed in the afternoon for at least two more hours of work.

32. Based on the context of part 1, why *most likely* did John do the ploughing?

   A. He does not want to go to school.

   B. He is trying to get rich before leaving home.

   C. He is strong enough to work, and his help was needed

   D. His father died at an early age.

   E. All of the above.

33. According to part 1, what *most likely* was the reason that farming was so difficult?

A. Many farmers could not afford a plough.

B. The land has many tree stumps that had to be removed.

C. In many families the men die at early ages.

D. Often the ploughs are too large for the ploughboy.

E. The farmers could not afford to hire men to help on the farm.

34. Based on the context of part 1, what is the meaning of the word *toiled*?

A. worked strenuously

B. chopped stumps

C. became injured

D. grunted

E. gave up

35. Based on the context of paragraph 1 in Part 2, what is the meaning of the word *keenest*?

A. unimportant

B. most intense, sharpest

C. saddest.

D. most unfair.

E. first

36. What was the main conflict in Part 2?

A. The author's desire to go to school versus his step-father's need for the author's financial help

B. The author's decision to go to day school or night school

C. The workers in the salt furnace versus the students

D. The conflict between the author's mother and step-father concerning the author's education

37. What is the literary point of view in both of these passages?

A. A third-person narrator describes the thoughts of a few characters.

B. A second-person narrator describes the thoughts and actions of the main character.

C. A third-person narrator describes the actions but not the thoughts of others

D. A first-person narrator describes all the thoughts and actions of others

E. A first-person narrator describes his own thoughts and actions.

38. In Part 2, what was the final decision made in regards to the author's education and job?

A. The author works early in the morning, goes to school, and then return to work.

B. The author goes to school a few months and then works a few months.

C. The author teaches himself.

D. The author works full-time and later on go to school.

E. The author works during the day and attends night school

Name _____ Date _____

The gods laid one buckskin on the ground with the head to the west: on this they placed the two ears of corn, with their tips to the east, and over the corn they spread the other buckskin with its head to the east. . . . Then they told the people to stand at a distance and allow the wind to enter. . . . Eight of the Mirage People came and walked around the objects on the ground. . . . When the Mirage People had finished their walk the upper buckskin was lifted; the ears of corn had disappeared, a man and a woman lay there in their stead.

—from *The Navajo Origin Legend,*
retold by Washington Matthews

39. On the basis of the information in the passage, you can conclude that Navajo legends

(A) recorded factual events in Navajo history

(B) contain little information about Navajo culture

(C) illustrate the fundamental beliefs of Navajo society

(D) were primarily used to entertain Navajo children

(E) show the value that the Navajo placed on material goods

40. What do the passage references to corn tell you about its importance to the Navajo?

(A) The Navajo never had enough corn.

(B) The Navajo viewed corn as a special treat.

(C) The Navajo placed great value on corn.

(D) The Navajo thought that corn came from the Mirage People.

(E) The Navajo relied on the wind to provide them with corn.

We wear the mask that grins and lies,
It hides our cheeks and shades our eyes—
This debt we pay to human guile;
With torn and bleeding hearts we smile,
And mouth with myriad subtleties.

Why should the world be overwise,
In counting all our tears and sighs?
Nay, let them only see us, while
      We wear the mask.

We smile, but, O great Christ, our cries
To thee from tortured souls arise.
We sing, but oh the clay is vile
Beneath our feet, and long the mile;
But let the world dream otherwise,
      We wear the mask!

—"We Wear the Mask,"
by Paul Laurence Dunbar

41. Which words *best* describe the speaker of the poem?

(A) angry, defiant

(B) vain, self-centered

(C) selfish, narrow-minded

(D) optimistic, energetic

(E) matter-of-fact, resigned

42. The people in this poem struggle against

(A) indifference

(B) pride

(C) gender equality

(D) prejudice

(E) loneliness

What do the text of a law and the minutes from a legislative meeting have in common? They are examples of public documents, official government papers that affect everyone living in a particular area of a state or nation. These documents are referred to as public because they concern laws and issues that all citizens have a stake in. For this reason, these documents are made available for average citizens to read, analyze, and discuss.

The Emancipation Proclamation is a public document from 1863. It signed into law President Abraham Lincoln's proclamation that "all persons held as slaves" within the rebellious Southern states were freed. Many historians believe that this public document altered the nature of the Civil War.

43. Why might it have been important for people to have access to the text of the Emancipation Proclamation?

   (A) People needed to understand the details of the law.

   (B) People needed relief from the Civil War.

   (C) People needed to feel close to their President.

   (D) People needed to have a say in their government.

   (E) People needed to know both sides of the slavery issue.

44. Which of the following is an example of a public document?

   (A) transcript of a network news program

   (B) United States census report

   (C) diary of a colonial American

   (D) brochure for a travel company

   (E) directions for assembling a bookcase

WRITING

Directions: *The sentences below contain errors in grammar, usage, word choice, and idiom. Parts of each sentence are underlined and lettered. Decide which underlined part contains the error, and mark its letter on your answer sheet. If the sentence is correct as it stands, mark (E) on your answer sheet. No sentence contains more than one error.*

45. The <u>son</u> of Jewish <u>immigrants</u> <u>Billy Joel</u>
        (A)   **(B)**   **(C)**
grew up in <u>Hicksville, New York</u>. <u>No error</u>
          (D)   **(E)**

46. Joel <u>fell in love</u> with <u>classical</u> music when
        (A)   **(B)**
he was four, <u>but</u> he soon <u>began</u> to take
         (C)   **(D)**
piano lessons. <u>No error</u>
          (E)

47. <u>When Joel was a child</u>, his engineer
      (A)
father <u>left</u> the family, forcing his mother
     (B)
to <u>raise</u> her two children on a <u>secretarys</u>
    (C)   **(D)**
salary. <u>No error</u>
     (E)

48. Although the family was <u>poor and didn't</u>
              (A)
<u>have much money</u>, Joel had a <u>rich cultural</u>
                    (B)
<u>life</u> learning to play the piano and
<u>going to classical concerts</u> with his
         (C)
<u>grandfather</u>. <u>No error</u>
    (D)   **(E)**

49. <u>He</u> also <u>box</u> and <u>spent</u> time with <u>friends</u>.
  (A)   **(B)**   **(C)**   **(D)**
<u>No error</u>
  (E)

50. Joel <u>began to dream</u> of becoming a
       (A)
professional musician <u>and playing</u>
             (B)
<u>professionally</u> <u>after</u> he saw the Beatles
  (C)
<u>perform</u> on *The Ed Sullivan Show*.
  (D)
<u>No error</u>
  (E)

51. <u>When</u> he <u>was</u> just fourteen, Joel <u>joined</u>
  (A)   **(B)**   **(C)**
his first band, <u>and it was called</u> The
           (D)
Echoes. <u>No error</u>
      (E)

52. <u>At the age of sixteen</u>, Joel became the
    (A)
<u>pianist</u> <u>at</u> a local band called the <u>Hassles</u>.
  (B)   **(C)**   **(D)**
<u>No error</u>
  (E)

53. He worked <u>a lot</u> of late nights, <u>earned</u>
         (A)   **(B)**
money <u>that</u> helped <u>his mother</u> pay the
    (C)   **(D)**
mortgage. <u>No error</u>
      (E)

54. Joel had trouble <u>and difficulty</u> balancing
           (A)
school and work, <u>and as a result</u> of his
          (B)
many <u>absences</u>, was <u>not able</u> to graduate
    (C)   **(D)**
with his class. <u>No error</u>
      (E)

55. <u>As</u> Joel tried to <u>break</u> into the music
   (A)   (B)

business, he <u>had</u> to work other jobs to
         (C)

make <u>end's meet</u>. <u>No error</u>
     (D)   (E)

56. He <u>reviews</u> music for a music magazine,
     (A)

<u>helped</u> paint a <u>country club</u>, and worked
 (B)   (C)

in a factory, <u>all while working on his</u>
            (D)

music. <u>No error</u>
    (E)

57. <u>In 1972</u>, Joel <u>signed</u> his <u>very first ever</u>
  (A)   (B)   (C)

<u>recording contract</u>. <u>No error</u>
  (D)   (E)

58. His first album <u>was</u> a failure, <u>and</u> his
       (A)   (B)

second album, released in 1973, was the

<u>hugely</u> <u>successful</u> *Piano Man*. <u>No error</u>
 (C)   (D)   (E)

59. <u>Hit song after hit song</u> has followed, <u>yet</u>
  (A)   (B)

Joel warns people against <u>assessing</u> him
          (C)

as a "pop meister who just <u>churns out</u>
           (D)

these hit singles." <u>No error</u>
       (E)

60. <u>Unlike</u> many pop artists, Joel <u>have</u>
  (A)   (B)

tackled a <u>range of social issues</u> from
    (C)

unemployment to the legacy of the

<u>Vietnam War</u>. <u>No error</u>
  (D)   (E)

61. In the late <u>1980s</u>, Joel toured Russia,
     (A)

playing songs <u>what</u> <u>emphasized</u>
     (B)   (C)

similarities <u>between</u> people despite
    (D)

political divisions. <u>No error</u>
       (E)

62. <u>More recently</u> he has <u>lectured</u> at colleges
  (A)   (B)

to help young <u>musicians</u> learn from his
     (C)

<u>experiences</u>. <u>No error</u>
 (D)   (E)

63. <u>Even though</u> Billy Joel has won some of
  (A)

the world's <u>mostly</u> <u>prestigious</u> music
   (B)   (C)

awards, he <u>continues</u> to write and
    (D)

produce new music. <u>No error</u>
      (E)

64. <u>Who</u> knows <u>what</u> he <u>will surprise</u> us <u>by</u>
 (A)   (B)   (C)   (D)
next? <u>No error</u>
   (E)

Directions: *The sentences below contain problems in grammar, sentence construction, word choice, and punctuation. Part or all of each sentence is underlined. Select the lettered answer that contains the best version of the underlined section. Answer (A) always repeats the original underlined section exactly. If the sentence is correct as it stands, select (A).*

65. Looking to the future is a natural part of the human **experience, much** of the technology that has become widespread since 1945—television and computers in particular—shows us a brighter future.

   (A) experience, much

   (B) experience—much

   (C) experience; much

   (D) experience. Much

   (E) experience much

66. The new technology does make life **more easy and more pleasant.**

   (A) more easy and more pleasant.

   (B) more easy and pleasant.

   (C) more easy and pleasanter.

   (D) more easier and pleasant.

   (E) easier and more pleasant.

67. Paradoxically, it also introduces complexities **that had been unknown** in earlier days.

   (A) that had been unknown

   (B) which was unknown

   (C) that was unknown

   (D) which were unknown

   (E) that were unknown

68. The years from the end of World War II to the present day **have been** a time of change.

   (A) have been

   (B) has been

   (C) will have been

   (D) is

   (E) are

69. Great strides have been made in civil rights and **woman's rights**.

   (A) woman's rights.

   (B) woman rights.

   (C) women rights.

   (D) women's rights.

   (E) womans' rights.

70. Popular entertainment **has changed dramatically**, not just in presentation (from radio to television, from phonographs to CDs).

   (A) has changed dramatically,

   (B) has changed dramatic,

   (C) has changed drama,

   (D) is dramatic,

   (E) is drama,

71. These changes and others have had **an affect** on American literature.

   (A) an affect

   (B) an effect

   (C) a affect

   (D) affects

   (E) affect

72. Their effect seems somehow less dramatic than the changes themselves, **although**.

   (A) although.

   (B) consequently.

   (C) however.

   (D) even though.

   (E) subsequently.

73. After World War II, Americans wanted life to return **back to normal**.

   (A) back to normal.

   (B) at normality.

   (C) to normal.

   (D) back to the way it was.

   (E) normally.

Name _____ Date _____

(1) Just as fears of witchcraft once besieged the citizens of colonial Massachusetts, the fear of communists in the United States government <u>obsess</u> millions of Americans after World War II. (2) The man most responsible for this fear was Senator Joseph R. McCarthy.

(3) McCarthy (1908–1957) was elected to the United States Senate from Wisconsin in 1946. (4) He gained national attention in 1950. (5) At that time, he claimed that many communists occupied influential government positions. (6) Throughout history, government officials, and other people in the public eye, have been targets of ridiculous accusations. (7) McCarthy had little evidence, but his charges raised a national outcry. (8) The federal government launched security probes, employees about whom doubts arose were fired, and McCarthy even accused the Eisenhower administration of treason.

(9) McCarthy's fall was as abrupt as his rise. (10) During a televised investigation of the United States Army, his behavior <u>was a turn-off to many</u>. (11) In 1954, the Senate censured him for "contemptuous" conduct. (12) He died three years later. (13) An atmosphere of reckless accusations of disloyalty is still called "McCarthyism," especially accusations not backed by evidence.

74. Which of the following should be used in place of the underlined word in Sentence 1?

(A) obsessed

(B) had obsessed

(C) will obsess

(D) may obsess

(E) is going to obsess

75. Which is the *best* way to combine Sentences 4 and 5?

(A) In 1950, he both gained national attention and claimed that many communists occupied influential government positions.

(B) In 1950, when he claimed that many communists occupied influential government positions, he gained national attention.

(C) He gained national attention in 1950, which was when he claimed that many communists occupied influential government positions.

(D) He gained national attention when, in 1950, he claimed that many communists occupied influential government positions.

(E) He gained national attention when he claimed in 1950 that many communists occupied influential government positions.

76. **Which of the following editorial changes would help focus attention on the main idea of the second paragraph?**

    (A) Move Sentence 3 to the end of the first paragraph.

    (B) Delete Sentence 6.

    (C) Add some examples after Sentence 6 about how people reacted.

    (D) Combine Sentences 7 and 8 by changing the period after "outcry" to a comma and adding the conjunction "and."

    (E) Move Sentence 7 to the beginning of the paragraph.

77. **Which of the following contains a misplaced modifier?**

    (A) Sentence 1

    (B) Sentence 4

    (C) Sentence 9

    (D) Sentence 11

    (E) Sentence 13

78. **Which is the *best* revision of Sentence 8?**

    (A) The federal government launched security probes, employees about whom doubts arose were fired, and then McCarthy went so far as to even accuse the Eisenhower administration of treason.

    (B) The federal government launched security probes, and employees about whom doubts arose were fired. McCarthy even accused the Eisenhower administration of treason.

    (C) The federal government launched security probes, and employees about whom doubts arose were fired, but McCarthy even accused the Eisenhower administration of treason.

    (D) The federal government launched security probes, and employees about whom doubts arose were fired; yet McCarthy even accused the Eisenhower administration of treason.

    (E) The federal government launched security probes. Employees about whom doubts arose were fired. McCarthy even accused the Eisenhower administration of treason.

79. **Which is the *best* revision of the underlined part of Sentence 10?**

    (A) was a turning off to many

    (B) turned off many

    (C) alienated many

    (D) dismissed many

    (E) bored many

Prompt 1

Directions: *Think carefully about the issue presented in the following passage and the assignment below.*

In an effort to curb truancy, your city council is considering citing parents as well as children when children skip school. For a first offense, parent and child would each be fined $50; each would be fined $75 for a second offense. Third and subsequent offenses could carry jail time for the parent.

Assignment: What is your position on this issue? Plan and write an essay in which you develop your point of view on this issue. Support your position with reasoning and examples taken from your reading, studies, experience, or observations.

Prompt 2

Directions: *Think carefully about the issue presented in the following passages and the assignment below.*

To ensure the safety of students, teachers, and administrators, some school districts in the United States employ police officers to patrol schools during the school day. Suppose that the school board in your district is considering doing the same.

Assignment: Are you in favor of or against having police officers in your school? Plan and write an essay in which you develop your point of view on this issue. Support your position with reasoning and examples taken from your reading, studies, experience, or observations.

Name _____ Date _____

Answer Sheet: Screening Test

1. Ⓐ Ⓑ Ⓒ Ⓓ	15. Ⓐ Ⓑ Ⓒ Ⓓ
2. Ⓕ Ⓖ Ⓗ Ⓙ	16. Ⓕ Ⓖ Ⓗ Ⓙ
3. Ⓐ Ⓑ Ⓒ Ⓓ	17. Ⓐ Ⓑ Ⓒ Ⓓ
4. Ⓕ Ⓖ Ⓗ Ⓙ	18. Ⓕ Ⓖ Ⓗ Ⓙ
5. Ⓐ Ⓑ Ⓒ Ⓓ	19. Ⓐ Ⓑ Ⓒ Ⓓ
6. Ⓕ Ⓖ Ⓗ Ⓙ	20. Ⓕ Ⓖ Ⓗ Ⓙ
7. Ⓐ Ⓑ Ⓒ Ⓓ	21. Ⓐ Ⓑ Ⓒ Ⓓ
8. Ⓕ Ⓖ Ⓗ Ⓙ	22. Ⓕ Ⓖ Ⓗ Ⓙ
9. Ⓐ Ⓑ Ⓒ Ⓓ	23. Ⓐ Ⓑ Ⓒ Ⓓ
10. Ⓕ Ⓖ Ⓗ Ⓙ	24. Ⓕ Ⓖ Ⓗ Ⓙ
11. Ⓐ Ⓑ Ⓒ Ⓓ	
12. Ⓕ Ⓖ Ⓗ Ⓙ	
13. Ⓐ Ⓑ Ⓒ Ⓓ	
14. Ⓕ Ⓖ Ⓗ Ⓙ	

Name _____ Date _____

Answer Sheet

Practice Test 1

1. Ⓐ Ⓑ Ⓒ Ⓓ
2. Ⓐ Ⓑ Ⓒ Ⓓ
3. Ⓐ Ⓑ Ⓒ Ⓓ
4. Ⓐ Ⓑ Ⓒ Ⓓ
5. Ⓐ Ⓑ Ⓒ Ⓓ
6. Ⓐ Ⓑ Ⓒ Ⓓ
7. Ⓐ Ⓑ Ⓒ Ⓓ
8. Ⓐ Ⓑ Ⓒ Ⓓ
9. Ⓐ Ⓑ Ⓒ Ⓓ
10. Ⓐ Ⓑ Ⓒ Ⓓ
11. Ⓐ Ⓑ Ⓒ Ⓓ
12. Ⓐ Ⓑ Ⓒ Ⓓ
13. Ⓐ Ⓑ Ⓒ Ⓓ
14. Ⓐ Ⓑ Ⓒ Ⓓ
15. Ⓐ Ⓑ Ⓒ Ⓓ
16. Ⓐ Ⓑ Ⓒ Ⓓ
17. Ⓐ Ⓑ Ⓒ Ⓓ
18. Ⓐ Ⓑ Ⓒ Ⓓ
19. Ⓐ Ⓑ Ⓒ Ⓓ
20. Ⓐ Ⓑ Ⓒ Ⓓ
21. Ⓐ Ⓑ Ⓒ Ⓓ
22. Ⓐ Ⓑ Ⓒ Ⓓ
23. Ⓐ Ⓑ Ⓒ Ⓓ
24. Ⓐ Ⓑ Ⓒ Ⓓ
25. Ⓐ Ⓑ Ⓒ Ⓓ
26. Ⓐ Ⓑ Ⓒ Ⓓ
27. Ⓐ Ⓑ Ⓒ Ⓓ
28. Ⓐ Ⓑ Ⓒ Ⓓ
29. Ⓐ Ⓑ Ⓒ Ⓓ
30. Ⓐ Ⓑ Ⓒ Ⓓ

Practice Test 2

1. Ⓐ Ⓑ Ⓒ Ⓓ
2. Ⓐ Ⓑ Ⓒ Ⓓ
3. Ⓐ Ⓑ Ⓒ Ⓓ
4. Ⓐ Ⓑ Ⓒ Ⓓ
5. Ⓐ Ⓑ Ⓒ Ⓓ
6. Ⓐ Ⓑ Ⓒ Ⓓ
7. Ⓐ Ⓑ Ⓒ Ⓓ
8. Ⓐ Ⓑ Ⓒ Ⓓ
9. Ⓐ Ⓑ Ⓒ Ⓓ
10. Ⓐ Ⓑ Ⓒ Ⓓ
11. Ⓐ Ⓑ Ⓒ Ⓓ
12. Ⓐ Ⓑ Ⓒ Ⓓ
13. Ⓐ Ⓑ Ⓒ Ⓓ
14. Ⓐ Ⓑ Ⓒ Ⓓ
15. Ⓐ Ⓑ Ⓒ Ⓓ
16. Ⓐ Ⓑ Ⓒ Ⓓ
17. Ⓐ Ⓑ Ⓒ Ⓓ
18. Ⓐ Ⓑ Ⓒ Ⓓ
19. Ⓐ Ⓑ Ⓒ Ⓓ
20. Ⓐ Ⓑ Ⓒ Ⓓ
21. Ⓐ Ⓑ Ⓒ Ⓓ
22. Ⓐ Ⓑ Ⓒ Ⓓ
23. Ⓐ Ⓑ Ⓒ Ⓓ
24. Ⓐ Ⓑ Ⓒ Ⓓ
25. Ⓐ Ⓑ Ⓒ Ⓓ
26. Ⓐ Ⓑ Ⓒ Ⓓ
27. Ⓐ Ⓑ Ⓒ Ⓓ

Answer Sheet for SAT/ACT

1. Ⓐ Ⓑ Ⓒ Ⓓ Ⓔ	17. Ⓐ Ⓑ Ⓒ Ⓓ Ⓔ	33. Ⓐ Ⓑ Ⓒ Ⓓ Ⓔ	49. Ⓐ Ⓑ Ⓒ Ⓓ Ⓔ	65. Ⓐ Ⓑ Ⓒ Ⓓ Ⓔ
2. Ⓐ Ⓑ Ⓒ Ⓓ Ⓔ	18. Ⓐ Ⓑ Ⓒ Ⓓ Ⓔ	34. Ⓐ Ⓑ Ⓒ Ⓓ Ⓔ	50. Ⓐ Ⓑ Ⓒ Ⓓ Ⓔ	66. Ⓐ Ⓑ Ⓒ Ⓓ Ⓔ
3. Ⓐ Ⓑ Ⓒ Ⓓ Ⓔ	19. Ⓐ Ⓑ Ⓒ Ⓓ Ⓔ	35. Ⓐ Ⓑ Ⓒ Ⓓ Ⓔ	51. Ⓐ Ⓑ Ⓒ Ⓓ Ⓔ	67. Ⓐ Ⓑ Ⓒ Ⓓ Ⓔ
4. Ⓐ Ⓑ Ⓒ Ⓓ Ⓔ	20. Ⓐ Ⓑ Ⓒ Ⓓ Ⓔ	36. Ⓐ Ⓑ Ⓒ Ⓓ Ⓔ	52. Ⓐ Ⓑ Ⓒ Ⓓ Ⓔ	68. Ⓐ Ⓑ Ⓒ Ⓓ Ⓔ
5. Ⓐ Ⓑ Ⓒ Ⓓ Ⓔ	21. Ⓐ Ⓑ Ⓒ Ⓓ Ⓔ	37. Ⓐ Ⓑ Ⓒ Ⓓ Ⓔ	53. Ⓐ Ⓑ Ⓒ Ⓓ Ⓔ	69. Ⓐ Ⓑ Ⓒ Ⓓ Ⓔ
6. Ⓐ Ⓑ Ⓒ Ⓓ Ⓔ	22. Ⓐ Ⓑ Ⓒ Ⓓ Ⓔ	38. Ⓐ Ⓑ Ⓒ Ⓓ Ⓔ	54. Ⓐ Ⓑ Ⓒ Ⓓ Ⓔ	70. Ⓐ Ⓑ Ⓒ Ⓓ Ⓔ
7. Ⓐ Ⓑ Ⓒ Ⓓ Ⓔ	23. Ⓐ Ⓑ Ⓒ Ⓓ Ⓔ	39. Ⓐ Ⓑ Ⓒ Ⓓ Ⓔ	55. Ⓐ Ⓑ Ⓒ Ⓓ Ⓔ	71. Ⓐ Ⓑ Ⓒ Ⓓ Ⓔ
8. Ⓐ Ⓑ Ⓒ Ⓓ Ⓔ	24. Ⓐ Ⓑ Ⓒ Ⓓ Ⓔ	40. Ⓐ Ⓑ Ⓒ Ⓓ Ⓔ	56. Ⓐ Ⓑ Ⓒ Ⓓ Ⓔ	72. Ⓐ Ⓑ Ⓒ Ⓓ Ⓔ
9. Ⓐ Ⓑ Ⓒ Ⓓ Ⓔ	25. Ⓐ Ⓑ Ⓒ Ⓓ Ⓔ	41. Ⓐ Ⓑ Ⓒ Ⓓ Ⓔ	57. Ⓐ Ⓑ Ⓒ Ⓓ Ⓔ	73. Ⓐ Ⓑ Ⓒ Ⓓ Ⓔ
10. Ⓐ Ⓑ Ⓒ Ⓓ Ⓔ	26. Ⓐ Ⓑ Ⓒ Ⓓ Ⓔ	42. Ⓐ Ⓑ Ⓒ Ⓓ Ⓔ	58. Ⓐ Ⓑ Ⓒ Ⓓ Ⓔ	74. Ⓐ Ⓑ Ⓒ Ⓓ Ⓔ
11. Ⓐ Ⓑ Ⓒ Ⓓ Ⓔ	27. Ⓐ Ⓑ Ⓒ Ⓓ Ⓔ	43. Ⓐ Ⓑ Ⓒ Ⓓ Ⓔ	59. Ⓐ Ⓑ Ⓒ Ⓓ Ⓔ	75. Ⓐ Ⓑ Ⓒ Ⓓ Ⓔ
12. Ⓐ Ⓑ Ⓒ Ⓓ Ⓔ	28. Ⓐ Ⓑ Ⓒ Ⓓ Ⓔ	44. Ⓐ Ⓑ Ⓒ Ⓓ Ⓔ	60. Ⓐ Ⓑ Ⓒ Ⓓ Ⓔ	76. Ⓐ Ⓑ Ⓒ Ⓓ Ⓔ
13. Ⓐ Ⓑ Ⓒ Ⓓ Ⓔ	29. Ⓐ Ⓑ Ⓒ Ⓓ Ⓔ	45. Ⓐ Ⓑ Ⓒ Ⓓ Ⓔ	61. Ⓐ Ⓑ Ⓒ Ⓓ Ⓔ	77. Ⓐ Ⓑ Ⓒ Ⓓ Ⓔ
14. Ⓐ Ⓑ Ⓒ Ⓓ Ⓔ	30. Ⓐ Ⓑ Ⓒ Ⓓ Ⓔ	46. Ⓐ Ⓑ Ⓒ Ⓓ Ⓔ	62. Ⓐ Ⓑ Ⓒ Ⓓ Ⓔ	78. Ⓐ Ⓑ Ⓒ Ⓓ Ⓔ
15. Ⓐ Ⓑ Ⓒ Ⓓ Ⓔ	31. Ⓐ Ⓑ Ⓒ Ⓓ Ⓔ	47. Ⓐ Ⓑ Ⓒ Ⓓ Ⓔ	63. Ⓐ Ⓑ Ⓒ Ⓓ Ⓔ	79. Ⓐ Ⓑ Ⓒ Ⓓ Ⓔ
16. Ⓐ Ⓑ Ⓒ Ⓓ Ⓔ	32. Ⓐ Ⓑ Ⓒ Ⓓ Ⓔ	48. Ⓐ Ⓑ Ⓒ Ⓓ Ⓔ	64. Ⓐ Ⓑ Ⓒ Ⓓ Ⓔ	

Answer Sheet

Short Answer/Essay

_____

_____

_____

_____

_____

_____

_____

_____

_____

_____

_____

_____

_____

_____

_____

_____

_____

_____

_____

_____

_____

_____

_____

_____

_____

_____

_____

_____

Answer Sheet

Short Answer/Essay

_____

_____

_____

_____

_____

_____

_____

_____

_____

_____

_____

_____

_____

_____

_____

_____

_____

_____

_____

_____

_____

_____

_____

_____

_____

_____